W0081441

Praise for *Be a Man About It*

'An absolutely fascinating enquiry into the nature of masculinity, coming at a time when it's really needed. Hats off to George Bell'.

—Stephen Fry
UK comedian, actor, writer, and presenter

'An essential read for our generation of men, rewriting the rules in a way that's honest, freeing, and makes me excited for our future'.

—Tj Power
Sunday Times bestselling author of The DOSE Effect, *and neuroscientist*

'Powerful. Moving. Necessary.

George Bell's book about being a man, manhood, and masculinity is a much-needed and precious resource.

Working on the front line and in the trenches of mental health care services, including within the National Health Service (NHS), as a consultant psychiatrist, I have seen time and time again how toxic constructs of masculinity contribute to the epidemic of suicidal behaviours in boys and men.

It is difficult not to be deeply touched by George's compassion, intellect, and wisdom that permeate throughout this book. *Be a Man About It* tackles a taboo topic with delicacy and panache and provides a blueprint for boys and men in particular to navigate the precarious territory of masculinity – a landscape fraught with peril, challenges, obstacles, and barriers.

This is such an important contribution to the literature, helping to fill a void that has existed for far too long'.

—Dr Ahmed Hankir
MBChB, MRCPsych, consultant psychiatrist, author of Breakthrough: A Story of Hope, Resilience, and Mental Health Recovery, *World Health Organization award-winning doctor*

'*Be a Man About It* isn't some macho pep talk or a pity parade, it's a deeply human look at what happens when men are taught to bury everything. If you've ever felt like you're quietly falling apart, start here'.

—Gavin Oattes
International keynote speaker and bestselling author

'*Be a Man About It* is a powerful reminder that vulnerability is strength, not a weakness. A guide for men – and those who care about them'.

—Dwain Chambers
British athlete

'A soaring assessment of the state of modern masculinity which helps us understand why we are where we are today, before grounding us again with the seeds to cultivate an improved masculinity that works for boys and men from now and into the future'.

—Dr Naveen Puri
Medical Director, Bupa UK Insurance

'With sensitivity and insight, George offers both personal per-spective and practical guidance, making this a vital resource for anyone navigating mental health challenges – whether their own or someone else's. This is more than a book; it's a lifeline'.

—Alice Hendy MBE
Founder of R;pple Suicide Prevention Charity

'This brilliant book offers a refreshing and accessible exploration of masculinity. Its breadth draws you in with ease and makes it a must read for everyone, because conversations about masculinity touch us all'.

—Amelia Wrighton
Co-founder and CEO of Suicide&Co

'*Be a Man About It* is an honest, powerful, and much-needed book that lifts the lid on the pressures and challenges men face today. I found myself relating to so many of the real-life experiences shared, and I was equally encouraged by the science and expert insight that back them up. It doesn't shy away from difficult or taboo subjects – subjects that desperately need to be spoken about. This is not just a book for men who might be struggling, lonely, or feeling lost, but also for women who want to better understand the men in their lives. Direct, raw, and deeply human, this book is a must-read'.

—Andrew Jenkins
Finalist of the BBC's The Traitors, *and motivational speaker*

'A beautiful weaving of research, biology, experts, and personal experience on how you, as a man, can live a happier, healthier, and more productive life in all of the areas that matter to you. But unlike many books about men, George offers a clear path forward not just for men, but for society as a whole'.

—David Chambers
Men's dating and relationship coach

'This book is well written and highly readable. It deals with a much-needed subject – masculinity – and how men perceive themselves as men. It rightly redefines masculinity as being vulnerable about one's physical and mental health, being open and transparent in conversations about potentially sensitive health issues, and asking for help when needed rather than burying their heads in the sand. I would recommend this book to all men, especially those that find it difficult to show vulnerability in their emotions and in talking about problems with their physical, mental, and sexual health'.

—Dr Prasanna Sooriakumaran
*Professor of Urology and a
lead clinical advisor in men's health*

'A powerful and emotive read that will break down so many barriers that men place around their and others' mental health and well-being. George Bell has written a narrative with compassion and an openness, a style that will offer hope and courage to so many. This book will give men validation, relief, and encouragement to challenge the current theme of "say nothing". A book of hope that will simply save lives'.

—Gary Hayes
Ex-military and police, Anti-Terrorism Unit

'I hope one day to walk into a bookshop and see a "masculinity" section. This book would be in it, with I hope many more to come. This is much-needed writing about the male experience and we need a lot more of it. Chapeau to George and the men who've shared their stories with him'.

—James Routledge
Author of Mental Health at Work

'This should be required reading for every man. *Be a Man About It* isn't just another book on masculinity, it's a clear and compassionate roadmap toward healthier men, stronger relationships, and a better world'.

—Jeremy Lipkowitz
Men's porn addiction coach

'Masculinity is a tough topic to tackle right now, and George has done an incredible job of balancing statistics, respecting other groups, and showing real care with the information he shares. Highly recommend for everyone'.

—Katie Maycock
Wellbeing consultant and burnout coach

'This book is powerful, honest, and long overdue. It tackles the real, often unspoken pressures men face and offers a new, healthier framework for masculinity. It's not about blaming or shaming, it's about understanding, and redefining what it truly means to be a man in today's world. Every man (and everyone who loves one) should read this'.

—Mark Ormrod MBE
Royal Marines veteran, author, speaker, and resilience coach

'In this wonderful book you will find great wisdom in not only the challenges of manhood but the challenges of how not to be shaped into clones of other people's definitions of manhood. As Bell guides us, when we choose to discover ourselves, what it is to have a "male mind" and its challenges we discover the courage and wisdom to recognise that at the heart of all of us is the desire to feel connected, cared for and caring, to live this short and turbulent life, to be helpful not harmful to make a difference in the world for the better'.

—Paul Gilbert OBE
Psychologist and founder of Compassion Focused Therapy

'A must read for anyone interested in men's health. George's insights are refreshingly honest with practical solutions, offering a much-needed challenge to the modern concept of masculinity'.

—Dr Ravi Lukha
Medical Director, Bupa UK Insurance

'*Be a Man About It* is a powerful read that tackles head-on the pressures men face today. Bell challenges outdated stereotypes and offers a fresh, compassionate vision of masculinity – one that embraces openness, emotional honesty, and connection. This book is a call to action to rethink what it means to be a man and to create a culture where everyone can truly thrive'.

—Professor Rory O'Connor
Professor of Health Psychology and Director of Suicidal Behaviour Research Laboratory at the University of Glasgow

'Required reading for all young men unsure of their place in the world. It is the book I wish I had when I was struggling'.

—Ryan Hopkins
Author of 52 Weeks of Wellbeing

'This book manages to be both insightful and very readable and, most important, puts forward some solutions we can all engage with. I wholeheartedly recommend it'.

—Dr Tim Woodman
Medical Director, Policy and Cancer Services, Bupa UKI

'A must-read dive into the pressures and complexities that men face today, and a showcase that the term masculinity isn't binary'.

—Tommy Hatto
Actor, model, and speaker

'George brings such genuine warmth and thoughtful curiosity to the exploration of the issues facing masculinity right now. As he reminds us, there is no rule book for being a man, no easy to follow blueprint that points in the right direction. Maybe this book starts to change all that'.

—Wendy Robinson
Director of Services at Campaign Against Living Miserably (CALM)

'With a rare blend of expert insight and powerful personal stories, *Be a Man About It* offers a fresh and much-needed commentary on masculinity'.

—Dr Dan Nicolau
Physician at King's College London

'At last, a book that doesn't shy away from the fact that male masculinity is a topic that has its place and needs an open conversation. From the author's own lived experience and extensive research, this book challenges those who subscribe to the "man-up" culture to consider what really are the challenges men face in society today. It might no longer be a "man's world" in the old-fashioned sense but this book's suggestion that we adapt to a more flexible version of masculinity, means that men will feel less displaced and better understand how they fit into the new world order of things. With 12 men dying by suicide in the UK every single day, this book provides plenty of reasons to give more men hope'.

—Steve Phillip
Founder of The Jordan Legacy CIC

'I feel like what *Miseducation*, the Lauryn Hill album, was to women is what this book is going to be for men. A bible that helps men navigate life and answers most of the questions that keep us up at night. It's very much needed and it's going to affect generations to come'.

—Kenneth Erhahon (Shocka)
Music artist

'This is a necessary exploration of modern masculinity. Written from the heart with an honest, compassionate, and balanced look at how we can offer a path towards healthier identities for men in our society. We are reminded how "suppression and silence can be killers", a resonating phrase that captures why change is so urgently needed. Can we collectively start to make a conscious shift to expand our definition of masculinity for the better?'

—Dr James Stevenson
Lead physician, Bupa Health Clinics

"BE A MAN ABOUT IT"

"

'Absolutely fascinating'
STEPHEN FRY

BE A MAN ABOUT IT

"

Building a healthier idea of masculinity

GEORGE BELL

CAPSTONE
A Wiley Brand

This edition first published 2026

© 2026 by John Wiley & Sons, Ltd.

All rights reserved, including rights for text and data mining and training of artificial intelligence technologies or similar technologies. No part of this publication may be reproduced, stored in a retrieval system, or transmitted, in any form or by any means, electronic, mechanical, photocopying, recording or otherwise, except as permitted by law. Advice on how to obtain permission to reuse material from this title is available at http://www.wiley.com/go/permissions.

The right of George Bell to be identified as the author of the editorial material in this work has been asserted in accordance with law.

Registered Offices
John Wiley & Sons, Inc., 111 River Street, Hoboken, NJ 07030, USA
John Wiley & Sons Ltd, New Era House, 8 Oldlands Way, Bognor Regis, West Sussex, PO22 9NQ, UK

For details of our global editorial offices, customer services, and more information about Wiley products visit us at www.wiley.com.

The manufacturer's authorized representative according to the EU General Product Safety Regulation is Wiley-VCH GmbH, Boschstr. 12, 69469 Weinheim, Germany, e-mail: Product_Safety@wiley.com.

Wiley also publishes its books in a variety of electronic formats and by print-on-demand. Some content that appears in standard print versions of this book may not be available in other formats.

Trademarks: Wiley and the Wiley logo are trademarks or registered trademarks of John Wiley & Sons, Inc. and/or its affiliates in the United States and other countries and may not be used without written permission. All other trademarks are the property of their respective owners. John Wiley & Sons, Inc. is not associated with any product or vendor mentioned in this book.

Limit of Liability/Disclaimer of Warranty
While the publisher and the authors have used their best efforts in preparing this work, including a review of the content of the work, neither the publisher nor the authors make any representations or warranties with respect to the accuracy or completeness of the contents of this work and specifically disclaim all warranties, including without limitation any implied warranties of merchantability or fitness for a particular purpose. No warranty may be created or extended by sales representatives, written sales materials or promotional statements for this work. The fact that an organization, website, or product is referred to in this work as a citation and/or potential source of further information does not mean that the publisher and authors endorse the information or services the organization, website, or product may provide or recommendations it may make. This work is sold with the understanding that the publisher is not engaged in rendering professional services. The advice and strategies contained herein may not be suitable for your situation. You should consult with a specialist where appropriate. Further, readers should be aware that websites listed in this work may have changed or disappeared between when this work was written and when it is read. Neither the publisher nor authors shall be liable for any loss of profit or any other commercial damages, including but not limited to special, incidental, consequential, or other damages.

Library of Congress Cataloging-in-Publication Data is Available:

ISBN 9781907326134 (Cloth)
ISBN 9781907326141 (ePDF)
ISBN 9781907326165 (ePub)

COVER DESIGN: PAUL MCCARTHY
COVER ART: © GETTY IMAGES | JASENKA ARBANAS

Set in 12/15pts and Sabon LT Std by Straive, Chennai, India.
Printed and bound by CPI Group (UK) Ltd, Croydon, CR0 4YY

C9781907326134_161225

Contents

Masculinity (noun); the characteristics that are traditionally thought to be typical of or suitable for men – *Cambridge Dictionary*

Introduction

Men are allowed to be one of two things: mad, or fine.

— *Bill Burr, comedian*

Men are under pressure.

That can be a punchy thing to write in this day and age, but ignoring it doesn't make it any less true.

There are many opposing beliefs about masculinity permeating throughout our society. Some say that masculinity is facing a crisis. Others argue it's *always* been facing a crisis. One side is trying to crush a masculinity that they label as 'toxic', while the other is rushing to defend its honour.

Some are arguing for better rights for men, others argue that men have no place to voice those rights in the face of historical oppression caused to other groups, primarily by men. And there's a certain segment that will get enraged at even the mere mention of the word 'masculinity', as though the concept itself is so fragile that a single whisper is enough to bring the whole thing tumbling down.

Much of the debate has become bitter and binary, an us-versus-them mindset in which there are no winners. Men blaming women, women blaming men. Men blaming men, even. In amongst all this squabbling amongst ourselves, we've lost our ability to see nuance, grey areas, and messy middles. We've lost sight of the *true* problem – that many men are under immense pressure, some systemic, some internalised. And many are cracking beneath it all.

As I've embarked on my journey of sharing more about masculinity and trying to draw attention to this problem, some have taken it as an affront to the way of life they've always known. I regularly receive private messages and public comments from people who seem certain that I'm on some sort of self-indulgent noble crusade, and that masculinity doesn't need saving from itself; it simply needs saving from supposed attention-seekers like me.

One such message read 'why can't you leave men alone? They're doing just fine'. This single sentence epitomises our approach to a problem which continues to grow; we bury our heads in the sand thinking that if we can't see a problem, then there isn't one.

Of course, many men *are* doing just fine, some are doing great even. But the broader picture of data pulled from various countries, continents and globally, tells a worrying story. On average, men have a global lower life expectancy than women by around four to five years,[1] they're more likely to die from non-sex-specific cancers[2] and cardiovascular disease,[3] more likely to be homeless,[4] struggle with substance abuse,[5] and be both the victims and the perpetrators of homicide.[6]

They're more likely to go missing,[7] be sectioned,[8] die from workplace accidents,[9] and have lower academic achievements than their female counterparts.[10] Men make up the majority of prison populations around the world, often exceeding 90%. In the UK alone, men account for around 96% of the prison population.[11]

Men are also more likely to die by suicide, with around 75% of suicides in Canada,[12] the US[13] and the UK[14] being men. Globally, on average a man dies by suicide roughly every single minute of every single day.[15] By the time you finish this chapter, depending on your reading speed, at least 10 men around the world will have taken their own life.

There's always context and caveats to statistics, and the reasons are complex. But there's plenty there to build a compelling enough counterargument as to why leaving men well alone might not be the best course of action. But just *why* are the statistics around men so damning?

For so long, traditional masculinity has been equated with action, adventure, strength, the external. And this isn't a bad thing, many of these ideals and values are things that men not only cherish, but have served them greatly throughout many points in history.

But in many ways we've also made masculinity into something too rigid and unmalleable, losing sight of the fact that much of masculinity, and humanity itself, can be flexible. Traditional masculinity is one that values emotional suppression, rather than expression, and the avoidance of deep interpersonal connections. These habits and behaviours are things that many men have been taught, and then internalised and reinforced.

And that's one of the saddest things that we've led many men to believe; that their emotions are something to be feared and suppressed, not welcomed, understood, and used as a tool for growth, resilience, and change.

We often tell men to push these emotions to one side – believing we're building them up to be strong and not realising that we're simply strapping a tight, uncomfortable mask around their faces while a pressure cooker builds inside them. Many boys and men have grown up believing silence brings strength, not realising that this silence rarely means resolution. It can often mean suffering. Sometimes even suicide.

And yet we push ahead with our much-touted, golden cure for any male malaise. And that is to tell a man to simply be, well, more of a man. As though the fix for a broken leg is to run on it more and bash it with a hammer.

The thing about pressure is you can only have so much of it before it *has* to be released somewhere, and the thing containing it explodes. What we're seeing in some of the damning statistics around men is this pressure exploding – in the form of substance abuse, gambling and sex addictions, porn use, withdrawal, a growing loneliness epidemic, a flocking towards harmful influencers, sexual dysfunction issues, eating issues, mental health issues, suicide, and plenty more.

As a society we see only what's happening above the surface – men becoming withdrawn, men who aren't holding it together, and we read about the extremes in the media. It's easy to see these external acts and criticise the collective man as 'bad' and in urgent need of 'fixing'.

And it's the perception of only the external that can give rise to tired, outdated stereotypes about men. That they're one-dimensional, simple, and lazy. That they're emotionally inept, unless it's anger and violence. That they're often something to be feared, not celebrated.

Currently, there aren't many positive messages in public discourse about men, with this discourse focusing on extremes, toxicity, and stories of men taking a dramatic swing to radicalism and right-leaning politics. Many, particularly younger generations, feel blamed for a patriarchal system that they've had no hand in building, yet feel negatively impacted by.

But there is a huge slice of the pie we often miss that contains a lot of good men trying to do good for themselves and others, who support equality and progression, and who are trying to expand the definition of what it means to be a man. Too often, public narratives fall into a trap of being unable to separate the collective image of man from individual men.

In her book, *The Will to Change: Men, Masculinity and Love*, the American author, bell hooks, wrote: 'The crisis facing men is not the crisis of masculinity, it is the crisis of patriarchal masculinity. Until we make this distinction clear, men will continue to fear that any critique of patriarchy represents a threat'.[16] In other words, it's not masculinity itself that is harmful or toxic; it's the rigid, power-driven version of it that has been passed down and reinforced that needs examining.

I'm conscious that as I write this, those from other groups who have felt oppression for decades, maybe even centuries, because of their sex, sexuality, race or anything else, may feel a certain resistance to a man talking about the need for male rights. I once received a comment that said 'how convenient that men have "discovered" oppression now that it only impacts them'.

I want to acknowledge the struggles and battles that many of these other groups have faced and continue to face. In most cases, the system *has* been built by men, to benefit men, and abused by men. It's caused deeply systemic issues which have impacted a lot of people.

But it's important to remember that while the system has often been built and abused by men, the spoils are not shared equally among them. Many men are feeling the negative effects of a patriarchal system too, and so I don't believe in making this a gender war with one side against the other, or dismissing any-one's struggle or pain. It's possible to hold support for more than one person and group at the same time, and there's more strength in unity than division.

And men need this support. Because a quote that stuck with me during my research said 'when bad things happen to women or because of women, we often look at the environment and society around them as the cause. But when bad things happen to men or because of men, we often only look at the individual and ask "what's wrong with him?"'

The truth is, no one is born *wanting* to become an addict, a criminal, a suicide statistic. If we keep spending all our time fishing men out of the bottom of the river, rather than going upstream and asking why they're falling in in the first place, you can bet we'll have to keep digging early graves for our brothers, fathers, sons, friends. Ourselves, even.

And that's where we're not focusing enough; the environment around men. Because for so long men have, in essence, had so many advantages compared to other groups, we've not stopped to ask how they're *really* doing. In many cases, it's not a masculinity crisis that we have; it's much more than that. It's deeply entangled with a poverty crisis. A political crisis. A social media and technology crisis. A mental health crisis. A poor education crisis. A historical and societal crisis which is telling us how we *should* live. We're often blamed for how we feel, with little regard to the context that has made us feel that way in the first place.

None of this excuses individual acts of wrongdoing, and I give nobody, regardless of gender, a get-out-of-jail-free card. But we're so focused on surface-level actions that we're missing what's happening below that surface; a lot of men who are desperately trying to swim against a tidal wave of learnt behaviours: emotional suppression, and silence. Human-made male traditions are dragging them under the water and outdated cultural beliefs are pushing them down further.

There's no rule book for being a bloke, no easy-to-follow blueprint that points us in the right direction. And most young boys aren't getting sat down by their dads to talk about emotions, erections, and anything else that comes with being a man. And so this social conditioning, male tradition, and emotional suppression is passed down from generation to generation like an ill-fitting, unwanted hand-me-down.

We're told to toughen up, but a bit too much and it's toxic. We're told to soften, but too much of that and it's weak and unattractive. Who do we listen to? For men who have been so used to having one role, one way of being, one place in society, it's an absolute orchestra of noise, building to a crescendo of opinion at breakneck speed that can very often cost them their lives.

What's the price of inaction? That we continue to perpetuate the very issue that we want to avoid: helping men and boys feel understood, valued, and accepted.

So how do we do it? Where pressure can reach breaking point, it can also be released in healthier ways too. The river is going to keep flowing whether we like it or not; it's up to us to decide which way we want to send it.

There are three core things I believe will help:

- **Recognise that men are facing a challenge**. Many people don't want us to talk about it, but the statistics are over-whelmingly compelling; too many men are dying before their time or facing dozens of health, work, and life-related challenges. Ignoring it doesn't make it go away, and we can hold space for caring about this at the same time as the causes of others.
- **Understand that suppression and silence can be killers**. We have tricked many men into believing that emotions are to be feared, and shunning these emotions will make them stronger. But often all it does is shackle them to the ground. In many cases, emotional suppression, rigid mas-culine norms and social conditioning are the things tear-ing men down, building the pressure within them. What if we started to teach men not to control emotions them-selves, but to control their *response* to their emotions?

- **Expand our definition of masculinity**. It's not masculinity that's toxic, it's our rigid definition of it. For too long we've treated it as a fixed fate rather than what it really is – expandable, flexible, and existing on a spectrum. It's not about traditional masculinity versus this new wave, it's about recognising that often too much of anything in abundance isn't a good thing and the key lies in balance and a forgotten middle ground.

The saddest part of my research is also the part that carries the most hope. So much of what men are hamstrung by is social conditioning, cultural constructs, and male tradition. We may label it as biology and the natural order of things, but this isn't the case. It's sad because it means *we're* the ones perpetuating the problem. But it's also hopeful, because it means that it's within our hands to enact change.

I don't believe that men are broken or a problem that needs to be fixed, I believe that the system they're operating within often makes them feel that way. And there are plenty of systemic issues that exist, changes we need to make in boardrooms, classrooms, and governmental offices.

But we also have the power, responsibility, and agency to start changing things immediately, today, for ourselves. Our influences, our beliefs, and our language. Our actions, habits, and connections with other groups.

Too often we don't celebrate men for the great things they could be, but rather focus on the stereotypical traits they *might* be. Men do want to talk, to have belonging, connection, and community. They want to feel valued and give value, to have purpose and to be wanted. Men have a *lot* to give, in their work, their relationships, and in their contributions to the world.

I've seen some of the very best of men and seen the wonderful things they're capable of. There are a lot of good men out there. Some who have been conditioned into hiding some of those parts of themselves.

This isn't all men, and things do seem to be improving generationally. But, there *is* a problem that needs our attention. We only have to look at the statistics downstream in health challenges and life expectancy to see where some of this problem is rising. And if we give the solution the attention and space it deserves, we'll find that there is a lot of good within men still to emerge. It's on all of us to help bring that out.

Grand epiphanies that radically change someone's life rarely happen from one book alone and in an instant. I'd love for this book to do that, but I hope to at least expand your worldview and perspective, and hope that you'll find something here, however large or small that may be. Maybe a moment of clarity. Maybe a little hope. Maybe the start of a conversation you've been waiting 10 years to have. Something. That's how change starts.

A Bit About Me

This book isn't about me, and while I will occasionally drop in the odd nugget about my experiences, I want the focus to remain firmly on the collective man. However, I want to share a bit about myself, why I'm writing this book, and, in case you're wondering, what gives me the right to be asking people to read the following chapters.

At the age of 21, I was entering the years unofficially dubbed 'the best years of your life'. The message from everyone was one of fun, growth, and opportunity. I was about to step out into the big wide world, one that I could supposedly make my oyster.

The trouble for me was that I was in the middle of a quarter-life crisis, grappling with my identity and spending the majority of my waking hours battling against suicidal thoughts. I hid it like an absolute champ too; nobody around me had a clue what was going on.

And those masculine traits of strength and resilience that men are told to have? I worked them like a pro, putting on a happy, confident mask, pushing everything down to the bottom. I managed to land myself a job with a former Dragon from *Dragon's Den*, beating hundreds of other applicants in the process, despite the fact I was still trying to beat my own mind at the same time.

Even on the way to my second-stage group interview with 10 other candidates in the same room, I was thinking about suicide as I waited for my train. Once in the interview room I switched on my confident, exuberant, masculine self, and did what I needed to do to beat the competition and get the job. Because that's what we do, right?

I can talk about this subject because I've lived it. I know what it's like to feel the pressure of being a man, to have to fit in, to not show emotion, to do what needs to be done because that's what we've been told to do. And to fear weakness as though it were a cancer. It's that societal pressure that kick-started my journey with mental health issues.

There's a bit of an unwritten rule when it comes to being a bloke around the things you must or mustn't do. Generally speaking, your manliness will be measured by the weights you can bench, the number of women you sleep with, the sports team you follow, and the speed at which you can drink pints. (And never half-pints, of course.) Not forgetting that you also mustn't, at any point, discuss your emotions. Vulnerability should be banished and emotional suppression upheld.

There is nothing wrong with people who value these things, but often it's presented as the *only* way to do masculinity. So you can imagine the trouble I had stepping into an all-boys school as a skinny, quiet kid that didn't like sport, liked doing his homework and, at that age, was fairly terrified of girls. And I was a sensitive kid to boot. Nice one George, good start.

You can probably guess where this is going – I was bullied. It followed me around corridors, in classrooms, and out of school on social media. It felt pretty relentless. What happens when, as a young kid trying to understand yourself, you're getting told daily that, essentially, you're not man enough? Well, of course I was going to have issues with my identity later down the line.

And that's how I ended up in that place, with my issues, right before my interviews with the former Dragon's team. Depressed, anxious, and so sure that my only way out was going to be suicide. I thought landing the job would fix everything for me, because on the *outside* I was 'successful' now. What I had yet to realise was that the problem was a mental one, and there was a whole bunch of struggle that followed, and things got worse before they got better.

I was left in a place where I eventually had to quit my job, and barely left the house, cutting off my friends and the outside world. Family and friends would be arranging plans for the following months and years, while I told myself I wouldn't be around to see them.

Nobody ever thinks this will happen to them. Until it does. I certainly didn't. No man wakes up thinking that's where his life will head, often until it's too late. No kid is born destined to get mental health issues or struggle with their identity.

Others will think that only the weak can suffer with a mental health issue. But coming out the other side of that inner battle showed me I have several of those traditional masculine traits in abundance. It takes some real strength and resilience to drag yourself back from the brink when the thing trying to push you over is your own mind.

I saw a quote from the writer, Katherine MacKenett, that stuck with me. 'Every time I witness a strong person, I want to know: What dark did you conquer in your story? Mountains do not rise without earthquakes'.

My experience with mental health issues fundamentally changed me as a person and I haven't been the same since. And I'd wager that anyone who has been through something similar will tell you the same. It's like being unplugged from the Matrix.

I've been strong and resilient, but I've also struggled with my mental health and emotions. I've been through therapy, I've done the classic 'lad' things to try to fit in, I've gone too far the other way and tried to become 'enlightened'. I've tried meditation, journaling, tech-detoxes, diets, courses, coaching, and all other things (fad or otherwise) in the pursuit of being the optimal version of myself.

What I learnt along the way is that often we can have too much of all of this stuff. Was I a better person when I focused only on meditation, self-help books, and growth, cutting out time socialising, Netflix, relaxing? And trying to reject traditional masculinity?

I'm not so sure. Really, these things didn't help me do the thing I actually needed to do – get a better understanding of myself and what my definition of being a man was. And that was a crucial realisation for me. So many things that have happened in my life – jobs I took in London, nights out I went on, things I said and did – a lot of it was influenced or caused by an imbalanced relationship with my own sense of masculinity.

For a long time, my story was that I suffered with, and then recovered from, mental health issues. I thought that was the depth of the story. But as I started to explore more of masculinity, I asked myself the question: 'would I have suffered with mental health issues if I'd had a more comfortable sense of masculinity from a younger age?' Mental health issues are complex, so it's impossible to tell, but honestly in my heart, the answer feels like no.

And so I realised that my relationship to my own sense of masculinity has acted like a soundtrack to my life, always there, always playing. Sometimes it's acted like a guide, leading me to things I've enjoyed and things that have served me. Other times it acted more like a puppeteer, controlling me in ways that satisfied a perception of masculinity in other people's eyes, rather than things I actually wanted in my life. Whatever the relationship was, it was always hanging over me in every decision, every act.

And that's not abnormal. We bring our identity to the things we do. But when it feels like we have two identities playing off of each other, competing with each other? Problems can arise. It took me a long time to realise that soundtrack was there, and even longer to realise I wasn't always following along to the same tune.

I learnt, too late, that masculinity can be flexible, where for so long I believed it to be fixed. I had to discover where what I had previously learnt may not be serving me, the impact it was having, and then take the personal responsibility to change those things in my life. And that's how I've structured this book:

- **Part One:** What's got men to where we are. The historical, biological, and societal context that's building an internal pressure cooker.
- **Part Two:** Where that pressure is reaching breaking point. Taboos that we don't talk about, things that men are struggling with, the conversations that we don't want to have.
- **Part Three:** What an expanded kind of masculinity looks like, and how we can all start to release that pressure in healthier ways.

I've worked in the mental health space for 10 years, supporting global businesses such as Just Eat, Red Bull, Bupa, Aviva, and

NatWest. I've included research and data where necessary, and I've interviewed over 40 people for this book, both experts and people with powerful stories – army veterans, professors, sports stars, people who have faced addiction, people who have lost others or nearly lost themselves. All to highlight the challenges men face, but also why trying to force all men into one definition of masculinity doesn't make sense.

Masculinity is a broad topic, one that could easily fill 15 volumes. So I've had to be selective with what I cover, knowing that masculinity is shaped by culture, upbringing, race, class, sexuality, identity, and plenty more. While I haven't been able to explore all of these in depth, please know that I strongly believe in people being able to live the life that they want to, full of respect, dignity, and humanity, regardless of their beliefs, gender identity, race, sexuality, or any other factor, and this book is for anyone exploring masculinity, whatever that means for you and whatever your personal definition is.

I know this is a highly contentious topic, and I've tried to be as genuinely balanced, fair, and inclusive as I can. I don't believe in attacking specific groups and I don't believe in blame, shame, or men versus women. This book isn't about elevating men, it's about elevating everyone. Any part or passage where there is a perceived feeling that I'm elevating men above others, or dismissing the experience of others, I promise this isn't my intention. You might not agree with everything I say, but my hope is that by the end of this book we can both agree that *something* needs to change.

This is a book for men and women. Men to better understand themselves and women to better understand the men in their lives. I've written about this through the lens of masculinity, but many of these things will apply to women too.

Finally, this book isn't a substitute for proper medical advice, and if you're facing a challenge, please do speak to a medical professional. I've signposted some brilliant organisations at the back.

Not everything in this book will be relevant to you, but I'd urge you to read it all. Often the things that happen to men do so because of lack of education, and so stigma continues to thrive. And who knows, there might be a single line, maybe even a single word, that gets you to sit up and think 'that's me' or 'that's what I think my partner is going through' and that's enough for me. That's what I was searching for all those years ago.

Part One

The Pressure Cooker

We tell our men to 'man up' and 'be a man about it', thinking we're doing them a service by toughening them. What we don't realise is that while they may stand taller on the outside, many on the inside are shrinking. Life experiences and emotions don't disappear simply because we want them to; they build quietly, a strain slowly rising.

It acts like a pressure cooker in men, the contents inside bubbling and boiling away. But you'd never leave a pressure cooker on indefinitely and unattended, else it's certain to reach a breaking point, even explode perhaps. Too much pressure applied to most things causes them to break. And while a nice and often-shared quote about 'diamonds being formed under immense pressure' perhaps provides a small slice of motivation, the reality is that humans aren't gemstones, and need to be able to recognise when pressure is healthy, and when it's harmful.

This pressure cooker isn't one that a man has invented himself, for himself. It's often been forced into his hands from the moment he was born with the weight of historic, biological, and societal baggage. But it's one he internalises and then continues to reinforce, sometimes knowingly, sometimes unknowingly.

Too often, what we assume to be biological, predetermined facts about men are in fact heavily influenced by cultural norms and historical beliefs, created at a moment in time by a select group of people to suit a certain agenda. We sometimes use what we assume to be predetermination as a lazy excuse to absolve ourselves of responsibility to enact change. The thing about pressure, and this is just as true with men, is that it *can* be released, healthily and safely. But we can only start to do this by understanding what's fuelling it.

1
The Biology of Masculinity

> *Masculine and feminine roles are not biologically fixed but socially constructed*
>
> *—Judith Butler, philosopher*

Human biology and physiology is an incredibly complex subject, and this isn't a book that's going to explore that in depth. But to understand what men are coming up against, it's critical that we have a top-level understanding of our biology. Too often we treat masculinity as a fixed concept, a singular blueprint that's rigid and immovable, suggesting there is only one path down which a man is fated to travel: he's either 'masculine' or he's not. This isn't the case.

Nature and Nurture

At the risk of sounding simplistic, there are clear distinctions in the biological makeups between males and females, with a string of genetic, structural, chemical, and hormonal differences. For example, men generally produce higher levels of testosterone while women tend to produce more estrogen. At a very basic level, some studies suggest that men's higher level of testosterone may be one reason they have an increased sex drive or engage in more risk-taking behaviour.

Our immunological structure can be another difference. Women tend to have stronger immune responses and so are better at fighting off infections, but this can also make them more susceptible to developing autoimmune conditions. Men, on the other hand, show stronger early immune responses, which can lead to more severe symptoms. This means that man flu really is a thing!

These are only two examples which provide a small snapshot, but I use them to highlight the fact that there *are* biological differences between males and females which may have influenced, to some degree, the ways in which we've drawn up our definitions of masculinity and femininity.

What muddies the water somewhat, and this is crucial, is that biology and sex isn't clear cut and binary, but instead operates more on a continuum. The differences discussed, among many others, exist as *averages*. If you took every single man and woman on the planet, you would, for example, find that *some* women will have higher levels of testosterone than *some* men. This is important to note because with this alone, assuming that all men fit into one singular box of what it means to 'be a man' is scientifically and biologically inaccurate.

And yet in some ways, this is how we've oversimplified our approach to masculinity and femininity, making them binary opposites rather than part of the same continuum. As humans, we like to use socially constructed labels to simplify things. It can help us understand concepts and bring order to our worldview. Sometimes this is useful, but sometimes labels can be incredibly reductive, limiting our understanding and perpetuating unnecessary stereotypes.

Labels can often develop into cultural generalisations and status quo, ones that we accept at face value without questioning them too much. And so we have created neat little boxes labelled 'masculine' and 'feminine', with separate, clearly defined characteristics being applied to each box. It's a binary process, where boys and men are placed into one box, girls and women into another, with both needing to fit the characteristics of their predefined label. Generally, they look like this:

Masculine:

- Strong
- Tough
- Resilient
- Independent
- Rational
- Protective
- Providing

Feminine:

- Emotional
- Sensitive
- Dependent
- Submissive
- Domestic
- Compassionate
- Caregiving/nurturing

We've already established that there are biological reasonings that have influenced how these traits may have been separated out, and science does help to tell part of the story. For example, where we know that men tend to be naturally stronger than women, it can make sense to see why 'strength' is labelled as 'masculine'. It might help to explain why more men get sent to wars or undertake more manual labour jobs. If men historically and primarily assumed the role of the hunter, it may explain why 'providing' is seen as a man's role.

But how well do these things hold up in the modern age? If men were the only providers, then why do women work too? If you were to lock the majority of men in a cage with a female kickboxer, I'd love to see them argue that strength isn't for women. This is an extreme example and one that's a little facetious, but if we can have even one instance of men or women exhibiting traits from the opposing 'box', then doesn't it make these neat opposing boxes a little confining?

And so the trouble arises when we can't see past this separation, ignoring all nuance and unique humanness, and forcing people into these boxes rather than seeing them on a continuum of averages. For example, how often do you hear a man called a 'girl' for showing emotion, or a muscular woman called 'butch'? Men are told to 'get back to work' and women are told to 'get back to the kitchen'.

We do this because if we see a man or woman exhibiting traits from the 'other' box, it's easier for us to label it, rather than just taking it for what it is: something that person enjoys doing or is a natural part of their personality or identity that might be different to our own. *Rather than understand them for who they are, we understand them through our bias, experience, and eyes.*

It can also give rise to harmful stereotypes about men where they can be seen as simple and lazy, stupid even; emotionally inept, angry, and nothing more than a 'brain below the belt'. These stereotypes and labels rob men of their agency to change or be anything other than what we assume they 'should be'. It's often the people that sit at the extremes of the continuum that we see, where we hear in the media about the most violent men, and so it becomes easy to associate men with violence and aggression, missing the fact that there are a great deal of men who sit much farther away from that on the continuum.

And sometimes we take these stereotypes as fact, perpetuating and sharing faulty life lessons and knowledge, men assuming they *must* operate a certain way in order to fit a certain perception. Take the 'alpha male', an idea originating from studies on wolves, which argued that there is an aggressive, dominant leader, one who battles for control of the group. Many human males today do what they can to align with being 'alpha', while rejecting 'beta' qualities of weakness, passivity, and submissiveness.

However, this study was conducted on captive wolves, not wild ones, and so the basis of the study was flawed as it wasn't natural behaviour being examined. The researchers and primatologists who inadvertently helped popularise the term 'alpha male', later stressed for a different interpretation of the phrase.

In studying other animal groups, such as wild wolves and chimpanzees, they found that many groups operated as family-led units who rose to leadership positions through a mix of both dominance *and* strategic and deliberate social bonding and empathy. They used this compassion to help maintain their position. Clearly, these animals have a good grip on the need to find flexibility between 'masculine' and 'feminine' traits, realising there is balance in both. This isn't to suggest that there is *no* existence of dominant males, but in many species the term 'alpha male' is overly simplistic and doesn't reflect the true nature of fluid hierarchies.

Everything discussed here serves as an interesting debate around masculine and feminine traits. Perhaps they're not as easily separated as we once believed, and perhaps what we're simply talking about are 'human' traits, a spectrum along which you will find averages and extremes, but not polar opposites between the sexes. Different countries and cultures recognise a different number of genders and, particularly in recent years, we've seen a growing visibility of people identifying as transgender, whose gender identity is different to the one they were assigned at birth. These are reminders that the boundaries between 'masculine' and 'feminine' aren't always as clear-cut as we often assume, and people experience them more fluidly and to different degrees. Whatever people's personal beliefs on gender roles and gender identities, the very fact that there is such fierce debate, a multitude of beliefs and viewpoints, and no singular agreement around the world, surely shows that this is all far less simple than we sometimes make it.

I highlight all of this to show that masculinity isn't a fixed concept, but rather something people experience differently. Averages, extremes, and continuums aside, the piece I'm most interested in is to what extent these traits are biological certainties, and what level of influence do human-made, cultural possibilities have? Is there a neatly painted line between them? What are men destined to be and do, and what are they moulded into? And, importantly, what can be changed?

I spoke with Dr Dan Nicolau, a mathematician, engineer, and physician at King's College London, about this very subject as I attempted to unpick the complicated boundaries around sex, gender, biology, and culture. For example, I put it to Dr Nicolau that maybe men take more risks not because of biology, but because of culturally enforced emotional suppression, where this spills out into riskier behaviours. 'Maybe it's our job to take more risks', he replied. It took me back a bit, but he continued:

in other animals, that's their job. Someone has to take risks, if we didn't we'd still be living in trees. And it may be that the cost for that is that you lose a lot of males to things like violence. So it could be baked into our DNA. I'm not saying we shouldn't combat it, and as a doctor it's my job to combat it, but it may be that there's a very strong evolutionary reason for it.

For example, there's a species of underground Somalian mole rat, who split the boys in half; builders, and then soldiers who protect the queen for life so, clearly, the naked mole rat genome has decided it's okay to sacrifice half the guys who become soldiers. And genetically we're not miles apart from mole rats, we're one evolutionary step away, so perhaps human males are more predisposed to this too.

While this example is illustrative, Dr Nicolau raises an interesting point: you only have to turn back the dial a hundred years or so where we *were* operating under remarkably similar circumstances. Generally, men went off to war and died, while protecting their women back home who nurtured the offspring. While there is a lot of nuance as to the reasons why, perhaps it's only our ability to engage in debates on equality and morality that has moved us further away from those underground Somalian mole rats.

Clearly, there isn't a neatly painted line between biology and social constructs and if I'd hoped to find one, I'd be disappointed. But the very fact that it *is* so murky shows why our rigid approach to masculinity is faulty.

Dr Louann Brizendine, in her book *The Male Brain,* wrote:

---

our understanding of essential gender differences is crucial because biology does not tell the whole story. While the distinction between boy and girl brains begins biologically, recent research shows that this is only the beginning. The brain's architecture is not set in stone at birth or by the end of childhood, as was once believed, but continues to change throughout life . . . our brains are more plastic and changeable than scientists believed a decade ago.[17]

What this tells us is that biology does lay strong groundwork for humans and creates natural predisposed leanings towards certain behaviours. We can't dismiss this, and it tells an important part of the story. However, much of this isn't fixed or binary, and it's often society, conditioning, and tradition that shapes us and builds the rest of the house on biology's foundations. This means that our gender identity and roles are much more flexible and fluid. Judith Butler, an American philosopher and gender studies scholar and author of the book, *Gender Trouble,* argues that masculine and feminine roles are not biologically fixed but socially constructed.[18]

The piece that I'm most concerned with is emotional expression in men or, rather, the lack of it. Emotional *suppression* seems to be a bedrock of traditional masculinity, and one which I believe plays a huge role in many of the devastating statistics around men. We tell men to be strong, to be resilient, to 'man up' and to avoid vulnerability. So how much of the trait 'emotional suppression' is a biological certainty, and how much of it is cultural and human-made?

Bottled Up: Emotional Suppression Versus Emotional Expression

Neurologically, studies and science have shown that there is little evidence to suggest that men are any less emotional than women,[19] and that both women *and* men experience emotions intensely. The differences between men and women tend to lie in the expression of these emotions, not the capacity to experience them.

There's evidence to show that the positive emotional expression gap between boys and girls is much smaller at a younger age, and this gap widens as children grow,[20] with it seeming to get stamped out of boys around puberty, due to a mixture of hormones *and* social conditioning. But still, both have similar emotional processing systems within the brain and feel the same emotions. In its simplest terms, what this means is that our insistence for men to reject their emotions is telling them to reject a normal part of their human experience.

And this is where we often go wrong with masculinity and men. We tell men to control their emotions and to be more 'stoic', but the modern use of stoicism in popular culture seems to have been bent out of shape to fit more traditional masculine ideals.

The original philosophy of Stoicism, founded in roughly 300 BCE was built on emotional *control* as a bedrock, not suppression. Suppression is to ignore something, to push it to one side, down somewhere deep to never be explored. But *control* is something entirely different; in order to control something, we have to understand it, and have the mental tools and models to take an appropriate response. Stoicism does value calmness and composure, but not at the expense of feeling, rather as the destination to arrive at only by understanding our feelings. To know what an incredible meal tastes like, we have to have experienced a bad one. To understand true joy, we need an understanding of grief or suffering.

Crying becomes the ultimate act which sits in the crosshairs of those who value rigid traditional masculine values. At its most basic level, crying is a natural human response. It's a human capability, not a sex-specific one, and if men had no need for crying at all, it's highly likely it would have been stamped out of us from an evolutionary standpoint. It's actually good for us, with evidence showing it acts like a natural painkiller and mood booster to the body, and some researchers argue that it's crucial for our social and moral functioning.[21]

There is some suggestion that differing levels of hormones between the sexes may influence the expression of emotions, and this may be evolutionary. For example, one argument is that perhaps men who, primarily assumed the role of hunters, needed better emotional control when out in the wild. But this is more speculative than scientific.

And, importantly, our hormones don't inhibit our capacity to *feel* these emotions, instead impacting intensity, thresholds, and expression. For example, it's thought that testosterone doesn't cause emotional suppression itself, but modulates responses, particularly influenced by the environment and social situation. In his research on crying, most notably his work *Why Only Humans Weep*, Ad Vingerhoets argues that our expression of crying can be heavily influenced by social norms and learnt behaviours, which often dictate frequency and appropriateness of the act.[22]

As we have already examined, much of the case with 'masculine' and 'feminine' traits can be explained through biology, but this alone doesn't tell the whole story. It may set thresholds and foundations, but these are often shaped by human-made cultural conditioning, and influenced by our environment into a learned and taught behaviour. And this is just the same with emotional suppression, where boys and men are conditioned out of expression and are told 'that's the way you're meant to be'.

The biggest tragedy for me is that our emotions are there to help us feel the things we experience in life. When we lose someone, we grieve and cry because we cared, because we loved. In some ways, the harder we grieve, the more we loved. And so crying can be considered an act of love, and to suppress that is to suppress the meaning that someone or something held in your life.

Men have the capacity to both show and feel compassion, to love, to have purpose and to feel things just as deeply and strongly as their female counterparts. But their inner struggle, passion, desire, ability to feel empathy, and so on, is often lost and squashed down by the weight of social constructs and stereotypes which we falsely label as the biological natural order to things.

What we fail to see is that emotions, just like crying, are neither 'good' nor 'bad', they're simply sources of information, a way for our bodies to process things. Humans have labelled them positively and negatively, missing the valuable role that they play for humans, regardless of gender. They act as our internal compass, and to disregard them is like going on a thousand-mile road trip and throwing away your map.

Men become desperate to dissociate from emotions they perceive as weak and to sweep their problems under a rug. What most don't realise is that this acts like a pressure cooker, slowly building, that pressure having to release eventually, as steam hisses out of the cracks and nuts and bolts begin to ping off.

The Body Keeps the Score, a groundbreaking book from author Bessel van der Kolk, shows how memories, experiences, and emotions, when not properly processed, can leave lasting imprints on both the brain and the body.[23] If we don't process and resolve things, they don't disappear. They store and build. Cultural norms might tell you that pushing your problems to one side will solve them, but you can bet your body is keeping score of everything, silently, subtly. Carl Jung, the Swiss psychotherapist, famously said 'what you resist, not only persists, but will grow in size'.

If we don't release this pressure safely and in a healthy way, then it will find its own way of coming out. It's not a leap to suggest that this pressure comes out into many of the devastating health and life issues we see with men: addiction, homelessness, violence, premature deaths from things like cancer and cardiovascular disease due to avoidance of health-care pathways, or suicides even.

Men have been taught for so long to not turn inward and to reject their natural, biological emotions. In short, it's often not biology killing men, it's pride and emotional suppression, masks that have been strapped onto them. We tell men to 'man up', often not realising that all we're doing is bringing them down.

Someone that I spoke to for this book told me that their brother has lost five best friends to suicide. *Five.* But he has never spoken about it, and when she tries to get him to talk about it, he shuts down and withdraws. He has one best friend left, who's in and out of hospital with substance abuse. She said that 'he just sees it as part of life. He's absolute tunnel vision, he won't talk about it. It's just the norm'.

The emotion that many men do seem most comfortable with is anger. Why? There are biological reasons for this. For example, higher testosterone levels in boys can influence how they respond to a perceived threat or challenge, although it doesn't cause violence in and of itself. Men may like how anger feels, as their muscles tighten and toughen, versus anxiety or crying where we feel physically more vulnerable. For other men, it's the emotion they most understand or know, and where other emotions can feel alien, anger may bring a sense of safety and comfort.

Many tend to agree that boys are taught from a young age to suppress their emotions of sadness and vulnerability, whereas strength, on the other hand, equals social status. And so the one emotion they may be taught to express is anger. Is it any surprise that once boys grow into men, many of them end up in pointless brawls after a few beers at the pub? Most believe that strong communication comes from the fist, primal and animalistic, not the mouth.

A group of people I knew back home discovered this the hard way. Two best friends got into a scrap over nothing after a night at the pub. One threw a punch, and his best mate fell to the curb, cracked his head and died instantly. The one who threw the punch ended up with a prison sentence for manslaughter. A friendship group ripped apart in an instant, all because of one punch. All because those boys who became men had been taught it was better to settle their differences with aggression and anger, rather than communication.

We see this play out in the world of sports. This is how a lot of men connect, it may remind them of their childhood, it's how many bond with their fathers, and it leans into traditional masculine values of strength, physicality, and competition. Where many men perhaps are unable to process and voice emotions, I believe that sport is a vehicle for this.

For anybody saying men can't do emotion, you only have to see men engaging with sports to know this isn't true. They'll cry, shout, scream, hug. . . you name it. But this is likely because it's become culturally accepted for men to show emotion in these places, while it isn't elsewhere.

And perhaps it's this pent-up nature of emotion that can see an overly tribalistic, angry nature arise in sports. Opposing sets of fans threatening each other, fighting each other, for no other reason than simply supporting a different team. Homophobic and racist chants around the crowds, the raucous mob mentality taking over. There's even a link between sports teams losing and an increase in domestic abuse.

Some will say 'this is just what men do'. But I come back to the point that the brain is mouldable. I've never thrown a punch in my life because I've been taught that violence and aggression isn't the solution to problems. This behaviour is learnt and socialised, not ingrained in us, even if we may be more predisposed to it. Men may have a more natural leaning towards aggression or anger, and we have to learn this is something we need to help men to channel, regulate, and sometimes even celebrate, otherwise it can have nasty, potentially violent, consequences.

The trouble, as I see it, is that we too often conflate biological certainties with human-made cultural constructs and male tradition, and often don't have or apply the right level of education, critical thinking or awareness to be able to distinguish the two. We make 'man' or 'woman' into two opposing, binary fields, trying to neatly squeeze each and every human into one. But it's clear that much of what we assume to be a predetermined certainty often isn't this black and white and the reality is that the human experience is much more flexible than we allow it to be. Our insistence on putting things into two neat boxes is no more dangerous for men than with culturally conditioned emotional suppression.

So this is what is helpful to understand about men and vulnerability if we want to start to work back some of the terrible statistics around men. A path forward is in helping men to understand that humanity isn't fixed and to understand the range of emotions that they can experience. To understand that these emotions are natural human responses and can be channelled into positive pursuits. To help men understand why these emotions present themselves, which situations trigger what for them, and give them better language and vocabulary in describing them. All to help them to overcome the shame, fear, and stigma that will be puppeteering their bodies and their emotions. Only *then* will we get men to talk more openly. Much easier said than done, of course. But that's what we're up against.

Professor Paul Gilbert OBE, a clinical psychologist and founder of Compassion-Focused Therapy (CFT), has a career in psychology spanning over 50 years and has been cited almost 80,000 times. So he knows more about human emotions and the brain than most! There was a line he said to me that summarised the entire challenge we face with masculinity. One of his clients, a military veteran, saw a close friend die after stepping on a landmine. He suppressed the emotion of that experience for years, eventually telling Professor Gilbert in one of their sessions, 'I've always had the courage to die, but never to cry'.

Key Summary

- **Nothing is absolute:** There are biological differences between sexes which explain certain behaviours, but these exist as averages, not absolutes. Biology is complex, and there are many factors at play, but what we do know is that biology alone doesn't tell the entire story and social conditioning plays a huge role.

- **Not so distinctive:** There is less obvious distinction between 'masculine' and 'feminine' traits than we like to think, with science showing men can feel emotions just as intensely as women.
- **Neither 'good' nor 'bad':** Emotions are natural human responses and information to the body. Rejecting these simply stores them in the body, which builds like a pressure cooker.

2
The History of Masculinity

Men have been absolutely and utterly conned by history

—*Professor Paul Gilbert OBE, psychologist*

We tend to have a wonderful habit of looking back only a few decades when informing our present. Knowing that masculinity isn't a fixed concept, how have perceptions of it changed over time? Are we using centuries and millennia to inform our thinking, or only decades? Even less, perhaps?

When we talk about the 'history of man', we're often referring to humanity as a whole, 'mankind'. Depending on how you want to look at it, this phrasing could inform why so much of our history focuses specifically on the stories of men, with women often playing a side character to the acts of good or bad that men have done throughout our relatively short lifespan in the universe.

History books and lessons tend to focus on wars and conflicts, generally caused by men and involving men – Hitler and Churchill, Stalin and Roosevelt, Alexander the Great, Julius Caesar. The dropping of the nuclear bombs on Japan. Or they focus on leaders and creators, inventors like Thomas Edison and Alexander Bell. I even did an entire university module on Robin Hood, a man for whom no definitive proof exists that he was even real.

Women felt like the supporting cast to these men. Perhaps being a man, I was biased to only being interested in learning about other men, but my most vivid memory of women throughout history was seeing them on propaganda posters, ushering their husbands off to war while they stayed home, arms around the children. Is this a fair reflection of women's role throughout history or have men always been the ones at the forefront, the strong leaders, the noble providers?

We rightly celebrate the achievements of the male codebreaker Alan Turing, now immortalised in the Hollywood film *The Imitation Game*. But I don't remember learning that, at its peak, around 75% of the employees at Bletchley Park were women, sitting in a range of crucial roles, and the sheer scale of women's involvement is often overlooked. Or about Elizabeth Friedman, dubbed 'the Mother of Cryptology', much of whose work was often attributed to men, sometimes intentionally. Perhaps the most famous women I remember learning about during my school years were Rosa Parks and the Suffragettes, but we learnt about them through their acts of defiance against a system created by men. How often do we learn about women for their own acts of invention, philosophy, or exploration?

Granted, women were given less chances to do these things under patriarchal systems, and so there may be fewer stories. But that in itself exposes the problem of troublesome cultural beliefs, policies, and norms throughout our past.

There's a phrase, sometimes attributed to Winston Churchill, that says 'history is written by the victors'. But I would add to that: 'history is written by those in power', and more often than not, those in power have been men, and they have shaped the narrative. But not all men have been in power, and it's both men and women that have been unduly affected by the prevailing narrative.

There have been fairly clear gender roles throughout history, at least in Western history. While there are caveats based on class, location, and time period, men generally dominated public and political life in the ancient periods, holding roles as priests, scribes, and merchants, while women were often consigned to domestic duties, child-rearing, and roles of sub-ordination. That divide persisted with male roles evolving to landowners, knights, and clergymen, while women often had limited legal status, tied to male guardianship. Men were often celebrated as multi-talented, while women weren't seen as thinkers or weren't always properly acknowledged for their contributions. The waves of feminism through the nine-teenth, twentieth and twenty-first centuries have pushed back on this inequality, but despite many wins, it's clear that these gender roles have persisted into boardrooms and politi-cal offices.

As with our knowledge on predetermined biological traits, sometimes our knowledge on history and our predetermined gender roles can be built on shaky ground too. We believe that these gender roles have persisted because men are the 'hunters' and women are the 'gatherers'. We tell ourselves men *should* be at the forefront in today's society because that has always been their role, and they're the 'natural' leaders. However, recent archaeological findings have found that this is not as clear-cut as previously thought, with many women playing a much greater role in hunting. One article, titled 'The Myth of Man the Hunter', which compiled data from 63 different foraging societies around the globe, found that 79% of them had documentation on women hunting.[24] This is only one example, but where else have we let historical myths inform our present-day reality?

Given so much of our history often places men at the centre, sometimes at the expense of women and sometimes based on myth, I began to ask myself; what did I learn about masculinity, if anything, and was it accurate?

In truth there is a gaping hole in my perception and education of men in this regard. I learnt little behind the titles, royalties and leadership. The struggles they faced, the emotional burdens they carried, the grief and loss they suffered. What they talked about with their friends at the pub, tavern, or tabernas. I remember learning about Churchill's depression, what he referred to as his 'black dog', but it was wrapped up in commentary of wartime leadership and resilience, rather than a deep dissection of mental health struggle itself.

We've often been presented with a two-dimensional view of people throughout history, like a filtered social media page – which is to be expected when some lived so long ago – but we've often always focused on the external rather than the internal. When the only stories we get served up are those of strength, honour, and glorious death, is it any wonder that we believe these things mark the true measure of a man?

Perhaps it's because as a society, these are generally the things we value with masculinity. Power, strength, and authority. There's little room for heroic, noble stories of empathy, compassion, and humanness.

Stories of struggle within our present are often treated as the punchline to a joke or a tabloid scoop. Although things are slowly changing in this regard, we see how gossip, banter, and paparazzi treat those struggling, and it reminds us that this struggle doesn't belong in our present, much like it doesn't belong in the history books.

Hollywood *does* give us stories of emotional men, but it's often wrapped around computer-generated images (CGI), battles, and muscles. Maximus Decimus Meridius's grief in *Gladiator* is powerful, but would the film have done so well if it wasn't about a fight to the death?

In my interview with Professor Paul Gilbert OBE, the part that struck me most was when he said:

Men have been absolutely and utterly conned by history. We developed empires run by elites, and these elites go to war with each other. The only way you're going to get to go to war is if you have males who prepare to sacrifice themselves. The only way you're going to do that is to get males to deny that they've got vulnerabilities or that they're frightened.

We also know that certainly in the early days, a lot of the wars, like with the Vikings, they're all high on drugs or pissed out of their brains because it was so scary for so many of them, but you don't see that in Hollywood.

So we've been absolutely conned by the elites to have this idea of toughness so that we never acknowledge our pain, which allows us to be good fighters. But actually, you know, we're human beings. And the greatest courage comes from not only recognising that we're human, but recognising our vulnerabilities. Instead, it has been forced onto men that they aren't allowed to acknowledge the reality of the sufferings in life.

It was often those in power, of course, who also decided that women didn't need the vote, segregated people because of their race, conducted witch trials, and chemically castrated people for being gay. What came before, and what persists now, didn't always come because it was right – in many cases it came because it suited the agenda of a small group of people.

The narrative that's been shaped, is it one that still serves us? Well, considering that the world seems to be eternally at war, despite being taught of its horror in schools, I'm not sure we're learning our lessons. It seems to me that our history can restrict and minimise us. It *should* be there to teach us and guide us, and while it has the power to liberate, often it's used to shame men into submission and silence.

We're told that our grandfathers had it tougher during world wars, blackouts, and rationing, and we're asked what right do we have to feel sad in the face of those who came before, suffering such unimaginable turmoil? But we're talking about a time when emotional suppression was even more rife, and the absence of them talking about their pain doesn't mean they didn't suffer. This is not to dismiss or discredit the strong wartime resilience that this generation displayed, but it's also important not to play 'whataboutism' with someone's experiences, as you will *always* be able to find someone who has it 'worse' than you, and that doesn't invalidate your pain.

We know these history books can sometimes give us a narrow view, and when it comes to things like mental health, so much of our thinking and advancement is so new and so recent, that if we let ourselves be guided in this by history alone, we're sure to stray off path and get lost.

Are there any examples of a different narrative throughout history, one that also shows the value of vulnerability and compassion alongside war and power? Because the truth is, whether it's 2025, 1954 or 100 BCE, men will have loved, laughed, lost, wept, fought, raged, and experienced every other emotion under the sun.

Homer's epic *Iliad* and *The Odyssey*, written around the late eighth or early seventh BCE, featured strong heroes who fought and went to battle, but cried, and cried often. Professor Gilbert told me 'indeed, the very idea of Greek tragedies at the time have their clue in the name; they're tragic. They were designed to have audiences come together and experience sorrow and grief, and to cry together, to share that experience'.

There was also the compassionate Good Samaritan in the Bible, or the wise Buddha, alive sometime between the sixth and fourth centuries BCE, whose teachings said that acknowledgement of suffering and pain is a critical step in the path to enlightenment. Confucius, a philosopher, lived in a patriarchal Chinese society, meaning most of his students were likely men, and his teachings were embedded with the need for compassion and emotional regulation.

These are only a snapshot, and there are many more examples throughout texts and cultures. But these alone are illustrative enough of the point that, clearly, the way that we view men, mental health, and masculinity as a whole has changed throughout history and our concept of masculinity isn't as rigid as we like to make it. Recent history often paints us with one view on men, one that is based on valour and bravery, but it's clear that it's only one perception we've been served. While a focus on strength and emotional suppression may have suited elites throughout our history who needed to win wars, who is it serving now? And, more importantly, who gets to write the next chapter of our history?

Key Summary

- **Selective stories:** Our history books tend to lean towards stories that favour the 'traditional' view of masculinity. We are also painted one image which tends to negate the role of women.
- **Narrow education:** We learn little, if anything, about compassion, empathy, vulnerability, and other traits that make us human, particularly as these things didn't suit the agenda of the elites throughout history.
- **Historical flexibility:** Rolling back the clock a few hundred years, we can see that there *have* been more balanced views towards men and emotion, and so what is set now hasn't always been so.

3
The Present-Day Cost of Emotional Suppression

*Women outlive men everywhere in the world . . . of the 40 lead-
ing causes of death, 33 causes contribute more to reduced life
expectancy in men than women*

—*World Health Organisation*

We know that our biological and historical perception of masculinity is far less binary than we like to make it. Emotional suppression has served a small group throughout time, and it's become a fixed part of rigid masculine norms.

The present-day impact of this for men isn't a pretty one. As I write this, statistically the thing most likely to kill me is . . . myself. Suicide is one of the leading global causes of young male death, particularly in the age group 15–29,[25] and it's the biggest killer of men in the UK under the age of 50.[26]

Our response to this growing epidemic is generally to tell men to talk, often missing the fact that the thing that has led them there in the first place is a culturally conditioned route of emotional silence and suppression, or simply, not talking.

It has always broken my heart that all the wonderful things humans are capable of, all the advancements we make in so many areas of society, and we're still not able to create a world that hundreds of thousands of people want to stay within.

This is one lagging indicator of that pressure cooker building to an unbearable, unmanageable level, and the saddest part is that suicides are preventable, with the right, timely, evidence-based interventions.

The stats around suicide are the most poignant in highlighting the challenge that we're facing with masculinity. But, sadly, they represent only the tip of a rather ugly iceberg. Because there is consistent evidence across a huge range of areas which shows how men are facing poorer outcomes in many key areas.

As was already highlighted in the introduction to this book, men are more likely to have substance addictions, to be homeless, and to be both the perpetrator and victim of homicides. There are also concerning patterns emerging with men's health, where they're generally more likely to die from cancer, cardiovascular disease, respiratory disease, death in the workplace or at war. On average they have a three- to four-year shorter lifespan than women, and they're significantly more likely to have misconceptions around mental health *and* avoid seeking help for mental health.[27]

It's easy to find any study to suit an argument, and there are often a lot of nuances to them. For example, after a UK government callout in 2022 for members of the public to give feedback towards a new 10-year mental health plan, only around

19% of respondents were male.[28] It can make it hard to build the right picture when the source might not always be accurate.

Statistics will vary depending on geographical location, demographic, socio-economic background, and a host of other variables. Demographics themselves as a whole can be a challenging way to break up groups, as one delightful study from BBH Labs found that generations actually have less in common with each other than Orangina drinkers, daily nut eaters, people who floss, and fans of crosswords.[29] What this means is that trying to box in masculinity and life experience by age alone isn't always effective.

And the reasons for these health and life challenges will never be clear-cut; there are a multitude of factors at play, including things like access to healthcare. So this isn't to say that emotional suppression and cultural attitudes alone are the chief perpetrators, but they're certainly playing their part.

Statistics themselves can be hard to relate to – nothing more than numbers on a page, gathering dust in an Excel sheet. I was almost one of these statistics myself. I've lost people and know plenty who have lost others who *are* part of these statistics already. Forever resigned to be a number in a government database, a name on a gravestone. But for those of us who carry the grief with us, a question will always linger of 'what if we'd caught something earlier?'

So instead of focusing on statistics, I want you to stop for a moment and focus on a man in your life, someone important to you. A father, brother, son, partner, yourself even. I want you to put everything you know and believe about masculinity to one side, and to simply focus on how it feels, *truly* feels, to think of them going before their time. What if tomorrow was your last day, when it didn't have to be, taken not by fate, but by outdated cultural tradition?

It's depressing, I know, but I do believe it's important that we sit with that discomfort. We often avoid the uncomfortable and bury our heads in the sand, but it's this very approach that costs men their lives. However, and this is the point I want to stress the most, we *can* do something about it. This doesn't have to be inevitable and many of these things are preventable.

A large number of studies point to perceptions of masculinity being a core driver in poor men's health and psychological factors. The data isn't completely well understood, but the evidence suggests that beliefs and lifestyle behaviours, influenced by traditional masculine traits, lead to an underutilisation of health services or more risk-taking behaviours like substance misuse, violence and aggression, or reckless driving.[30]

In short, in men's quest to adhere to the masculinity they've been taught is 'right', often that quest is leading them to a shorter lifespan. Many of the things I've covered aren't things wildly out of our control, biological certainties over which we have no power. Often it's happening because of *us*, because of inaction, misguided beliefs, and social conditioning.

I very much doubt that a coroner has ever ruled the cause of a man's death as 'didn't man up enough'. It's sometimes that very approach that has landed him on a coroner's table, before his time. What happens out in public, in pubs, on social media, in media tabloids, and so on, impacts men in private. Sometimes at the cost of their lives.

The conversation about masculinity might feel awkward. We might not want to have it. But the facts present a compelling picture of why it's one we can't ignore. These statistics are the lagging indicators of what's happening to men downstream. Importantly, it's well within our power to go upstream and stop men falling in.

Key Summary

- **Health impacts on men:** Across a range of areas, from physical health to mental health, educational prospects to crime, addictive behaviours to life expectancy, men consistently track worse than women.
- **The need for flexible masculinity:** Some studies point to the fact that an over-adherence to 'traditional masculine' values, including emotional suppression, is leading to many of these negative outcomes.
- **Time to act:** Many male deaths are premature and preventable.

Summary to Part One

Many of our history books often present one narrow view of men and the line between fixed biology and cultural conditioning is blurry at best, with it being more fluid than we often acknowledge. And it's having real-world consequences for our men today. But perhaps nothing has been more damaging to men than the emotional suppression we have taught them.

While there is evidence to suggest that biological differences *may* set the groundwork for this, the rest of the structure is built through cultural norms, reinforced by societal fallacies and myths.

We value this emotional suppression as a key traditional masculine trait. We tell men to ignore their natural emotions, for the unemotional man is the correct one, the one who is strong, powerful, in control. We rarely hear stories of emotional men throughout history, so why would we value them in our present?

We're so certain that this is the natural order to things, a path so well-travelled, that rarely does anyone stop to check the map and ask 'are we lost?' But all the while, a pressure cooker builds, slowly and silently. And where we value silence, suffering begins to thrive, sometimes with tragic consequences.

Part Two

When the Pressure Breaks

Much of the human experience happens on the surface. It's perceptible and physical. What we see is what we get. And so when the men in our lives show up loud, boisterous, and jovial, we take that at face value. Where many assume men are emotionally incompetent, what they miss is that often they're wearing a mask, one that has sometimes been forcibly strapped onto them from a young age, so young that they don't even *know* they're wearing one.

Meanwhile, under the surface, any emotions, troubles, or struggles are left simmering on a low heat, fuelled by the weight of historic, biological, and societal baggage that is keeping a lid firmly shut on vulnerability. Eventually, that pressure reaches breaking point and causes a number of behaviours which can be seen as unhealthy.

There are six key behaviours where I believe we're seeing this happen:

1. Neglecting health
2. Addictions

3. Disconnection and displacement
4. A need to perform
5. Carrying of shame
6. Avoiding trauma and wounds

We know what's happening downstream, the lagging indicators: homelessness, addictions, violence, crime, premature death, and suicide. We see the statistics. We see the media headlines. But rarely do we get to see the *real* people behind the stories and the studies.

There are lots of books and articles that look at general statistics and studies conducted over decades or the compiling of data which can be easy to disassociate from. And these things have great value. But I've taken a different approach and focused on individual stories and experiences.

Individuals who, so desperate to fit into the box of 'traditional masculinity', pushed away their emotions and struggles into the shadows until their pressure cooker exploded, turning into addictions, pain and years of life missed. Unspoken truths, hidden taboos, stigmatised experiences. Things that led to a life less fulfilled and almost a shorter one. Men from all walks of life with different classes, upbringings, sexualities, countries, and – importantly – experiences.

Stories are one of the most powerful tools we have and I believe they'll highlight *why* a rigid approach to masculinity isn't helping our men, it's harming them.

These breaking points aren't always clear-cut and linear. Some people might experience several. One may have caused another. Some we may be aware of, some it may be the first time we've heard of it. We can't always paint a neat line from A to B on how something started and what's going to come next.

This isn't an exhaustive list, but is illustrative of a growing problem. Not everything will relate to you, but I'd urge you to read them all. Often it's lack of knowledge that keeps conversations hidden in the shadows.

When I was at my lowest, I felt like I was the only person in the world facing the things that I did, and I carried around my shame like a spectre haunting me in every interaction. It wasn't governmental statistics and white papers I sought solace in, it was real stories from real people. This was where I found my hope and, most importantly, my understanding. Because we can't fix something until we understand what the problem is. By having these conversations, we can begin to take the masks off of our men and ourselves.

4

Breaking Point #1:
The Hidden Cost
to Health Avoidance

Men are caught in a dangerous Venn diagram of shame, suppression, and poor education. The resulting centre of that diagram is a neglection of health, both body and mind, which is having devastating consequences.

Movember has found that in the UK, roughly 15 men die prematurely every single hour.[31] As I write this, that's at least 106,000 men who will die prematurely before this book is published, and that's only in one country. These deaths aren't biological certainties, they're often preventable, treatable, and avoidable.

We can't eliminate premature death entirely, but what we *do* have control over are some of the factors that are causing it. One of these is emotional suppression. It's not a leap to say that strict adherence to traditional masculinity, therefore, is killing men.

I spoke to several doctors and professors to ask: why are men ignoring their health and how much of that comes down to the stories they've been told about being a man?

When Men Ignore Their Bodies

If our bodies are cars, then women go for regular MOTs. Men don't.

—Dr Tim Woodman, Medical Director for Policy and Cancer Services at Bupa UK Insurance

Physiologically and biologically there are many areas that differ between sexes, but we share the experience of our bodies changing as we grow older. Both sexes face things like puberty, growth spurts, and the awkwardness of unplanned erections or unexpected menstrual bleeding. These things are a natural part of growing older, as are aches, pains, and illnesses.

And yet despite these shared experiences, it's well documented that females are much more likely to use healthcare pathways than their male counterparts.[32] I knew that the mask of masculinity was no doubt playing a part, and I explored this deeper with Dr Naveen Puri, Medical Director for Bupa UK Insurance and who has over 20 years' experience as a GP. He told me:

Girls are medicalised from a very young age, in that they develop a familiarity with medical settings and healthcare. In the UK, we have national screening programmes, but they're mostly for women who from their early 20s are invited every few years to go to their GP surgery to have a cervical test to screen for cervical cancer. Even from a much younger age, they're immediately aware of their bodily functions, with some girls as young as nine starting to have menstrual bleeds, or periods. They may be getting support from a GP, and they're likely speaking to their mums or carers or teachers about it too and getting a living education on things like how to use sanitary products or how to stem the flow of blood.

So in some ways, girls may quickly become used to their bodies, their health, and speaking about it. But do boys get this same education? Rarely. In the UK, the first screening programmes which men can access aren't until much later in life, around the age of 40. And yet the highest risk age group for testicular cancer is between 18 and 34,[33] so it does beg the question why men aren't screened earlier, and whether there are systemic issues that aren't helping men and may reinforce the perception in them that they shouldn't be engaging in healthcare services.

And where girls may be having conversations with their mothers about their bodies, are boys doing the same with their fathers on things like erections? Naveen continued, 'I once had to console a boy who came to me because he'd suddenly ejaculated for the first time and he thought his penis was broken! Which shows that boys aren't being taught about how their bodies work, or familiarised with medical settings where they could safely ask questions about their bodies in a way that they should'.

'What's the impact of this lack of education for boys?' I asked Naveen.

Sadly, it's far-reaching. If we take sex and sexual function as an example, their education comes from places like the school playground, through masculine banter or porn. Sex becomes associated with something that's a little bit taboo and a little bit shameful. And we see where this develops later in life; at the extremes we see men who aren't respectful of women during sex; unhealthy use of pornography or even porn addiction; issues like erectile dysfunction and performance anxiety. They develop body dysmorphia or confidence issues from the unrealistic images they see on porn. All because boys and men haven't had enough comfortable conversations around sex and sexual function.

And this is the critical challenge with our health. Poor education in our youth gets combined with shame, embarrassment, and emotional suppression, at a time when our brains are developing the most, and can quite easily come back to haunt us later in life.

As I was researching for this book, I came across one health-related term I hadn't heard before, the 'andropause' – the gradual decline in testosterone levels in men that starts around the age of 30–40. It is sometimes unhelpfully referred to as 'the male menopause', but these comparisons are simplistic and incorrect. Menopause involves a much more sudden and rapid hormonal shift, while for men, their testosterone declines gradually, at the rate of about 1% per year. And so for most men, it's simply a natural part of ageing that doesn't typically require medical tests or treatment. That being said, it can still coincide with a number of emotional, physical, and sexual effects in men such as erectile dysfunction, muscle loss, depression, and decreased motivation – all things which feel like the antithesis to much of the traditional view of masculinity.

While these male hormone changes don't always cause these symptoms, and aren't always responsible if symptoms are present, we can see the challenge that some men may face where their bodies go through a hormonal change, one they may not be aware of, and one that can have an impact on a range of areas that affects their sense of masculinity.

Where is this being taught to men? It certainly wasn't a part of my education. Knowing I'd never heard of the andropause until I started my research for this book, I conducted an (admittedly small) survey among people in my circle, and asked whether they were aware men may face hormonal-related challenges as they grow older. More than one person laughed while they waited for the punchline to what they assumed was a joke! Not a single person had heard of the andropause. If we treat these male hormone changes as a joke, then what else have we been trained to dismiss?

Dr Tim Woodman, Medical Director for Policy and Cancer Services at Bupa UK Insurance, told me that, sadly, when a woman comes to his GP surgery, he thinks little of it. But when a man walks in, it's an immediate alarm bell, because it usually means something has become serious and has gone past preventative.

While Dr Ravi Lukha, Medical Director for Bupa UK Insurance, told me that the reality of this for a lot of men means that they're having to go to A&E to treat things that could have been prevented earlier in a GP surgery. 'The worst place someone can present themselves with something like cancer is at A&E. Because if the symptoms have got bad enough that you have to go to A&E . . . it can often be too late'.

The fact that even our doctors and GPs are alarmed when a man steps into their surgeries speaks volumes about the perception that is held around men and health – that they do too little, too late, and don't talk about it enough.

Traditional masculinity and emotional suppression tells us that seeking support for our health is weak. That there's 'nothing wrong' and if we push it to one side, it'll go away. And the consequences of this are deeply ingrained and hard to undo.

Dr Tim Woodman himself is testament to this. He's been a medical doctor for over 40 years, with in-depth experience of cancer. He would know better than most people how to spot the signs of cancer and how to prevent it. But even he ignored warning symptoms:

> *I stuck my head in the sand and basically thought it's nothing, it'll pass. It didn't, and it was my wife who said you really need to get this sorted. I went to the doctors and got told I had advanced prostate cancer, and it was too late for any local treatment by this point. So we had to chuck the kitchen sink at it over the course of about fifteen months, and that itself has come with a huge range of impacts on my masculinity!*

Thankfully, Tim's cancer was caught, in large part due to his wife who pushed him to get treatment. But I had to ask him why, why did he delay going? And why do so many men follow this pattern? 'If our bodies are cars, then women go in for regular MOTs. Men don't. They wait until the car is broken and has to be written off before doing anything about it'.

The fact that a doctor with four decades of experience ignored his own symptoms highlights the gravity of the challenge facing men. All human bodies change and healthcare pathways are open to all. It's often a belief and tradition that's stopping men seeking the help that they might need. Rigid masculine traditions have quietly shaped this behaviour for many decades.

> **Reflection**
>
> *Do you feel like a part of your identity gets challenged when you think about needing support with your health? Where do those beliefs come from?*

When the Mind Is Left Behind

Women seek help, men die

—Jules Angst and Celile Ernst, psychiatrists

It's not only the physical where the breaking point of emotional suppression is making men neglect their health, but the mental too. I remember hearing stories from my youth of adults suffering with mental health issues, even taking their own lives. My vivid memory is one of gratitude that I didn't have 'any of that mental health stuff'. I packed my bags for school, my physical education kit in tow, constantly reminded just how important it was to maintain our physical health. School social status was even decided based on who could best kick a ball around the playground.

But mental health? That certainly wasn't something any of us learnt about. It didn't even cross my mind that I *needed* to learn about it. Nobody ever explicitly taught me that I had mental health; I knew that I had a brain, but to me that was just the physical.

I had to suffer a mental health crisis to get the education I needed, and sadly I know there will be plenty of people still out there that don't know they have mental health. I'm not talking about mental ill health, I'm talking purely about the health of our mind, which has ups *and* downs.

I still to this day hear people say 'I suffered with mental health' when referring to a mental health issue, rather than 'I suffered with mental *ill* health'. It's a critical distinction. We don't say 'I suffered with physical health', which as a statement, makes no sense. We say 'I suffered with *poor* physical health'.

We're also often very specific with our language when it comes to physical health and say things like 'I broke my leg playing football and now need to be in a cast for five months'. But with mental health, everything gets lumped together, good and bad, and with very limited vocabulary.

While we *have* made great progress on mental health in general in recent years, there hasn't been the same level of progress in the niche of men's mental health. Many men still do whatever they can to disassociate themselves from mental health and the heavy baggage that it comes with. And I believe it's clear and simple to see why.

Traditional masculinity and mental health repel like opposing magnets. Dr Ravi Lukha and I spoke about this in depth, and he said that the added complexity of mental health is something that many men struggle to process and work through.

For men, many often think simply like this: A, I twisted my knee, B, my knee is in pain, C, let me see if I can fix it, which might include a bit of a surgery, and I'll be better in a few months. It's a very clear, linear journey without any stigma. In fact, it's almost a badge of honour, because you can say, look at me, I've got an injury because I'm physically active. But mental health? Because of the stigma, the complexity, the lack of ABC journey, it doesn't work like that.

Where many men's brains may work in a linear fashion, craving clear-cut direction, the messy, loopy, somewhat nebulous journey of mental health can feel scary. Add centuries of shame on top of that and you can see why so many are quick to reject it.

While of course it's too over-generalised to suggest this is *all* men, if we were to take Dr Lukha's example and apply it to mental health, it might go something like this: A, I was bullied as a child. So B, I have trouble dealing with difficult situations. Then C, I'm struggling with money issues.

How often as men are we taught to sit with these situations and difficult emotions, and to process these paths? We rarely are, and so many of us push the difficult feelings away, sure that's the fix, but really two roads are present. We can take road D, which is about processing our emotions, perhaps speaking to a therapist and working through it. Or, we can take road E, which is allowing the pressure to seep out elsewhere. It could be an addiction, a fight, suicide even.

For many men who act out, commit crimes, withdraw, or end their lives, it may stem from being stuck in the messy middle of mental health, but they may never have been taught to accept that middle and *how* to work through it.

There is evidence to suggest that men and women may process mental health issues differently, with men more likely to externalise it and display anger, aggression, substance abuse, or risk-taking behaviour.[34] We often see these external acts alone, and perhaps even punish them, overlooking the possibility that these might be masking what is going on under the surface and missing the fact that many men have been conditioned into responding this way.

A man, when faced with an emotional battle – a battle that he has been told for years, maybe decades, makes him weak – and feels his masculinity is threatened, is he going to threaten that *even more* by opening up? By telling his friends, by going to a therapist, and having a cry? In most cases, unlikely. He's going to do things that have the perception of being more masculine. It doesn't matter what turmoil he's feeling on the inside, as long as externally he can present an image of a man that's not only holding it together, but a man whose masculinity is to be admired. And this is the additional context that we often miss going on below the surface.

There are numerous conditions and experiences that fall under the umbrellas of mental health and mental ill health, each with their own unique set of circumstances, that will impact people differently based on their own contextual life situations. But the point is, men haven't been conditioned enough to be comfortable with these things and to process them in the right way. The cost when we don't do that, when we slip into that messy middle, when we don't know how to address it and work our way out, can lead us down a tragic path.

When Men Can't Talk

A popularised quote around men's resistance to help-seeking is 'women seek help, men die'. While it lacks nuance, there is sadly a huge degree of truth to it, even if over-generalised. If you're a man living in the UK under the age of 50, the biggest threat to your life is yourself. Suicide is a leading cause of death for men around the world and there is a huge gender disparity in the figures.

Amelia Wrighton, the co-founder and CEO of Suicide&Co, a suicide bereavement support charity, highlighted the problem of suicide more generally to me: '36,000 people are newly bereaved by suicide every year in the UK. And things aren't getting better, the suicide rate has gone up for the first time in 20 years, increasing by 7.6% in 2023 from 2022 alone'. This isn't a globally specific statistic, however, and suicide rates do fluctuate by region.

We generally have a troublesome relationship with how we handle suicide, and Amelia highlighted the challenge to me, in both society and healthcare systems:

I have so many sad stories of neighbours crossing the street to avoid someone recently bereaved by suicide. Parents not wanting their children to go and play with a family impacted by suicide. How can we ever change things if this is our approach?

And the system itself isn't set up as well for handling mental health, particularly suicide. If you lose someone suddenly and tragically to physical health, there are pathways for that. If you're in a traumatic incident, there are pathways for that. If someone is murdered, there are investigations and avenues for that. But when it comes to suicide? It just doesn't really have that. There's a systemic lack of support and referral pathways.

This is particularly true for men, where in the mental health world, most therapists are female. Immediately this creates a barrier for men who want to speak to another man. We know that men are less likely to seek support than women, which could be because more traditional therapeutic approaches are focused on deep exploration of emotion and the past, where many men may prefer a more solution- or action-orientated form of support, something like cognitive behavioural therapy, for example. Although many men won't know or understand the distinction between different types of therapy, and it'll all be lumped under one umbrella – one that they don't want to hold.

While a fairly simple equation could perhaps say 'well, less men are seeking support, so of course more are taking their own lives', this is overly simplistic. There is evidence that a number of men took their own lives *after* having contacted a frontline service,[35] so it's not like they're not reaching out. Many *are*, and for whatever reasons, are finding that those support structures aren't tailored to their needs.

So *why* are so many men taking their own lives? I spoke with Professor Rory O'Connor, a professor of health psychology who leads the Suicidal Behaviour Research Lab at the University of Glasgow. He's also the author of the book *When It Is Darkest: Why People Die by Suicide and What We Can Do to Prevent It*.

While Rory had initially registered to do his PhD on depression, a call from a professor with an opportunity to work on suicide research set Rory down a different path, and began his long career in the field. But this goes beyond just professional curiosity for Rory. It was some years later that the same professor who got Rory into this line of work, sadly took his own life, before one of his close friends who he undertook his PhD with, also took hers. 'So, although I've always been incredibly passionate about working in the area, both those experiences really floored me and reminded me of the challenge we face with suicide prevention on an individual level'.

With a career spanning the field for three decades, there are few people who know as much about suicide as Rory. Before diving specifically into masculinity, I asked Rory, at its most basic level, why people take their own lives.

He told me that suicide is, for many, the ultimate form of problem solving, as it ends the pain that they're feeling, pain that arises from a feeling of being trapped, defeated, humiliated, or a sense of great shame. 'The important thing to understand with people who become suicidal is that it's often not because they want to die, per se, but they want unbearable pain to end'.

Rory explained how many people experiencing suicidal thoughts believe that the world and those around them would be better off without them, and so suicide is far from a selfish act, and is actually an altruistic act in the eyes of many. And they get such tunnel vision that they can't see the devastation they'll leave behind.

Anyone who passes judgement on those taking their own lives is often doing so from a place of sound logic and a reasonable mind. Someone in the throes of suicidal thoughts isn't in the realm of logic; they view the world through a prism of pain. When I look back on my own experiences, it doesn't feel like George from the past, it almost feels like an entirely different person.

I asked Rory how best to describe the feeling of suicidal thoughts to someone who has never experienced them, and he said while everyone experiences it differently, some people describe it as if they're in a long, dark tunnel, one which has no light at the end. All they're feeling is overwhelming pain, pain which is often internalised, making it harder to see and articulate. And they believe they're going to be stuck in that tunnel forever, caught in a vicious cycle of despair.

So why is it, I put to Rory, that more women report issues with mental health, and yet more men take their own lives? Why is the male suicide rate so devastatingly high? And what responsibility does masculinity hold for all of this?

'In every country around the world, the number of males taking their own lives outpaces that of women. Part of that is down to the fact that women tend to use less lethal suicidal methods, whereas men choose more lethal means, which are more likely to end in death'. To Rory's point, there are numerous studies which show that women are 1.2–4 times more likely to attempt suicide,[36] depending on which source you look at, and yet more men take their own lives.

Rory continued, 'but men are also less likely to seek help for mental health issues. And, of course, the third reason is that masculine norms play into it. Men have been brought up in a society of emotional suppression, not expression which is, of course, associated with a higher suicide risk.'

As he explained to me, the biggest risk group in the UK right now for suicide is middle-aged men. Another masculine norm, the fear of interpersonal connections, is playing its part in this. Many men experiencing a midlife crisis find it coincides with a breakdown of a relationship or marriage, and many men invest a huge portion of their interpersonal support into this one person, rather than building close bonds with others around them. So when a relationship breaks down, they don't have that support network there.

As we discussed it further, it was clear how masculinity, or at least traditionally held beliefs around it, could be leading to more men taking their own lives. That lack of interpersonal connections leads to loneliness, isolation, and emotional dysregulation. Suicide, by its very nature and as Rory has already said, brings about feelings of shame, embarrassment, and failure. These are feelings which men have a particularly hard time dealing with, because they go against everything that they've been biologically and socially conditioned to believe about themselves – that they must be strong, competitive, attractive, and a leader. And so the feelings of shame perpetuate and fester.

The Stories Behind the Statistics

Some estimates say that when someone takes their own life, roughly 135 people are impacted in some form. I had powerful, emotive conversations with two amazing and inspirational individuals who spoke of the personal impact that being bereaved by suicide has had on them. The first was Steve Phillip, whose son, Jordan, took his own life at the age of 34.

Jordan was 6ft tall, good looking, the sort of person who lit up a room when he walked into it. In 2019, I was away running a workshop for a business, and Jordan and I were exchanging messages. I arrived quite late, I told him I'd get a bite to eat and asked if he wanted to chat when I got back. He said 'don't worry about it, sounds like you've had a long day, we'll catch up later if that's okay'. And that was the last message I ever received.

The suicide note that Jordan left behind read 'please know that this was the only way for me to stop the thoughts that were literally showing me no way out'. Steve described Jordan as someone that didn't open too much about his struggles, and when Steve checked in on him, the response was normally 'I'm fine'. A response that I'm sure a lot of men can relate to.

After he was gone, we found his journals where he shared how he was really feeling. He berated himself a lot for past mistakes he'd made. But he was doing a lot of work on himself too, and there were journal entries about how tomorrow would be a better day. Even the day before he took his own life, the journal entry was a really positive note. And I could just see that he was still fighting so hard. Jordan never opened up to us about how he was really feeling, and I wish he had. But from reading his journals, I know it's a myth that men can't process how they're feeling. It's a myth that they don't want to talk. They just need the right space and the right environment.

This perfectly encapsulates the challenge men face in the modern world. A mask of emotional suppression is forced onto their faces, but all it's doing is trapping their voices and pushing down their experiences. Most men *do* want to connect, to talk, to feel a sense of belonging. Often we just never know what's going on below the surface. This is what happened to Caroline Roodhouse, who was bereaved by suicide in 2018 when her husband, Steve, took his own life, leaving behind two young girls, only nine and two. As she recounts in her book on the experience, *Daddy Blackbird*, the police arrived at her house with 15 unforgettable words, 'We've found him. He's not alive. And it's clear he has done it to himself'.

He left behind no note, no paper trail that explained why he did what he did. Caroline has theories, fragments she's pieced together from various conversations. But really, she and her girls are left with unanswered questions and, in Caroline's words, a 'box of rage'.

I blamed him when the washing machine broke. If he'd been here, it wouldn't have broken, and when the car breaks down, and when I can't pay the bills . . . these things wouldn't have happened if he was here. Everything is his fault, which clearly isn't fair, but there's a degree of truth in it.

Over time that box of rage has shrunk, as Caroline began to learn that it was the grief reacting and talking, not logic. And so the focus of our conversation was on the kind of man he was: a good, caring husband, a loving father. One who, like any of us, went through the normal ups and downs of life. He was someone that ex-colleagues described as an amazing leader, who built them up, helped them achieve new positions. But he also never talked about things like the death of his parents, and seemed to put all his energy into helping others, leaving 'nothing left in the tank for himself'.

There was one story Caroline shared that struck a real chord with me, and stayed with me for days:

I remember when one of my daughters was four or five, and came bursting into my room, saying 'Mummy, I know what I want for my birthday!'

'And I said, brilliant! What is it?'

'I want my dad back.'

It breaks my heart that so many people leave this world thinking that there was no other option. There was a quote that stuck with me during my own journey that gave me a small kick of inspiration: 'Suicide is a permanent solution to a temporary problem.'

There was enough there to make me dig deep, to feel sure that there had to be some hope and chance of recovery lodged somewhere. But I almost reached a point where I thought this was my *only* solution, because for a long time, talking and seeking help was simply a non-starter. Because that's not what men do, or so we're told. It was only when someone in my life questioned me on my abnormal behaviour that I felt I had to be honest about what was really happening below the surface. And then she forced me to seek medical help. If this hadn't happened, I genuinely don't know if I'd still be here today. It seems crazy looking back to think that I almost traded my life to stay inside the boundary of an imaginary box titled 'masculine'. Because that was what I was taught men do.

My pressure cooker almost exploded in the worst way imaginable, but luckily I got the help I needed. Many men don't, whether that's for their mental or physical health. And that needs to urgently change, otherwise we will keep seeing too many loved ones go before their time.

Please know that suicide is preventable. If you're struggling or know someone that is, there are resources available – if you're in the UK please call the Samaritans for free on 116 123; or if you're outside of the UK, please visit Befrienders Worldwide or Find a Helpline, both global directories which can help you find the right support.

*If you're worried about someone's mental health, ask them directly 'have you thought about suicide?' Be direct, not indirect. All the evidence tells us this **does not** increase the risk of suicide, but actually can be the first step in someone seeking help.*

Reflection

What does mental health mean to you? A weakness to hide, or something you can proactively and proudly work on?

Key Summary and Reflections

- **Neglection of health:** Emotional suppression and traditional masculinity are causing many men to either entirely avoid medical pathways, or access them too late.

- **Premature deaths:** Statistically, many men are dying prematurely around the globe, with cardiovascular disease, cancer and suicide some of the leading causes of death and a huge gender disparity in many of the figures.
- **Limited education:** Our education around male health is limited, and many boys and men are getting their education from places that increase shame, stigma, or embarrassment.
- **Putting pride to one side:** Every doctor I spoke to told me that the embarrassment around seeking help exists only in the patient's mind. Whatever is going on for that person, the doctor has seen it dozens of times before, sometimes on the same day! Please don't let pride or embarrassment stop you seeking help.

5
Breaking Point #2: Addictions

Not only is emotional suppression causing men to neglect their health, both body and mind, but it's also causing men to release pressure not through connection, but coping. For many men, that comes in the form of addictions.

Men are consistently at higher risk of addictions, with the Office for National Statistics (ONS) reporting that men in England and Wales are more than twice as likely to die from drug misuse than women.[37]

There is a whole range of reasons someone may develop an addiction. There's a strong genetic element to it, while some argue that men's higher levels of testosterone can increase their risk-taking behaviour. Others say that they may exhibit higher sensitivity to reward-granting activities, while some say it's influenced by strong cultural norms.

What's incredibly important to note is that an addiction is far from a 'choice' or a moral failing, as addictions are categorised as a brain disease. Sadly, I think this is where we can often muddy the water with men and addictions.

We focus on the man with the addiction, but don't always zoom out and ask what has led him down that path. This isn't to draw attention away from the devastating impact that people with an addiction can have on those around them, but we don't seem to always ask whether it's perhaps not the man alone who has an issue, but it is in fact systemic issues and rigid masculine norms that have failed him.

For many men, an addiction is a symptom, not a cause. It's their way of releasing pressure and covering up pain that they might not even know they have. Nick Conn, the founder and CEO of Help4Addiction, an alcohol and drug rehab advisory service, said to me 'drugs, alcohol, gambling, sex, porn . . . whatever the addiction is, that's not somebody's problem. That's their solution.'

Many things become an addiction for men, it could be pornography, masturbation, or sex. Others overwork, obsess over fitness, or become addicted to shopping. Some turn to alcohol, drugs, and gambling. One can even develop an addiction to scratchcards. Many of these don't have official addiction pathways, while others, like working, may be glorified, masking what's happening underneath.

Mark Griffiths, Distinguished Professor of Behavioural Addictions and one of the world-leading voices on addiction who has published hundreds of papers on the subject, told me that he believes *anything* can be classed as an addiction. 'I've got six criteria that I use. I don't care what the behaviour is, if it fits into my six criteria, then I class it as an addiction. These are salience, mood modification, tolerance, withdrawal symptoms, conflict and relapse'.

Mark readily admits that he is sometimes at odds with other academics in the addiction community, as he gets accused of watering down the concept by saying that anything can be one, if it fits into his criteria.

But I agree with Mark's definition, particularly through the lens of men and masculinity. Where men may have for so long been conditioned to ignore their natural emotions, their pain, their struggle, their everyday life experiences, or simply sitting with their thoughts, they instead throw themselves into activities, actions, and hobbies as a way of dealing with it. If they're doing this, whether consciously or subconsciously, at the detriment to a normal life and to avoid pain or confronting issues, then it's not healthy, and it can be an addiction.

Addictions can have a devastating impact and cost people money, jobs, relationships, sometimes even their lives. It doesn't only impact the sufferer, but the people around them too, who also sometimes knowingly or unknowingly become enablers in that person's addiction.

While I can't cover every addiction, the next few chapters will show how some men, who have reached breaking point inside, turn to vices as a way of coping. We must start to consider not only the accountability an individual needs to take, but also where society has failed them too. For many men, addictions are the result of a path that rigid societal norms have forced them down.

The more that we tell men to man up and to suppress their emotions, the more that we'll be sending them down paths like the ones here.

Substance Abuse: Addicted to the Escape

What I didn't realise was the problem was in my head

—*Nick Conn, CEO, Help4Addiction*

When we think of addictions, it's substance abuse that we're most often thinking and talking about. Indeed, it's the addiction that most support systems and healthcare pathways are set up to treat, and it's only in recent years that we've begun to expand our understanding and support for other addictions.

From 2023 to 2024, over 310,000 people were treated for a substance abuse problem in the UK, and these were just the ones we know about.[38] More than two-thirds of this number were men. The World Health Organisation found that, globally, 3.2 million people died in 2019 due to alcohol and drug use, with also over two-thirds being men,[39] showing that the disproportionate gender divide tracks globally.

I spoke with Nick Conn, CEO of Help4Addiction, and asked him what led him to the role he now holds.

Nick tells me.

I'm a recovered addict and have been clean for 16 years. Nobody is born an addict. But I got introduced to cocaine and it was just as I found out I'd passed my exams to be accepted into the police. So it was kind of a celebration, and as soon as I took it, I thought "this is how I'm meant to feel. This was the medicine I'd been searching for my whole life". From then on, I was constantly chasing that feeling. I got into the police and I was staying at Hendon, the police training academy. It's obviously very

*high security, so I was coming outside to meet my dealers to
bring drugs back in.*

But things progressed rapidly for Nick, who had to leave the
police and left for another country to get away from everything. 'Because you think, if I can get away from where I'm at,
then the problem would go away and I'd stop taking drugs, but
what I didn't realise is that the problem was in my head'.

As Dr Ravi Lukha previously said to me, this speaks to how
many men approach their health. If there is a simple, clear, linear fix for an issue, men often seem more comfortable with
that and inclined to do something. But when it becomes messy,
less clear, and involves an emotional or psychological fix, they
can resist and reject it. Or, they assume that everything only
needs a physical fix, rather than one where they may have to
dig deeper. They've been conditioned into suppressing their
emotions, so it's no surprise that they suppress the idea of an
emotional fix for their issues.

Nick is lucky to still be here today. He ended up doing little
jobs for brothels in Berlin, and this escalated into full-blown
drug running across countries for the Albanian mafia. By his
own admission, he wasn't a bad person. But when the promise
of drugs is there for someone struggling with an addiction,
someone who feels such euphoria from the high, they're more
susceptible to do whatever is asked of them.

The problem for Nick? 'All of these drugs I was being given for
the services I was doing . . . turns out there was a tab being
built. I owed the mafia thousands, and I couldn't afford to pay'.
Nick fled, ended up homeless and lived like that for two weeks

before he told his family. When he finally did tell them, they got him into a hotel immediately, flew him back the next day, and that kick-started his journey into recovery and rehab.

Nick's story is obviously a dramatic one, one which would make (and has made) for great newspaper headlines. It's a story that most people with an addiction can't relate to. But what lies underneath it all is something that I believe most people with an addiction *can* relate to, particularly men, and why substance abuse can be so prevalent. Why did Nick's addiction start? He said that as soon as he took cocaine, he knew this was how he 'was meant to feel'. Because what he felt *before* that was a crippling sense of low self-esteem.

Not to oversimplify Nick's powerful story, but if we distill everything – the addiction, leaving the police, drug running for the mafia – it all started with low self-esteem. And one that he struggled to talk about, by his own admission, because of his masculinity. He was so convinced that he had to suppress this feeling to satisfy the conditions of masculinity, that it was easier to turn to drugs than to open up. And then he felt like the kind of man he believed he was meant to be, one that was more attractive to women and more successful. He kept chasing that feeling, a feeling which became an addiction in itself, a self-fulfilling cycle.

Addictions rarely exist in a vacuum, and we know that they are often a solution and a symptom, and for Nick the real issue was low self-esteem. Research shows a strong link between low self-esteem and unresolved trauma as being significant risk factors for developing a substance abuse.

As soon as Nick reached out to his family and was honest about what was going on, they got him home safely and into rehab. When Nick took off his mask of emotional suppression, all he found was love and support, and it kick-started his journey into releasing the pressure he'd been carrying for so long. Not everyone might have that network around them, or know how to reach out to them, and that's why it's on all of us to make the societal safety nets that much stronger.

Reflection

What do you turn to as a way of escaping when life feels overwhelming?

Gambling: Losing More Than Money

I lost about £7 or 8 million on gambling

—*Paul Merson, former Arsenal and England footballer*

Our understanding and acceptance of gambling as an addiction is relatively new, with it only having officially been classified as a 'Substance-Related and Addictive Disorder' in 2013. It's easy to think of addictions as involving only substances, putting things *into* our bodies. But as we know, addictions are often about coping with internal pain, and when that's the cause, an addiction can take many forms.

The reality of the dangers of gambling were brought to life for me by Paul Merson, former professional football player for Arsenal and England, now Sky Sports TV pundit. He candidly spoke about his struggles with addiction to drugs and alcohol, but it was gambling that he grappled the most with, leading to him almost taking his own life.

Paul said that 'the first time I walked into a gambling shop it was like walking into a spaceship, it just took all my anxiety away'. Similar to Nick Conn's story with substance addiction, it started with a desire to escape emotional pain and anxiety. Gambling was the symptom, anxiety was the cause.

Paul spoke of how any addiction is tough, but gambling can be ruthless, because nobody could see it. If we turned up to work after drinking a bottle of spirits, the signs might be more obvious – the smell, speech impediments, staggering. But with gambling, we could blow a whole month's wages on our phones on the train, and nobody would know.

It's no surprise people are driven to suicide, particularly around something like gambling addiction where you can lose an untold amount of money. In fact, it's been found that people suffering with a gambling addiction are two to three times more likely to attempt suicide than any other type of addiction.[40]

As a society we have a tricky relationship with things like gambling. You can't watch a sports match without seeing adverts from several different gambling businesses. They'll put a 'gamble responsibly' line somewhere in the small print, but this will do very little for the person with an addiction. So gambling is culturally accepted, and yet we shame the person with the addiction, not the culture that has led them there. And by shaming men into emotional suppression, we're doing what addiction wants – getting vulnerable people feeling isolated.

This isn't to criticise gambling or people who gamble, as for many it's an activity that they have a healthy relationship with, and one that they enjoy doing alone or with friends. But for someone who is vulnerable and gets caught in a spiral where they're always chasing that next win, it can have disastrous consequences.

It's happening in workplaces, pubs, homes even. Now, with easy access to technology and the advent of online gambling, the truth is that it can happen anywhere, at any time. Someone struggling with gambling might also turn to another vice, and they might struggle to tell those around them like their partner for deep fear that they'll leave them. And so the issue festers and gets worse.

Paul said: 'I lost about £7 or 8 million, but it's not about the money for me. I can get the money back, that's fine. What I can never get back is the time I lost. There's a photo of my kid at a school play, looking out at the crowd, looking for me. But I wasn't there, I was in the pub. I'll never get that time back'.

This isn't an isolated story, and Paul's experience brings the realities of gambling addiction to life. But what's happening underneath these stories? Researchers have been warning about its impact for many years. Professor Mark Griffiths has extensively studied gambling addiction over his 38 years in the space. 'There are over seventy different structural characteristics that you can find in gambling. Most of them don't have a major impact on addiction but there are some that are critical'.

For example, as Mark explained, one is event frequency. Addiction relies on constant rewards and high event frequencies – things like slot machines, which allow for continuous gambling and have been described as the 'crack cocaine of gambling'.

Another important characteristic is the psychology of the near miss. You may have just missed out on a line on a slot machine or maybe your accumulation bet on the football would have come in except for one result. You tell yourself you would have won, if only it hadn't been for that dodgy referee call. Gamblers don't continuously lose, they continuously nearly win.

The challenge that we discussed is how these things are getting easier to access. More gambling apps than ever, adverts everywhere you look. Loot boxes in games, in-play bets during matches, free bets – companies continue to squeeze every ounce of money that they can out of the market, and as more companies pop up, they come up with new, lucrative, and sometimes ridiculous ways to get people to part with their cash.

Where society may push away men who are struggling, there are companies ready to take advantage of someone's vulnerability and profit from it. If we don't help men to open up on their emotions, we may be causing them to open up their wallets instead.

People must take accountability for their addictions, but Paul finished with a quote that stuck with me, and one I believe can give hope to anyone who's struggling, as it was pivotal for his own recovery. 'I realised I wasn't a bad man trying to get good. I was a sick man trying to get well'.

This quote can apply to a lot of the things that we all go through. We can see ourselves as broken men, bad men, that have to stay quiet and fight and scramble our way back to being 'good'. And society takes us at face value and judges the external, all the while missing what's going on inside.

Maybe we all just need to realise that it's not always about trying to get good, it's about trying to get well. And for that to happen, we need to be able to talk about these things and remove shame from them. Because it's often not simply us that has a problem, it's the environment around us that's sick.

Reflection

What in your life have you been harsh on yourself for? Where did you need understanding instead of punishment?

Work: When Work Equals Worth

Our modern culture has glorified it [workaholism]

—Catherine Gildiner, author and clinical psychologist

The definition of a workaholic first appeared in Wayne E. Oates's work, becoming popularised in his book *Confessions of a Workaholic: The Facts About Work Addiction*, when he wrote that a workaholic is a 'person whose need for work has become so excessive that it creates noticeable disturbance or interference with their bodily health, personal happiness, interpersonal relations, and with his smooth social functioning'.[41]

Professor Griffiths believes it's important to make a distinction between workaholism and work addiction. 'Excessive does not mean addictive. You can work extremely hard and long hours, but if there are no negative impacts on your life outside of it, it's not an addiction. All work addicts are workaholics, but not all workaholics are work addicts'.

However, work addiction is not recognised as a mental issue, appearing in neither the DSM-5-TR (*Diagnostic and Statistical Manual of Mental Disorders*, Fifth Edition, Text Revision) or the ICD-11 (*International Classification of Diseases*, 11th Revision). Despite the fact that in some studies it's estimated in certain countries to affect up to almost 40% of the population.[42]

Why is this? I can only theorise that it's because working is seen as a good thing. And it is, of course. It brings purpose to our lives, food to the table, and money to the economy. But too much of anything normally isn't healthy.

The trouble is, hard or busy workers are idolised. The person with a busy calendar is an 'attractive' one, and we correlate hard workers with traits of intelligence, power, and control. The hustle culture of startups in recent years has added fuel to that fire, people glorifying grind over sleep, extremes over balance.

Work can feel like a particularly 'masculine' thing too. If we take the tenets of traditional masculinity, it's built around providing, protecting, status, control, and leadership. One or all of these are satisfied through work and it can give men the feeling of value and, of course, they get paid for doing so. Money itself, and the things it can buy, is often tied to masculine values of power and status, and can give people a shortcut to feeling like 'more of a man'.

Alongside these, I believe that there are other core reasons that a man may throw himself into work and develop an addiction with it. Many men have a deep wound of feeling not good enough, and they have insecurities, anxieties, and imposter syndrome. Overworking is a way of proving their masculinity to themselves and others, and avoiding sitting with that pain and discomfort.

This isn't to dismiss those that value working, and for some it can have a hugely positive impact on their mental health, giving them purpose and value. Work addiction becomes a problem, like any addiction, when overworking comes at the expense of other areas of their lives. Good sleep, healthy eating, time for resting or creativity. Chasing money over time with loved ones. Men can often get caught in a trap of overworking in order to provide for their relationship and family, falling blind to the fact that they're damaging these very things in the process of trying to provide for them.

It's challenging for men, because they're doing the things they think they *should* do and have been taught to do as a man: *provide, be the breadwinner, be successful and a leader.* All the while they're neglecting the rest of what makes us human: *connection, time with loved ones, time to do nothing.* Sadly, these things haven't been equated with the 'correct way to do masculinity'.

For a man who is struggling, work can be the ultimate vice; he can prove his masculinity not only to himself, but those around him. And if he doesn't get off the hamster wheel and stop, even for a moment, then he doesn't have to confront whatever might be going on inside.

Reflection

If work was no longer part of your status and identity, who would you be? And what would it look like for you to be 'good enough?'

Porn: When Sex Becomes a Scroll

Porn is the largest unsupervised experiment on men that we've ever had

—*Scott Galloway, American academic*

While work can be more of a socially accepted addiction, porn overuse is one of the most hidden. One US nationally representative sample found that 11% of males self-reported as having a porn addiction.[43] And this is just the men who report, this number is likely much higher. It's estimated that anywhere between 83% and 100% of male adolescents aged 11–16 in the UK have been exposed to porn.[44]

Wind the clock back 15 years and you had to go out of your way to access porn. It was relegated to magazines on the top shelf of newsagent stores. And now? Many social media algorithms are allowed to run mostly unchecked, with an increasing array of content being served up to people on a silver platter.

Porn is a highly addictive activity which, like many other addictive behaviours, causes a flood of dopamine in our brains. It's hardwired to make us feel pleasure, and in that moment, we feel great.

It's what comes after that is the problem. High spikes lead to deep crashes. Desensitisation occurs, and over time individuals may have to expose themselves to increasingly graphic content to chase the same high. You can end up physically rewiring the brain, which comes to learn that sexual pleasure comes from porn, not from the real thing.

It's a brutal, dangerous, and easily accessible cycle. There are even studies which show a direct correlation between increased access to and usage of porn with a rise in the number of people, mostly men, being charged with online child abuse offences.

This doesn't excuse accountability, but many men have said that they don't see themselves as having an interest in minors. However, the deeper they went down the rabbit hole of porn, the more graphic and illegal the content became to fuel their addiction.

So why are men drawn to porn? There are biological factors that suggest men are more visually stimulated, are more drawn to reward-driving activities, and have higher sexual desire than women. But there are deeply ingrained societal reasons too. Emotional suppression may make them turn to porn, where they can trigger a sexual reward without the need for emotional vulnerability. They can live out whatever fantasies they want and feel that they're playing their societal role as sexually active and interesting.

Porn is a multi-billion-dollar industry, with some adult creators making more in a year than even the most high-profile sports stars. Despite being such a money spinner, the reality is there is very little to no proper safeguarding in place around porn, where many websites have an age verification check that requires nothing more than the click of a button. There is very little to stop a nine-year-old pretending to be somebody much older, and once on the website, there is a limitless amount of content at his fingertips.

And so when you have men who have been taught to be emotionally suppressive, to be sexually explorative and to always be 'on', who perhaps might be having troubles in a relationship, what do you think they're going to do? They often don't know how to communicate how they're feeling, or even to understand what they're feeling, so they chase the quick, emotionally detached reward of porn.

Jeremy Lipkowitz, a former scientist, now works as a coach helping men to break free from porn addiction, and I reached out to him to get more insight on this topic. Jeremy's work was borne from his own story of compulsive porn addiction.

He told me: 'A porn addiction isn't just about porn, it's about escaping, numbing out, procrastinating, finding a way to avoid our emotions, the same with addictions to video games, alcohol, drugs, work . . . all the ways we escape'.

There's no binary equation of 'if you watch X minutes per day, you're addicted'. It's about the consequences it's having on your life. For Jeremy, this was the catalyst to making him stop. 'It was keeping me from real relationships, even with friends. Instead of going camping for a weekend with mates, I'd stay home to watch porn. I was just a normal young boy going through things that boys go through; I was teased, sometimes I didn't get my needs met as a kid, and porn made me feel good.'

I asked Jeremy if there are even any benefits to watching porn, and he explained that if it didn't have any positives, then people wouldn't develop an addiction around it. It can provide some comfort, relief, and distraction. It might help some people learn about their sexuality, although others would argue it tampers with it. You also don't have to worry about rejection in porn, but Jeremy said: 'is this even a benefit? Because your needs for intimacy and connection aren't really getting met, you're not engaging with real humanity. In my mind, the harms outweigh the benefits so drastically for 99.9% of the population'.

On an individual and generational level, porn is having a devastating and unseen impact. Scott Galloway, an American academic, said that 'porn is the largest unsupervised experiment on men that we've ever had'. So how *is* porn shaping the next generation of kids who have millions of hours of porn content at their fingertips?

From discussing the issue with Jeremy, it was clear that young boys are getting influenced in really harmful ways. Videos are becoming increasingly aggressive towards women and they're propagating stereotypes. A woman never turns down sex in porn, or if she does, it's shown as her playing hard to get. The message is that if the man pushes harder, she'll like it eventually. As Jeremy said, 'We're creating a generation of young men who think that sex means to choke a girl and make her cry. And girls are thinking that they need to be into this stuff'.

Jeremy was clear to stress that there is nothing wrong with these acts per se, as long as they're conducted by two consenting adults who are *genuinely* into those things, not just doing it because that's what they think sex *should* be. But the trouble is, we know that men aren't always getting proper education around these things from safe sources. Many are re-enacting what they see in porn because that's what they think they're *meant* to do. How many people know what they actually enjoy versus what they think they *should* enjoy? This is an issue which has existed long before the advent of porn, but porn has aggravated and confused it on a hugely dramatic scale.

And porn has impacts in other ways, as Jeremy said:

It is just so intensely stimulating on a dopaminergic level. There is an insane amount and variety of content. And it's like you're pushing a dopamine button with an intensity and velocity that we've never experienced. Your brain gets accustomed to it, and so to get to the same level of arousal you need more content, more extremes, more novelty. So when you have sex with a normal partner, your brain just doesn't recognise it. Things like erectile dysfunction and delayed ejaculation can be the result. And this can obviously have long-term negative consequences on normal, healthy relationships.

There is, of course, a moral issue at play here too, with the porn industry being inextricably linked with sex trafficking and the mistreatment and abuse of porn performers. Not to mention the amount of content that has themes of sexual assault or rape. By keeping that mask of emotional suppression on men, not only are we forcing them into harmful habits like porn addiction, which is rewiring their brains, but we're also helping to perpetuate much larger societal issues too.

I asked Jeremy, if someone understood all the issues and knew how to control them, would there be any benefits to watching porn? 'You do not need porn to live a happy, beautiful, thriving life. It's like saying that yes, some people can have a healthy relationship with heroin. But do you want to risk playing with fire?' The trouble for many men is that they don't know they're getting burnt. They're certain that opening up about their emotions is a blazing inferno, and so they carry their shame and pain into porn, not knowing that the real fire lies there. Often emotional expression can help put it out.

Reflection

How might porn be shaping the way you see sex, relationships or yourself?

Gaming: Living Virtually

Gaming disorder is a pattern of behaviour of such a nature and intensity that it results in marked distress or significant impairment in personal, family, social, educational or occupational functioning

—*World Health Organisation*

The first computer games date back to the 1950s and 1960s, but the industry has exploded since then, now worth hundreds of billions of dollars. Gaming can act as a place of solace and sanctuary for many men, but for others, it can quickly become an unhealthy behaviour.

For those who don't game, they may not understand the attraction. It can be seen as a nerdy activity for children, not grown adults. I regularly see online commentary from men shaming other men for gaming, or from women who regard gamers as unattractive or undateable. I can't say conclusively why, but I would hazard a guess that it flies in the face of 'traditional masculinity', as it's seen as lazy and built around inaction, versus what a man 'needs' to be – outside, active, and busy.

It again comes back to this external, perceptible image of how a man 'should' be, which is often highly superficial and materialistic. It also exposes much of the hypocrisy of our modern society. We criticise and shame some men who *have* found an activity that they enjoy, and something which might be good for their mental health, while also wondering why men don't open up more. It seems that much of society only wants men to open up as long as it's on the right terms and fits into the 'traditional masculine' perception.

For many, gaming is a hobby that can have a hugely positive impact on their mental health, give them creative escapism and bring them closer to friends. Professor Griffiths, who has written extensively on gaming addiction, including a paper titled 'The Educational Benefits of Videogames', said that 'there has been considerable success when games are designed to address a specific problem or to teach a certain skill. It has benefits educationally, cognitively, and it has psychomotor and therapeutic benefits'.

So while acknowledging the hugely rewarding and fun hobby for many people around the globe, we also have to acknowledge that it can lead to a harmful relationship. There are many reasons that men get so drawn to and addicted to games.

Where many men perhaps struggle to process and express emotions in the everyday world, and the stresses of life, work, and relationships can feel overwhelming and hard to regulate, gaming can sometimes give them an outlet and a place where they feel like they fit in. Many games are socially driven and offer solace to men who might feel isolated, and the extreme sense of competitiveness, reward, and progression is something that many male brains crave in plentiful measure.

The trouble is, of course, that anything in too much abundance can be harmful. And gaming, like gambling, is designed to keep us coming back for more. It's become increasingly sophisticated in recent years, with newer and more lucrative systems being created to keep gamers online for longer and parting with cash – reward systems, pay-to-win items, and loot boxes, some which act like virtual slot machines. It's gone so far in recent years that some games have been criticised by politicians as being 'online casinos designed to lure kids into spending money', essentially akin to gambling.

For those addicted to gaming, it's not just about playing a game. It's the emotional, social, and neurological escapism and dopamine hits that keep them coming back. But it can often be a stepping stone to plenty of other issues. Lack of exercise and sunlight, detachment from those around you, and dopamine desensitisation can stop real-world activities feeling as enjoyable. People have lost money, jobs, and relationships because of overgaming as they withdraw further, losing sense of their responsibilities and commitments.

A Reddit thread, titled StopGaming, is ranked in the top 3% of all threads by number of members. I scanned comments and read things like 'my husband's gaming addiction is going to end our marriage', and 'my husband games so much that I feel so lonely in my own home, like I'm living with a ghost'.

One personal story from another public forum, which I've anonymised, was from a man who wrote that he lost everything because of his gaming addiction – his family, his job, and his home. His wife and child were simply annoyances getting in the way and eventually he was fired for poor work performance, because he was gaming at work. As we know, one vice can lead to another, and this man began to use amphetamines to stay awake at night to game for longer.

As with any addiction, we cannot solely place the responsibility at the feet of individuals. While that is part of the picture, we also have to see that gaming can be a vice they turn to when they feel like the external world doesn't want them, and when their internal world is a tidal wave of emotions they don't understand.

It's easy to retreat to gaming because you feel like you don't have to try and prove your masculinity to anyone in there, you can be whoever you want to be. Maybe if we did a better job of making people feel like this in the real world, we wouldn't have as many issues as we do.

Reflection

What does gaming give you that you don't feel you get in the real world?

Key Summary and Reflections

- **Finding ways to cope:** By teaching men to suppress their emotions, many are finding other ways to cope and process. The river doesn't stop flowing, it simply looks for a new path. This often presents in addictions.
- **Looking at the bigger picture:** Addictions are a symptom, not a cause. We often criticise men because all we see is the addiction, but we miss what's happening underneath. They have a strong genetic element to them, but this

doesn't tell the whole story, and this is a societal problem. Addictions do not represent a moral failing.

- **The need for compassion and love:** If you think you're struggling with one of these, or you know someone who is, don't hate the person, hate the addiction. Practise self-compassion and self-love. Remember Paul Merson's quote – you're not a bad person trying to get good; you're a sick person trying to get better.

6

Breaking Point #3: Disconnection and Displacement

Traditional masculinity is one that champions independence, leadership, and competition. The antithesis to much of this, and indeed something that can be collectively frowned upon with men, is strong interpersonal connections, built on bonds of compassion, empathy, and vulnerability.

This is particularly the case in many father–son relationships or friendships between men. Traditional masculinity can fear or undervalue deep connections and so these relationships are often built around emotional distance, surface-level connection, and egotistical competition.

But humans are wired for real, deep connection, for community, for closeness with others. While we tell men to suppress their emotions and to reject interpersonal bonds, we are driving them to seek this connection from elsewhere. We saw this from the last breaking point where men may turn to addictions, meaningless one-night stands and porn, or retreat into gaming worlds where they feel more accepted.

Men are craving real connection, intimacy, and love. The mask he wears stops him admitting that, but all that does is allow loneliness to thrive. At the same time, the world is changing around him, where not only does he feel disconnected from it, but he feels displaced within it too. As gender roles and cultural values shift, some men can feel like they have no clear place left and this wedge of disconnection grows, keeping men divided, not united.

Technology: When Screens Replace Connection

There is an incredible evolutionary mismatch between how we are biologically hardwired and the technological society we operate within

—Tj Power, neuroscientist and author

I grew up on the cusp of technological advancements and video game explosion, so most of my childhood was spent mucking around with Lego, plastic lightsabers and bouncing on a trampoline for hours until my legs gave way. Now, technology and social media platforms have become a mainstay in our lives, with billions of people using them every single day.

These tools and platforms aren't inherently good or bad, and for a man who may be suppressing his emotions, technology can offer a lot of solace. But if we don't have a good, clear relationship with ourselves, our emotions, and our sense of masculinity, then they have the ability to control us, to heighten our insecurities and force us to withdraw from the world around us, sometimes without our knowledge. While men may be looking for solace, left unchecked this can quickly turn into seclusion.

I spoke with Tj Power, a neuroscientist and *Sunday Times* best-selling author of *The DOSE Effect*, who has made it his life's mission to make a difference in how society manages technology.

Technology as an Addiction

One of the most interesting topics that came up in my chat with both Power, and earlier, Dr Nicolau too, is on the development of the human brain, or rather, the relative lack of it. The human brain has developed over millennia, with very little major structural changes happening in the last 300,000 years. Technology, on the other hand, is growing at an exponential rate, with it generally being accepted that technological advancements in the last 100 years are greater than in the previous 10,000 years combined. Our brains simply cannot keep up with this speed of transformation; brains which were ultimately built to hunt, gather, and survive.

And hundreds of thousands of years ago, rewards would have been hard-gained. To get our dopamine hit, we may have had to spend hours trying to light a fire using a rock, cooking an animal we spent an equal amount of time hunting. Now we can short-circuit that same pleasure centre simply by lying in bed and scrolling through social media, and we begin to doom scroll for longer as we become desensitised to the hits, needing more platforms, more content, more scrolling to satisfy the urges.

We're facing something of a 'digital dementia', where we can't focus on a book, we can't stay present with our loved ones without our minds drifting, and our heart aches if we can't feel our phone in our pocket. There's a reason the Oxford University Press's Word of the Year in 2024 was 'brain rot'.[45]

Technology is sapping our motivation and energy, leaving us tired, burnt out, and unable to focus. But at the same time, the high levels of dopaminergic activity makes this an addiction just like any other.

Power said:

> *hundreds of thousands of years ago, humans had to make perhaps around 2500 decisions a day. That is what our brains are built for. Today? We're having to make about 35,000 decisions every single day. There is an incredible evolutionary mismatch between how we are biologically hardwired and the society we operate in, and our brains aren't built to cope. When it comes to phones, we really underestimate as a society how bad an addiction this is. It's exactly the same, if not more severe, than alcohol addiction, because of the increased frequency.*

This, of course, isn't purely a man's issue, it's a human issue and the impact of this somewhat hidden addiction on our bodies and minds is something we haven't fully yet seen play out. But the science on it is fairly clear. Dr Nicolau said to me:

> *the immune system can't distinguish between what's real and what isn't, so as we doom scroll our brains are rapidly accumulating data, including things that are racist, violent, highly sexual and more. Our bodies are constantly mounting immune defences to this and preparing us for a fight that never comes. It causes inflammation within our bodies, with cells then breaking down and needing to repair. This process is a primary cause of aging, so it's not a leap at all to say that, at a very simplistic level, technology is causing humans to age far quicker than they should.*

Dr Nicolau said that the reason this addiction can be so highly dangerous is because our bodies can't metabolise it like it can with substances. If you drink, smoke, or take drugs, your body will metabolise it and flush it out of our systems. But with social media and technology, these things stay buried in the brain, like a memory. The effect is permanent and once you see something, you can't unsee it.

Social media platforms form a particular outlet and place of solace, connecting people all over the world and giving them a way to share life updates. But these platforms aren't without peril. They're designed to be addictive and their currency is attention. At the time of writing this, social media giants are under investigation for unscrupulously and deliberately targeting and manipulating vulnerable adults and teenagers in times of crisis and during moments of psychological turmoil. A recent landmark ruling found for the first time that social media giants were partly accountable for the suicide of a 14-year-old girl who was served up hours of content around romanticised acts of self-harm. The coroner found that the individual died from an act of self-harm while 'suffering from depression and the negative effects of on-line content'.[46] The psychiatrist who was assigned to the case and had to view the content that the child watched had trouble sleeping properly for weeks after.

Troublesome influencers are gaining traction on these platforms too, with seductive and unregulated messages which draw people in, particularly young boys and men who aren't finding celebration in the outside world. And misinformation rules supreme. An investigation from *The Guardian* found that of the top 100 trending TikTok videos on mental health, over half contained misinformation and dubious advice.[47] This included things like eating an orange in the shower to reduce anxiety.

And so we can see the overwhelming intersection that not only men, but society as a whole, are up against. These tools and technologies that we constantly interact with are, in many cases, rewiring our brains, draining our energy, and feeding us misinformation. But what does this mean specifically for men? Men who, as we know, may be more predisposed to addictive behaviours, and, being told to be emotionally suppressive in the outside world, may be seeking solace online instead, as a way of dealing with their pain.

Swiping Past the Pain

Netflix's popular documentary, *The Social Dilemma,* which focused on the dangers of social media, summarised the issue best: 'We're training and conditioning a whole new generation of people that when we are uncomfortable or lonely or uncertain or afraid we have a digital pacifier for ourselves that is kind of atrophying our own ability to deal with that.'[48]

We are being given the ultimate get-out-of-jail-free card for life's difficult experiences and emotions, as technology gives us a tool for being able to avoid things we don't want to feel. And this isn't only things like mental health issues. At a very basic level, we're making ourselves unable to sit with our own thoughts, our boredom, our need to do nothing. For men, perhaps taught to not feel, taught to always be active and busy, technology simply becomes their new 'vice' for suppression and busyness. But the impact is far-reaching.

Why try to solve relationship challenges when an endless stream of attractive alternatives is a swipe away? While statistics vary, there is a general consensus that online searches for terms like 'virtual girlfriend' are increasing by hundreds of per cent year on year.[49] Some headlines even point to many men saying they could see themselves forming a deep emotional bond with these AI companions.

Power told me that we use our phones as a way of comforting our pain, but social media only moderately satisfies our human need for connection. It falsely deceives us into thinking we're seeing real people and real activities, doing these things ourselves, but isn't satisfying our biochemical need of *actually* doing these things. He said: 'If we eradicated social media entirely, within a few weeks you would see everyone being out and about way more and socialising'.

We have also developed a society that is incapable of processing things on our own, and so we share everything to our feeds – life updates, holidays, gym sessions, our plates of food. Some men may find themselves sharing specific updates in an attempt to perform or validate themselves against a particular sense of masculinity, taking comfort in the dopamine-generation of each like and comment. While on the other side, those scrolling through may compare, judge, and shame themselves.

This isn't everyone and I pass no judgement; many of us are guilty of this or have been in the past. But so much of what we and other people post online comes not from a place of sound self-awareness, but from a place of insecurity or low self-worth, all while our biochemical needs are only fleetingly satisfied.

Dr Nicolau said that 'for men in particular, they're likely to doom scroll for longer, because they have less self-control'. And what impact is this likely to have for men specifically, as they sift through untold amounts of content?

According to Power, we're creating a socially isolated lifestyle, one of passive consumption of content that's disrupting our capacity to be human. He told me that this social isolation isn't good for men, and that we're 'potentially creating a generation of young men who aren't necessarily great at contributing to their families and their work'.

It's this that leads Power to believe it can even be contributing to feelings of suicidal ideation in men. He explains that if we were to wind back the clock to ancestral times, boys would go out with other men and hunt, providing for the tribe. It was a hard day's work and the dopamine at the end of the day is the reward. But were there an equivalent of phones back then, and we were to stay in our huts scrolling, getting our dopamine hits instantly, we may likely become depressed because we're not part of the tribe. But we'd also be taking from the tribe, not partaking, and 'over a long period of time, our brains may actually begin to feel that the best thing to do would be to remove ourselves from the tribe. And I do wonder how much of this is happening for people today and leading to suicidal thoughts'.

He finished: 'of course, the reality is that suicide *isn't* the best thing to do, but I do believe that low levels of dopamine can effectively create depressive episodes, as we're meant to be doing effortful things, and many young boys aren't doing that'.

A Real-World Story

What happens when all of this comes together? The ability for men to withdraw, to avoid real-world discomfort and to take solace in the darker corners of the internet, finding toxic influencers and manipulative voices who can prey on the vulnerable, can have tragic consequences.

I spoke to Alice Hendy MBE, a cyber safety specialist who has worked with organisations such as the FBI, Microsoft, and GCHQ. The dangers of technology and the impact on men affected Alice in a much more personal way when in 2020, police officers arrived at Alice's house and informed her they had identified a body. It was her 21-year-old brother Josh, and he'd taken his own life.

With Alice's background in cyber security, she poured through Josh's devices, looking for any clues:

I found that about six months prior to him actually ending his life, he'd been going on the internet and searching for ways that he could do it. Some really harmful material was spun up. There was content encouraging and promoting suicide and self-harm. There were sites where people were giving Josh tips, giving him methods, giving him encouragement. He was given pain scales for each method of suicide to help him make a decision and he was told how long different methods would take. And he wasn't even having to go on the dark web to find that it was readily available to him.

This isn't an isolated problem. A UK-wide case study found that of the 544 suicides of young people between the ages of 10 and 19 between 2014 and 2016, almost a quarter (24%) had a suicide-related online experience. This includes searching for methods and posting suicidal ideas online.[50]

Alice's brother, Josh, had been struggling financially, and it was only after his death that Alice found he'd applied for 72 pay-day loans. He'd recently gone through a breakup too. Alice wonders how much Josh was struggling with these things, but his masculinity stopped him opening up, seeking help. Instead he was seeking harmful content in the dark corners of the internet.

After Josh's death, Alice saw a huge void in crisis intervention, and founded a suicide prevention tool called R;pple, online technology which anonymously interrupts individuals searching for harmful content online, and signposts them to support services instead.

We're on over two million devices around the world and we've intercepted over 120,000 harmful online searches. And these are crisis level searches, not just people looking for information about mental health. They are serious enough to be along the lines of 'I want to end my life'. We don't track what happens to a user after, however we've had thirty-two people approach us and tell us they were searching for something harmful and R;pple stopped them and they're now getting the support that they need and deserve. That's 32 lives we've helped to save.

How do you quantify a life? What is the positive cost of saving those 32 people? The impact that it has on their loved ones around them? The work that Alice and her team are doing is incredible, and shows the power of technology when we use it in the right ways. But it's hard not to miss the fact that R;pple has been founded in response to a devastating situation, and to put safeguards in place on platforms that, for whatever reasons, don't take enough steps to police themselves. For all the good work that R;pple does, it wasn't founded simply because of altruism, it was founded because of the very dangers of technology, and a safeguard that was desperately needed.

There is no denying that technology and social media platforms do a lot of good, and have connected the world in a way that was previously never even imaginable. And there's no point arguing for a world free of tech, we're way past that. But it acts like any drug or vice; that if we aren't in control of it, then it's bound to control us.

It's causing tiredness, addiction, and burnout on a mass level, but specifically for men, it acts as a tool to escape. Where they've been taught to emotionally suppress and to withdraw from interpersonal relationships, these platforms act as a place of solace, a place to avoid difficult emotions, a place to further disconnect from the world around them. As we saw with Alice's brother, Josh, it gave him a place to try to solve money issues, to find solutions to pain that he didn't think he could discuss with those around him. Technology isn't the problem, many people have a healthy and balanced relationship with it. But for men who don't know how to regulate themselves or their emotions, then it *can* become a real problem and allow their pressure cooker to rise.

Reflection

In what ways has technology made you feel more connected, and in what ways has it made you feel alone? Does the distinction between comfort and escape feel clear?

Men and a Growing Loneliness Epidemic

Where have all my friends gone?

—*Max Dickins, comedian and author*

This technological advancement feels like a bittersweet progression – two steps forward, two steps back. A few decades ago, if you had told people that soon they would have little devices in their pockets enabling them to theoretically get in touch with almost anyone on the planet at any time, they wouldn't have believed you.

However, the sombre reality is that while we've never been more connected, in some ways we've never felt further apart. We're seemingly more isolated, lonely, and exhausted than ever. Close friendships often exist primarily in phones rather than physical meet-ups, even though we maintain dozens, maybe hundreds, of 'friendships' through superficial social media followings. Getting a thumbs up on one of our selfies from someone we knew 14 years ago satisfies our short-term need for dopamine, but it doesn't satisfy our true human, biological need for connection.

Because that's what we're dealing with here – a biological need. Humans are social creatures that rely on cooperation and community for survival, while hormones are released during social interactions. Chronic loneliness, on the other hand, has been linked with a number of health issues and even premature death. Dr Vivek Murthy, the former surgeon-general of the United States, said that lack of social connections can 'increase the risk for premature death as much as smoking up to fifteen cigarettes a day'.[51]

Isabel Berwick is an editor at the *Financial Times* and, perhaps somewhat ironically, she and I have exchanged several messages over LinkedIn, but we've never met in person. She's taken a focus on the male loneliness epidemic, and in one of her articles, 'What's the problem with men?',[52] she notes that 'since 1990, the number of men reporting that they have no close friends has jumped from 3 per cent to 15 per cent'. That's a staggering increase.

She interviewed Max Dickins, the author of *Billy No Mates: How I Realised Men Have a Friendship Problem*. He began to research the topic when he realised that he had nobody he could ask to be best man at his wedding.

He poignantly said to Isabel that part of the male loneliness crisis has arisen from the collapse of 'the "third spaces" that used to support our friendships: the various contexts we spend our time that are neither home nor work – places like pubs, gyms, churches and parks'. Another of Isabel's guests, Scott Galloway, echoes this, that our move to an increasingly remote working world is pulling us away from workplaces where, as Scott says, we 'make friends and develop certain social skills'.

The conundrum for many men is that close interpersonal relationships, particularly with other men, are often frowned upon when we look through the lens of traditional masculinity. Any close bonds of compassion and vulnerability can often be labelled with homophobic slurs. So, men keep other people at arm's length, sure to satisfy society's expectation of them to be strong and independent. But this flies in the face of our ancient biological wiring, a system which predates any of this silly debate on masculinity by hundreds of thousands of years. We're imposing present-day constructs onto past-day realities, and the two aren't computing. The result is that a loneliness crisis is brewing among men.

Not that men will admit to this of course, because to admit to loneliness is to admit to vulnerability and is somewhat 'unmasculine' in this day and age. A UK study found that just under a quarter of men (24%) have nobody to turn to with their problems.[53]

They're staggeringly high numbers, and ones that felt heavy as I typed them. Part of my joy of writing this book is sharing it with those closest to me, and the sense of if I was doing this on my own, isolated, with nobody around me to cheer me on feels overwhelmingly sad.

Importantly, loneliness isn't only about having a physical lack of people around you. You could be in a room surrounded by people you call friends, or at home with dozens of people in your phonebook you could message, and still feel lonely. Loneliness can arise from the *type* of connection we have with these people where perhaps it's as shallow as an autumn puddle.

When I was at university, I had no shortage of faces moving in and out of my week, no shortage of notifications popping up on my phone. And yet it was one of the loneliest times I've ever felt, because I was carrying the burden of my mental health issues, which I didn't think I could share. I'd turn up to the social events loud, fun, and boisterous, because that's what men are meant to do, but I was hurting on the inside, and I knew that pain was waiting for me once I got back to my room. I felt a disconnect with those around me because the George they were seeing wasn't the George that was really showing up, he was just bloody good at hiding it. We often think of loneliness as only an elderly person's thing, but I believe that my story is not an uncommon one for many men around the globe who regularly feel the acute pang of loneliness.

Where men have been conditioned into emotional suppression, independence, and a need to not have to rely on others, it keeps a buffer between many of the connections they do develop. Where a lot of female friendships are built on strong emotional connections, male groups tend to be built around a sense of camaraderie, shared activities, competition, banter, and sport.

Men don't get close because perhaps they've never been taught to, because they don't know how to, or because they're worried it'll diminish their status in the group. Many men might have full calendars and plenty of people around them, but the lack of real depth to these bonds can allow loneliness to surface.

It's sad how often I hear stories, and have even experienced this myself, of when the first person in the group opens up about something, and they get a response like 'I've been going through something similar myself'. How long have both parties been wearing a mask, desperate for support, sitting right next to each other, but holding it in, worried about what the other one would say?

As we begin to unpick and work back some of these unhelpful stereotypes, we're beginning to see more and more people valued for their emotional confidence and expressibility. Tides are turning in this regard, and the more that we keep encouraging others to associate emotional expression as a sign of strong leadership, the more I hope we can reverse some of the terrible statistics around loneliness. It's no wonder that many are now labelling it an epidemic.[54] Rigid masculine norms have conditioned men into believing that needing others is a weakness, but this very belief is quietly breaking so many. In the same way our body needs fitness to stay strong, it also needs deep interpersonal connections. It's good for the body, the mind, and the soul. It's good for women *and* men, and it helps men release pressure in healthy, natural ways.

Reflection

What's one thing you've never told your friends, but wish you could?

The Seductive Pull of Harmful Influencers

These are callous, manipulative influencers . . . they willingly trick young men into believing that success is measured by money or dominance . . . and that the world – including women – is against them

—Gareth Southgate, former England football manager

There is a vacuum of disconnection where men feel misunderstood, even by themselves, and where they generally lack a good network of strong male role models. And people with seductive, harmful messages try to fill this void. These influencers are often master-marketeers, knowing how to dominate feeds and algorithms. Many of these role models and influencers fit neatly into the category of 'traditional masculinity' and exhibit these traits in spades.

People like Brian Johnson, also known as the Liver King, are a prime example. He has a physical shape that many men aspire to replicate, one of extreme muscularity, is wealthy, and promotes what he calls an 'ancestral lifestyle' of eating raw, unprocessed animal organs. Brian has over six million followers on TikTok at the time of writing, many of whom have likely bought into his diet to achieve his body, the physical representation of traditional masculinity.

The issue? Despite Brian claiming to have never taken steroids in order to achieve his physique, it was leaked that he was spending around $11,000 a month on performance-enhancing drugs. In essence, he lied to and manipulated his huge fan base.

He apologised once he was caught, and pointed to insecurities and self-esteem issues as part of the reason. There's nothing to be ashamed of for being a victim of poor self-esteem; we've seen plenty from this book how men often walk down dark avenues as a solution for low self-esteem.

But it becomes different when you're acting as a role model and potentially profiting from millions of people. This is what men are facing in the public – blindly following men who they aspire to be like, men who can hide secrets behind the algorithm, an algorithm which often rewards false information and increasingly sensationalist headlines.

Men get pushed towards these influencers for many reasons. One is to achieve this perception of traditional masculinity. Another is because of the lack of many other role models in their lives, particularly when social media algorithms reward extreme lifestyles. Another is that men are finding a lack of positive messages out there in public discourse, and they aren't often being made to feel proud for being a man.

Pride is a pleasurable emotion, and there is plenty of research that suggests a desire to feel pride is a natural human need. So when men, and particularly young boys who aren't perhaps as comfortable in their own skin yet, aren't seeing a lot of positive messages or reasons to feel pride about themselves, what do they do?

They might feel a great deal of shame and guilt swirl around inside them and go searching for that pride from someone who is offering it in abundance. Enter stage left harmful influencers who are filling the void that we're creating.

It's no surprise at all that men, particularly young boys, are turning to influencers like Andrew Tate. I might not agree with what he says, but I can understand why boys do. He has a lot of what the typical masculine man is meant to aspire to – money, fame, a good physique, and women around him. But more than that, he makes men feel proud to be male.

While facing serious allegations that include rape and human trafficking, which at the time of writing are allegations he denies, and holding views that are widely condemned as misogynistic, he has still amassed over ten million followers on the social media platform X. Role models are there to make us feel good about ourselves and make us feel that we can aspire to be more than we are now, or better versions of ourselves. Whether we like it or not, people like Andrew Tate are doing that for men. They have a seductive message that requires a great deal of critical thinking and self-awareness to push back on.

And when you have a group of people who feel lost, or angry, or are hurting inside, or who aspire to be more or better than they are right now, it's easy to doom scroll through these seductive messages and blame others, rather than sit with our discomfort and do the deep inner work. Our inner pressure is seeping out of the cracks, and influencers are ready to suck it up, whether for better or for worse.

Unfortunately, these messages are working. A report from Movember[55] found that of the over 3,000 young men they surveyed, those who followed current masculinity influencers were more likely to believe in traditional gender roles than those who don't. For example, 76% of those who *do* engage with these influencers believe men should be the heads of their families (versus 57% who don't engage).

Dr Zac Seidler, Global Director of Research at the charity Movember and who helped lead on the report, said of the findings: 'regressive views about the role of women were frighteningly prevalent, inflamed by influencers in this space building up resentment and a victim mentality'.

Our solution is often to criticise the influencers themselves, or to stoke a culture of fear about the men who follow them. Dr Seidler added that 'this freight train of a conversation on young men has sped so fast away from its starting point, fuelled by fear and alarmism it's forgotten who it's supposed to carry and where. Young men must be central in this movement, they must have a voice, they must co-create solutions'.

And this is the crux; we need to better understand the starting point of where the problem is. These influencers are not the problem, they are a symptom of the problem. Removing them does not remove the way that people are feeling, it doesn't remove people's hurt and people's need to feel pride. If people are flocking to these influencers, we have to stop and ask why. What is causing them to feel seen and heard by these people that they aren't getting elsewhere? How are we pushing them that way?

Trying to remove one influencer won't work, for another will simply take their place, like some kind of influencer whack-a-mole.

Other solutions like 'removing a child's access to social media' will also not solve the deeper, unresolved emotions. It would be helpful to go upstream and look at *why* they're able to dominate so much of our public discourse.

Dr Seidler summarised: 'everyone is obsessed with the radical, misogynistic, homophobic tropes of the world. It is a red herring. There is so much that sits beneath this iceberg, and lots of it is innocuous. The problem is the algorithm'.

And when men are culturally conditioned into suppressing emotions, to sit not with sadness but with rage, while often hearing criticism of men in public discourse, a void is created, and influencers, fuelled by this algorithm, are swooping in.

Reflection

What messages about being a man are you most drawn to, and are they empowering, divisive, or both?

The Dad Gap

I lost my dad's time, and I didn't think he loved me anymore

—*Andrew Jenkins, motivational speaker*

Disconnection doesn't just make us feel at odds with the world around us, but with the people in our lives too. We might spend untold amounts of time with them, but if we're wearing a mask the whole time, it's not really us that's there.

The strain of this is often felt most acutely between sons and fathers, both of whom have been told to keep emotionally distant and that their bond is one to be built on activity, not on love and compassion. Or it is built on love, but shown *through* activity, not through words and emotion. It's why I think sometimes the belief persists that fathers can be seen as absent or second-rate as caregivers when compared to mothers.

Things do seem to be changing, slowly. A 2022 YouGov poll found that the majority of respondents believed that fathers today play a greater role in the raising of children compared to the experience they had with their own fathers.[56]

But shame, stigma, and outdated beliefs can easily get passed down from generation to generation as fathers still wear their own masks of emotional suppression, given to them by the ones before them. What fathers might see as worthwhile life lessons for their sons on strength and manning up can, in fact, be costing their kids their lives.

It means that families often aren't building bonds of vulnerability and true connection. On the other side of the spectrum, there's a disconnect growing in today's world between children who may be more progressive around emotional expression and their parents, to whom it can be an alien concept.

Many boys, who are often eager to impress their fathers, are internalising lessons of toughness and independence. A study of 52 men aged 18–30 who had made a serious or near-fatal suicide attempt found that the men were:

generally from families where hegemonic ideals of masculinity, emphasising strength and emotional stoicism, were practiced. This gender environment, which was reinforced in the neighborhood, restricted behavior and the expression of feeling, shaped communication between fathers and sons and affected the father's ability to emotionally engage with his son. Fathers were significant figures in these men's lives and were role models for demonstrating masculinity practices but there was an absence of positive, nurturing, relationships between fathers and sons and this influenced the son's gender learning and his wellbeing.[57]

This is an admittedly small sample size which doesn't provide a bulletproof, ironclad argument that fathers should suddenly start baring their souls. And for those that end up attempting suicide, there is likely a complex web of things that have been at play that extends beyond just their relationship with their fathers.

But it has been found that the majority of mental health issues start in people when they are young. Studies conflict on the exact numbers, but a commonly used statistic is that around 50% of all mental health issues begin to present while someone is in their teenage years.[58] And in some ways, perhaps that's no surprise. When we're at our youngest is when we know ourselves the least. It's also when our brain is still developing and is the most susceptible to social influence, so parents play a defining role in shaping our beliefs and our life's direction.

Through my work in the mental health industry I've worked with lots of therapists, and one made a comment that stuck with me: 'the people who come to therapy do so because their parents never did, and issues get passed down from one generation to the next, until one person decides to break the cycle within their lineage'.

We know that emotional suppression is mostly a societal construct, a mask that we force onto men. And so all we're doing is handing these masks down through families, strapping our masks onto our children until their own children are old enough to get the same faulty life lesson. When all it does is stop families *truly* connecting.

An emotional, real-world example of this was brought to life for me when I spoke to Andrew Jenkins, a fan-favourite contestant on the BBC's *The Traitors*. Andrew was brought up in an old-school family with traditional leanings. 'We just didn't talk about feelings or emotions back then. I grew up in rugby clubs, gyms, and a culture of masculinity'.

And that was how Andrew connected with his father – through sports:

> *So there was a lot of competitiveness in my house, and me and my brothers all played rugby. I love rugby and I've had some great memories there. Nobody forced me to play. But my two older brothers had been playing the sport to a very good standard, and I saw them always getting my dad's attention. So did I play to fit more into my family, to get some of my dad's time? Probably.*

Everything changed for Andrew when he suffered a life-changing car accident. He was initially pronounced dead at the

119

scene, before being blue lighted to one hospital. They couldn't do anything for him, and he was transferred onto another. Police rushed to Andrew's parents' house, telling them they didn't have time to get changed. He was in such bad shape, they weren't even allowed to see him in the hospital.

The doctors were surprised that Andrew pulled through, but he was placed into a coma for four weeks. His family were told it was highly unlikely he'd be able to remember who they were or even speak, and he definitely wouldn't walk again. Not only did Andrew wake up, but he could speak, he recognised his family, and a few weeks later he walked out of the hospital.

The Andrew that I spoke to has managed to move on a great deal physically from the car crash. Some facial reconstruction surgery and hair transplants have repaired most of the damage to his face. He moves well and talks perfectly, with a thick Welsh accent I could listen to all day!

But it wasn't the physical remnants of the accident that have had such a long-lasting impact on Andrew's life. It was the emotional impact and the wedge it drove between his family bonds, the disconnect it caused.

My family were great and supportive, but once I was better we brushed it under the carpet. I put on a brave face and a mask, but inside I was hurting. My dad's love language is time. He never told us he loved us, but he showed it through his time. Anytime we played rugby, he would be there, come sleet, snow, rain, hurricane, he would be on the side of that pitch. We'd be talking about rugby before a match, we'd get home and still be talking about it.

But after my accident, I couldn't play rugby anymore. Every Sunday I'd be at my parents' house and my brothers and my dad were in one room, talking about the rugby matches they'd played in over the weekend, what had happened, and I had nothing to contribute. I lost my dad's time, and I didn't think he loved me anymore.

What Andrew talked through is reflected in so many male relationships, not even just parental, but as friends too. Men often bond over sport and other activities, and when that is stripped away, what's left? Men often don't know how to bond beyond that, deeper than that. And for Andrew, it meant that he felt like he'd lost his dad.

I asked Andrew how things are now, and he said:

I carried the emotional impact of that accident around for 25 years, wearing a mask. Me and my family never discussed it, but I was angry and resentful. So I started counselling and then all these years later I tracked down the surgeon that saved my life and went to see him. He told me I'm a miracle, that there were so many times I should have died. I realised how lucky I was to be alive, and so the next thing I did was go to my parents and sat them down to finally talk about the accident, a conversation we should have had over two decades ago. My mother told me she thinks about the accident every single day. Every knock she gets on the door, she thinks it's the police. She's carried that with her for all this time, and she'll probably take it to her grave.

And then Andrew, who has his own son, said 'the next thing I did was sit my son down in a coffee shop and we spent four and a half hours talking about it all. And then for the first time in my life, I told him that I loved him'.

I was really moved by Andrew's story, that he and his family had carried around the emotional burden of the accident for a quarter of a century, nobody talking about it or seeking help, because that's not what men do, right?

What was most notable throughout Andrew's story was how this dichotomy we've created of traditional masculinity versus modern masculinity means everyone loses. *Both* sides have a role to play. Andrew credits traditional masculine traits for getting him better, physically at least. To have the determination to be convinced you're going to walk again even when the doctors told you that you won't, takes some real inner strength and resilience.

But that same insistence and reliance on traditional masculinity became a ball and chain around Andrew's life, following him everywhere. It stopped him talking, it stopped him processing things with his family so that they could all heal. In trying to be strong, all that ended up happening was he spent 25 years of his life feeling angry, resentful, and like his dad no longer loved him, and they lost all that time together.

We all know that there is strength in strength, and Andrew is testament to that. But he's also testament to the fact that strength simply for perception's sake often isn't strength at all. He feels like he's lost 25 years with his family, particularly his dad, and for what? To tick a box that says 'masculine'? But who has this *really* served? Andrew's family had preserved their pride, but at the cost of time, love, and connection.

If Andrew hadn't been the one to grab the situation by the hands, not only would he and his parents forever have that wedge of disconnect between them, but it's likely he would have passed that resentment, pain, and anger down to his own son too. And so the generational cycle of an ideal of masculinity that is killing men would continue. It's on all of us to stop this cycle, and there's no better place to start than with our own families.

Reflection

Are there things you've never said to your parents, guardian, or loved one, but always wanted to? What's stopping you?

Key Summary and Reflections

- **The need for connection:** Our insistence for men to be strong, independent, and emotionally suppressive does not stop their deep, ancient biological need for human connection, intimacy, and belonging.
- **The trouble with technology:** Technology can give the illusion of connection, but it also helps men to avoid difficult emotions and become passive, and a way of connecting with influencers who may have harmful messages.
- **Influencers and the void:** Toxic influencers are not the problem, they are the symptom. Their messages are seductive because they make boys and men feel valued, celebrated, and worthy of something – messages that they often aren't getting enough from elsewhere. Influencers are filling a void that we have created.
- **What makes us human:** Connection doesn't make you less of a man. It makes you more of a human.

7
Breaking Point #4:
The Mask of Performance

When we feel disconnected from the world around us, the people in our lives, or even ourselves, life can feel performative. The mask of performance can come in many forms. Perhaps it's hiding parts of ourselves, perhaps it's competing with those around us, perhaps it's in how we present our external image to the world. It can be a physical competition or a subtle one, and we may try to perform in the boardroom, the bedroom and beyond.

Competition and performance is baked into male tradition and norms. To reject that is to reject something that many men enjoy and thrive on. And there is an argument to suggest it has biological roots too, although we know that social conditioning trains those roots to grow in a certain direction.

But sometimes that performance is for the perception of others, at the cost of inner peace. And when we're performing for others, not for ourselves, that pressure can build inside. What happens when men are performing for the world, but disconnected from themselves?

When Sex Becomes a Performance

We equip boys with no tools and a complete misunderstanding of romantic relationships and intimacy, leaving them to rely on ancient standards, fantasy-based edutainment, and misinformed perspectives to handle the world

—Dr Adi Jaffe, author and psychologist

For many men, there are few things in life where performance feels more critical than with sex. It becomes the ultimate act on which they believe they'll be judged. It can be a difficult topic to talk about because it carries such sensitivity, particularly when we talk about it in relation to masculinity. Generally speaking, the perception of the intersection between sex and masculinity isn't a good one.

Men are often stereotyped as lustful, unrestrained, and that the only thing they care about is sex. But this perception sadly also has a much larger, darker tinge to it. Many people, mostly women, have a negative story about a man. Being catcalled, objectified, stalked, assaulted, raped even. While any intelligent person knows that this isn't all men, it's enough men, happening so frequently, that there is a general nervousness around trusting men.

It's not been helped by books like *The Game*, where Neil Strauss partly teaches seduction as a skill so men can better pick up women. Some label it as helping men who feel shy, others label it as manipulative. Whatever our beliefs, it was wildly popular, and reinforced an assumption that men are primarily sex-driven. It says a lot that some years later, Neil's follow-up book, *The Truth*, focused on his unhealthy addiction to sex and the destruction that it caused in his relationships, having to go through therapy and rehab. I can't speak for Neil's circumstances, but I wonder if where *The Game* felt like the mask of performance, *The Truth* felt like the reality of the impact of that mask.

The fact is, sex can carry a lot of baggage for men. The perceived need to compete with their peers, the need to feel good enough and wanted. Feeling that they're 'successful' at the act itself, and the fears they hold over what gossip will spread if they aren't. Masculinity can often be equated with the number of sexual partners, and for some men, it can feel emasculating when he *doesn't* desire sex as much as his peers, or perhaps doesn't have sex as regularly. For some men, they feel uncomfortable if their partner has had more sexual partners; it might play on their insecurities.

For other men, it's a means of communication – where perhaps they struggle to express themselves verbally, sex can be a way that they express desire, attraction, and love. This can be frustrating for people and partners on the other side, where they might misunderstand a man's bid for emotional connection as 'men just being men'. Societally, love may be seen as something more 'serious', with sex just an act, but there is plenty of research that shows that feelings of love and sexual arousal are closely intertwined and share many of the same reward and emotional pathways in the brain.

What can sometimes be missed with men is that perhaps sex is their way of trying to connect, or perhaps it's their way of trying to communicate when they can't find the words, or don't know how to. For men who may equate so much of their self-worth with sex, a rejection can feel like a rejection not of the act itself, but of him as a person and as a man.

I write all of this with some heavy caveats and context. I don't excuse anyone, of any gender, who lacks self-control, respect, or the ability to understand 'no', and none of what may be happening under the surface listed above should be used as an excuse. Everyone must be held to account for their actions. I write about this to acknowledge what may be present for some men so we can begin to understand it and better communicate on it. Sex is such a focal point in many relationships, and yet often carries so much shame and misunderstanding. As a men's relationship and dating coach, David Chambers, who I interview more thoroughly later in this book, tells me that 'a lot of what it comes down to with sex is this deep wound that men carry of not being good enough, and so they struggle with rejection. A lot of this can be triggered through intimate experiences'.

And many men aren't great at communicating this. Rather than talk it through with their partner, they often wait until they're down the pub with their friends, making half-jokes about how they're 'not getting any'. Where the conversations should be happening at home, they're happening in a few pints with equally grumbly blokes. Some studies say that around a quarter of marriages end because of lack of physical intimacy, so it's obviously common. But rather than being dealt with, it often gets left at surface level stereotypes – 'men who want sex too much, women who don't want it enough'. While what's happening is both sides miss each other's bids for intimacy and connection and, perhaps, the wounds and insecurities that lie underneath.

Some of the issues around sex have legal roots too. In the UK, marital rape only became a crime in 1991. Before this, forced sex in a marriage wasn't considered illegal. The expectation was that people *had* to have sex because by that point, they were each other's 'property'. Many countries around the world still have incredibly ambiguous laws when it comes to this area.

So this means there are still plenty of people walking around in some countries who are legally being told that they can do what they want in a marriage. One way forward is by unpicking some of these ancient laws and policies at a societal level, alongside having better conversations in the bedroom too.

The mask of performance is one that a lot of men wear in the bedroom. For so many of them, feelings of self-worth, connection and communication may be tied up in sex. It becomes the ultimate performance for them because it's what they know and what they've been taught. They haven't been taught on school playgrounds that they'll be measured in how they treat others, in the respect and empathy they show. They've been taught that whoever has the biggest penis, whoever sleeps around the most, and whoever does it the best is the manliest. Sex shouldn't be such a performance, but many men treat it as one. And that's because they're not only trying to prove their sexual ability, but they're trying to prove that they're a man too.

Reflection

When have you felt the need to prove your self-worth to others through an act?

Sexuality, Labels, and Liberation

*The eighteen months I spent between realising that I was gay
and first telling someone was the worst time of my life*

—Matt Morton, former professional footballer

Sometimes a performance is about a physical act, a display of some nature. But sometimes it's much bigger than that – it's a mask that people wear around constantly as they lead a double life. Who people see on the outside may conflict with our identity on the inside. And this is sadly the case for many around the world who are struggling with their gender identity or sexuality when these things don't match up with accepted societal norms of masculinity.

One study found that 41% of transgender and non-conforming adults have reported attempting suicide at some point in their lives,[59] which some estimates place as being nine times higher than the general population. We only have to look at that to grasp the seriousness of the pressures that many are facing.

With sexuality, there appears to have been some progress. In 2023, the Office for National Statistics estimated that around 3.8% of the UK population over the age of 16 identified as gay, lesbian, or bisexual, an increase from 2.2% in 2018.[60] This is an increase of almost 73%; a monumental achievement that, at face value, shows we're heading in the right direction.

But do these numbers tell the whole story? It's not a stretch to say that it probably doesn't even come close. These numbers only capture those who have self-reported. What about those who don't feel comfortable doing so, or those who don't even realise that they're gay or bisexual? One study of the global population estimates that as much as 83% of sexual minorities around the world conceal their sexual orientation from all or most people.[61]

Traditionally, one of men's roles is assumed to be procreation, and it's the role most men have grown up believing they must fulfil. When we understand this clearly, it's also easy to understand why the reverse is so demonised.

Homophobic slurs and insults can be used so flippantly in our society that they have sadly become part of the modern vernacular. Some people using these slurs don't do so with malice, but often the homophobic roots of these slurs are forgotten or ignored.

But the impact remains, and when you really peel back the layers of the phrases and examine the roots, it doesn't paint a pretty picture. Same-sex relationships for men can carry certain unfair and outdated stereotypical connotations, getting equated with unmasculine traits or labelled effeminate. This is at odds with how many men have been taught is the 'proper' way to be. It perpetuates an unnecessary baggage of shame and stigma, and clearly these perceptions aren't correct or balanced. But it's often this perception that many hold and therefore push back on.

It's sad that we've weaponised sexuality in this way, and we have a troubled relationship with same-sex relationships around the globe, particularly when it meets the intersection of deeply religious cultures that perpetuate anything other than heterosexuality as immoral. Many countries still treat same-sex relationships in a much darker way where it's a criminal offence, sometimes punishable by death. This legal reinforcement of one way of being does very little to help us unpick rigid masculine norms and stereotypes.

But *why* is so much of society still so averse and prickly when it comes to same-sex relationship or attraction? I put that question to Matt Morton, a professional footballer who has been involved in football for almost 30 years, both as a player and a manager. He was also only one of the few men in the history of the UK's football structure to come out as openly gay, while still playing.

The first man was Justin Fashanu, way back in the 1990s, although I read that he did this because he feared he was about to be outed by a national newspaper. So it may have been more of a coerced coming out rather than doing it in his own time. Justin later tragically took his own life at the age of 37 while facing allegations of sexual assault, as he believed he wouldn't get a fair trial due to his sexuality, as written in his suicide note. The fact that this is one of the *only* examples prior to Matt shows not only how woefully society has handled people's sexuality, but also how hidden these conversations have been.

Clearly, Matt took a huge 'risk' by coming out – it simply wasn't something that was done at the time and, if we're honest, still isn't en masse. Why are we so far behind?

'We inherit behaviours and we inherit language', Morton said. 'If you grew up in a household that uses a lot of homophobic language, you're more likely to use it yourself. And for young boys, their dad is often the person they either aspire to be or to impress, and when they see him using that language with his mates, or shouting it at the telly, they're naturally going to imitate that. The bad news for that is that it's easily replicated. The good news is that it doesn't come from within'.

So many of the issues and stereotypes that have persisted, and men suffer because of, are things that have been inherited through generations of parents, teachers, bosses. And they've inherited their own language, traits, and beliefs from those who came before them, passed down often not through ill will, but simply because they don't know any better. The challenge, of course, is how this persists. Morton said:

Kids then take that language to the playground and it becomes something everyone else says and does. And then it becomes a habit. Homophobia was a lot darker not that long ago, in the 60s, 70s, 80s. We're more shocked now when we read a story about a gay couple getting attacked for holding their partner's hand. It still happens, but not daily like it used to. There was genuine hate. And hate often comes from fear, and that fear often comes from a lack of understanding or education.

We label what we don't understand and fear. People throw around homophobic slurs about things like crying because they don't understand crying themselves, and we see these conversations play out all the time, from playgrounds to boardrooms. It's often wrapped up in male banter, but it's important we look at *where* this banter is coming from. Is it coming from a place of our own lack of understanding and fear? Matt felt the impact of these stereotypes and labels when he first came out:

Some people close to me would say things like 'oh I never would have guessed' or 'I never thought you were gay', as if I should be wearing lipstick and have my nails painted. On the flip side,

---

because I've always cared about how I look, some people said
'I should have known, really.' I shaved my legs because I used to
model, I went to the gym, I got fake tans, and to some people it
was like 'oh yep, that's four of the six things on the gay check-
list, all I needed was another two and it would be definite'.

He explained that likely back in the day, when fewer people felt safe enough to come out, the ones that you knew about were the people probably less likely to have been able to hide it, and so may have exhibited a certain set of similar characteristics. The result of this is that it may have built up a stereotypical, narrow picture in our heads of what a gay man looks like. But Matt said, 'the reality is that you get all kinds of gay people, just like you get all kinds of straight people'.

Pride is often the movement that people most associate with advocating for the rights of those in the LGBTQ+ community, and it does fantastic work. But Matt raised an interesting point to me that if the *only* thing people outside of the community see is Pride, and things like, for example, a use of the colour pink in communications or a rainbow flag, then it might not break down those stereotypes as easily. 'Maybe we need a flag with a skull and crossbones instead! I'm being facetious, but we are dealing with such deeply ingrained stereotypes and pre-conceived ideas that will take a long time to break down'.

So how was it when Matt finally came out? 'A real mix of emotions.' His parents didn't take it as well as he'd have liked at first. He highlighted how being gay isn't the 'norm' that people expect. As Matt said, 'we're not at the point where you could just turn up to a party with another bloke and it not be spoken about. If you met a man tomorrow at an event and they started talking about their partner, your automatic assumption would be "oh, what's her name?" You aren't going to be thinking it's another man'.

And so Matt knew that, particularly in the football locker room environment he was in, that he had to come out. He went into it with a combative attitude, preparing himself for a fight of some nature: 'But there wasn't, the lads were just amazing. The build-up was the worst because of the dressing room culture, it wasn't toxic, but homophobic language was thrown around casually, including by myself, so I built a picture in my mind that maybe I wasn't going to be accepted'.

But Matt also explained that he felt lucky, because he was later on in his career and both his personality and his footballing ability had already been established: 'If I was 16 coming into that dressing room, I don't think I'd have done it. Assumptions would have been made about me and my footballing ability, because I was gay'.

The big question many people often arrive at when it comes to a huge life-altering event like this is 'what's changed? What's life like for you now?' Matt's response was the best I could have hoped for, when he said that in almost every single sense, nothing changed at all. It was the greatest irony that he spent all this time preparing for fights, thinking he may even have to move football clubs, but in the end, he found nothing but acceptance.

I'd spent my whole life thinking I was incapable of love, because I just couldn't fall in love with women. It wasn't until I was 30 that I realised I was gay, and the 18 months I spent between realising that and first telling someone was the worst time of my life. I felt like I was living a lie to everyone around me. So when I opened up and was accepted, and when I realised I could fall in love and be loved, it was amazing.

Morton finished with 'too many people sadly assume what will happen. So many men change careers, leave communities, even take their own lives, because they think they won't be accepted as gay if they open up. The message I want to put out is you'll be accepted. Maybe one team, whether a football team, friendship group or workplace won't accept you, but another one will'.

A UK survey from 2013 found that in the preceding year to the survey being conducted, 3% of gay men attempted to take their own life. This increased to 5% for black and minority ethnic men and 5% for bisexual men. In the same time period, the number for *all* men was 0.4%.[62] So we can see the huge disparity between issues that straight and gay/bisexual men face. Matt's story is, of course, one story, and the reality is there are many people from all walks of life who are not only leaving places like football clubs because of their sexuality, but they're leaving jobs, communities, and families too. Sometimes they're even heartbreakingly leaving this planet.

Why? There will be a multitude of reasons that are complex and intertwined. But you can bet that traditional masculine ideals and outdated societal beliefs and pressures play a huge part in it – men feeling such a deep sense of shame and a feeling that they won't be accepted. And so they keep their true feelings suppressed, as they've been told to, and keep their mask of performance strapped to their face. They're doing it well and, for that, society gives them a pat on the back. But they're not living the life they truly want to, and that mask keeps the pressure building.

> **Reflection**
>
> *Have you ever felt the need to prove your sexuality in order to prove your masculinity?*

Competition: The Race to Prove Yourself

I got back to fame. I got back to glory. I got back to number one in the world. And then I got caught and got a lifetime suspension from the sport I love

—*Dwain Chambers, former Olympic athlete*

From a biological, evolutionary standpoint, men can have an innate need to compete with each other. And there were historically, and arguably still are, good reasons for this. Our need to compete is deeply intertwined with survival and reproduction.

Way back in hunter-gatherer societies, men who were better able to hunt, secure food, and protect their group were more likely to attract mates and pass on their genes. And while sometimes men can get a bad rap for their need to compete, our bodies are almost partly *designed* to compete. It's been found that when we win a competition, our levels of testosterone rise. And higher testosterone levels can be perceived to mean a higher social status, and so a cycle is born where we compete to seem 'more attractive' than our peers, to push ourselves to win. This can surface in many ways, from sports competitions to simply making a joke at someone else's expense to put ourselves out on top.

However, it would be naive to think that our need to compete is purely down to biological conditioning, and so much is shaped by our environment. Competition is baked into the fabric of society, and that's not always a bad thing. We compete in our roles when it comes to performance and promotions, and we're competing with other businesses in the same industry. We love sports because teams can rise and fall through leagues, and we play video games to beat the competition, whether AI or real players. It can be fun and a good bonding experience, and competition can help to push each other to grow.

Competition often *feels* like a gender thing where, generally speaking, from a young age boys are encouraged to be competitive, while girls are encouraged to be more cooperative. The issue is when the need to win can cloud men's judgements, be that professionally or personally.

Knowing the value our society places on power and status, much of a man's self-worth can be tied to the perception of success, and many work harder, longer, and faster to be 'more of a man' in today's world.

Social media has swept in and what could have been the ultimate tool of connection has turned into the ultimate tool for competition and comparison. Every time you log on you'll be served up a smorgasbord of content that, whether consciously or not, we'll be comparing ourselves to. The perception of perfect lives, perfect partners, perfect homes, meals, and bodies. The jealousy that builds up within is partly down to the feeling of competition. And the algorithm fuels this. We're naturally drawn to the things that we're self-conscious about, so while we're told the algorithm is learning about stuff we 'like seeing', it's also learning to twist the doom scroll screw on our insecurities.

The feeling coming from getting ahead can become addictive, particularly when it feels like it's proving our masculinity, and sometimes it can drive us to do things that we might regret. This bending of morals to compete and win was the basis of my interview with Dwain Chambers, one of the fastest European sprinters in the history of athletics. He ran 100 m in 9.97 seconds and has won medals on both the European and international stage, holding numerous records. I spoke to Dwain when he was 46 years old, where he told me he still competes regularly, past his 'prime', because he loves it. This is a man that knows more than most about competition and being at the very top of the pyramid.

But he also knows a darker side to competition too, and how we can get caught up in needing to do things we'd later come to regret, in order to chase the high that comes from not only competing, but from winning. In 2003 Dwain was caught up in a performance-enhancing drug scandal when he tested positive for a banned substance. He was stripped of his medals, banned from athletics for two years and given a lifetime Olympics ban.

This is the story that grabbed the headlines, and it was easy to paint Dwain as the villain, which you can bet the media did. Dwain said to me, 'I didn't look in the mirror at myself, and didn't want to stay home on my own, because I didn't like myself. And then a penny dropped for me. What have I done?'

And although Dwain might have been painted as the villain, that wasn't the man that I spoke to. He was full of humility, and he spoke with unflinching honesty about why he did what he did, and why he now coaches others not to take the same path.

Dwain had led a fairly sheltered, strict childhood, where he wasn't allowed to play outside and engage with the other kids. He felt trapped, and when a coach at school noticed Dwain's natural talent and got him onto the running track, he finally felt free. He ran because he was fast but I also got the sense that he ran almost metaphorically, away from his childhood. His rise was rapid.

Within two years I was the fastest kid on the planet. All the built up frustration I had from childhood, I could use that energy on the track. And then as an athlete, your ego is filled by going out and performing in front of an audience. Your masculinity is displayed when you're in the warmup arena, parading around, like a lion in the Serengeti trying to impress a female.

And the feeling of the highs were addictive. For people in the general public who might not compete, it's the same adrenaline rush as your first kiss or passing your driving test. But in a sporting arena, hundreds of thousands of people cheering your name? It turns that little adrenaline rush into a flood. We become addicted to the cheering of the crowd. We feel almost god-like and are global superstars, we've got the money, the fame, the women. People recognise us on the streets. It's an addiction.

As Dwain talked, I could sense how addictive the feeling must have been. We place these masks of performance on our men, and there's no better place to perform than in sporting arenas, winning, with thousands shouting our name. But what about when those performances slip? Do we let the mask slip?

Dwain had gone from winning time and time again, from junior races to senior competitions. He was winning medal after medal, and the fame that came with it. And then, at the World Championships in 2001, he finished fifth. Suddenly, the public adulation he had, the parties he was invited to, it all disappeared, replaced by nothing more than a pat on the back. His agent told him that his contract was up.

Naturally, Dwain didn't want to lose that lifestyle, he didn't want to lose being at the top of the pyramid. Someone offered him a lifeline, a chance to stay at the summit, in the form of performance-enhancing drugs. He said:

I thought if I don't do this, I'm going to drop to number six in the world. I'll lose my contract, the praise will go, the money, fame, and women will go. So I took it. I got back to fame. I got back to glory. I got back to number one in the world. And then I got caught and got a lifetime suspension from the sport I love, an Olympic and Commonwealth ban and my reputation was in tatters. I had no idea how famous I'd become. No idea. And I ruined all of that.

But Dwain also stressed to me that he was glad he got caught: 'Because I wasn't going to stop, and I didn't like lying. The fame and the wins felt dirty, because they came with a heavy price. I hadn't earned them'.

Few of us can relate to the practical parts of Dwain's story. But we can relate to what lies underneath and behind that mask of performance. We compete in our everyday lives, whether it's micro-actions in the jokes we make in our groups to macro-actions around our appearance or in the workplace. And we can all relate to wanting to avoid pain and moving towards pleasure. Though his shortcut is an extreme example, Dwain, like many of us, didn't want to feel the shame of not winning, to lose the things around him that he felt made him a man: the women, the money, the fame.

There's nothing wrong with competition and indeed it can be a core part of masculinity. The trouble is when men are performing and competing not for themselves, but for the perception they want to achieve for others, or as a way of out-coping or outrunning insecurities. And when we can only achieve 'masculinity' by putting others down, cutting corners, or not being true to ourselves, then that feels like a pretty fragile brand of masculinity. But sadly this is a brand that we are promoting and co-creating when we don't also associate masculinity with compassion, connection, community, and humility.

Reflection

In what ways do you feel your worth is tied to your performance? Why?

Masculinity After Injury

It doesn't matter if you aren't the biggest bloke in the world or, in my case, only have one leg! If you're a decent bloke with good values, integrity, a good family man – that's masculinity for me

—Luke Tarrant, body image influencer

Much of a man's sense of masculinity is equated with his physical appearance, the body he displays to the world: strength, power, and a toned physique. What happens when that's taken away?

'Disability' is a broad term, and is highly complex and personal. It covers a huge range of things that can include physical, sensory, intellectual, mental, neurological, and chronic illnesses, and arises from interactions between a person's health condition and their environment. I've approached disability from a general perspective in this chapter, with the caveat that each person's experience will be highly subjective.

If we take the traditional view of masculinity, we know that it's associated with strength, power, autonomy, the ability to hunt, provide, lead, and take control. These are the traits that a man's mask of performance tells him he needs to shine against. Disability, on the other hand, can draw connotations of helplessness and dependence, and this perceived helplessness can get conflated with weakness.[63]

There are two incredible people that I spoke to who are doing inspiring work debunking and deconstructing this perception. The first of those is Mark Ormrod MBE, who in 2001, at the age of 17, realised his lifelong dream of becoming a Royal Marine. But what he couldn't have planned for was how dramatically his life was going to change when, on Christmas Eve of 2007, while on a routine foot patrol in Afghanistan, he stepped on and detonated an Improvised Explosive Device (IED). It instantly removed both of his legs above the knee and his right arm above the elbow.

Mark said to me:

---

in the Western world, we live in a bubble, we're very lucky. We're not really exposed to the brutality of the world until we experience it in the military. After my incident, I spent a week in intensive care and another five weeks in hospital. And then I was moved to a rehab centre and started my long road to recovery. I was discharged from the military in 2010, and that's when the next chapter of my life began, when I became a disabled adult, and someone without a plan for the first time ever.

Mark explained to me how tough it was in the beginning, being in a battle with himself and struggling to see the bigger picture. And what got him through it? 'I thought maybe I can't be a Royal Marine physically anymore, but I can mentally. One of the recruiting slogans at the time was "it's a mindset, 99.9% need not apply", and I just thought I need to take that mindset that got me through recruit training and apply it to my rehabilitation. And that made the difference for me'.

Another saying that they have in the military is 'no cuff too tough', which Mark explained to mean that no job or task is too demanding to overcome. It's obviously critical for a military mindset in some of the most inhospitable environments on the planet, but it's also clear to see that this is a saying we conflate with traditional masculinity too.

And this isn't always a bad thing. Clearly, there are times for this resilience, both in the military, and in everyday life. As Mark said, it was this mindset that helped him recover. The challenge, however, with traditional masculinity is how immalleable we make it, dismissing the need for a more flexible, expansive approach. I wondered how all of this changed for Mark after stepping on the IED – did his definition of masculinity change for himself, and how much of it was shaped by the military?

> *For me, being a man is about being the provider and the protector. We bring home the bread, we provide for our family, we protect our family. That's what I grew up believing, and I still do. Joining the military, you go from protecting your family to protecting your country. I believe in strength, fitness and looking after myself.*

If we look at this in simplistic terms, that paragraph aligns with the 'traditional' view of masculinity. But Mark didn't stop there, and explained that his sense of masculinity has changed, particularly after becoming a father. Knowing he had to care and nurture a child, he knew he needed a more expansive approach to masculinity.

> *I need to be the guy that can change nappies and go clothes shopping with the wife, but also the guy that can protect my family. Being a man can't always be 'just get on with it mate', you need to be able to listen, to understand, to be a bit more flexible as a bloke. And there's nothing wrong with that. The stuff I've been through, I've had to go through therapy, I've had to be vulnerable and raw. Does that make me less of a man? I don't think so.*

Mark's perception of masculinity was forged in his youth, shaped by the military, but then *had* to change after his accident. It's one that's maintained the good parts of traditional masculinity while bringing in a healthy, balanced edge.

And this was much the same as I found with Luke Tarrant too, who, while travelling around South America, was involved in a motorbike crash and ended up having to have his leg amputated: 'I woke up in hospital where they spent 24 hours trying to save my leg, before having to chop it off. I thought that was the worst bit, but then within another 24 hours I had sepsis. My organs started shutting down and things went from bad to a lot, lot worse. I was in critical care in Colombia when my parents arrived. In total I had to have eight surgeries on my left leg'.

Life has obviously changed a lot for Luke since the accident, who has chosen to see as many of the positives out of it as he can:

Cool things have happened to me since. We wouldn't be here talking about your book if it wasn't for the accident. I wouldn't have gained a load of Instagram followers and ended up at all these cool events.

But there have been some really tough moments. The first time I got back to my flat after release from hospital was tough. I couldn't fit through my bathroom door properly with the wheelchair and I realised how hard it was to do basic stuff like cook an egg. That was mentally savage.

Understandably there was a mental strain on Luke post-accident, but what I really wanted to know is how, if at all, it had impacted his sense of masculinity. He told me he'd always viewed himself as a tall, strong, physical bloke. 'And then suddenly I'm in a wheelchair with my mates having to push me around. I've gone from being taller than most people and looking down at them, to looking at their arses. That's the tough part for me, I hate relying on others. I have to ask others for help now, whereas before I was good just doing everything myself'.

And so that sense of masculinity has had to change. Where before it was about being strong and powerful, for Luke now it's about values. He told me of a friend of his, a former professional rugby player, who dove headfirst into a pool and broke his spine, paralysing himself. But he's managed to learn to walk again, and Luke says: 'I look at him and think he's just a total man. Because he talks about his problems and how he's feeling. He acts with integrity. It doesn't matter if you aren't the biggest bloke in the world or, in my case, only have one leg! If you're a decent bloke with good values, integrity, a good family man. That's masculinity for me'.

While this section has focused on physical disabilities, the intersection of masculinity and less visible disabilities – such as mental health issues or chronic illness – requires as much thought and attention. However, these two conversations brought the intersection of physical disability and traditional masculinity sharply into focus and the point here is that Mark and Luke haven't let their disabilities define them, and they've not let an outdated version of masculinity define them either.

Mark has gone on to be awarded an MBE, has competed in the Invictus Games, done Brazilian jiu-jitsu with Tom Hardy and featured in the 2020 Netflix documentary, *Heart of Invictus*. Luke has been candidly sharing his journey of recovery and adapting to his new life, right from videos of his post-amputation surgery in the hospital. He's regularly featured in the press, and has continued to travel the world, challenging himself to what's possible. Clearly, he hasn't let his disability define or limit him.

If I stick with purely traditional masculine traits, they've both actually ticked a lot of boxes. Fame, followers, achievements, medals, and awards. But it was the humility that shone through our conversations that stood out. These things weren't important to them as proof that they're men, they're important to them as proof that they weren't going to let their disabilities define them, that they could still go on to do great things, and that they could do it with compassion and empathy. That's real flexible, balanced masculinity to me. Toughness, resilience, and bouncing back after a setback, but also humbleness, softness, and the ability to ask for help when it's needed.

Their masks of performance have been removed, perhaps forced off from their accidents, but nonetheless, I felt I was seeing the *real* Mark and Luke because of it. Losing parts of their bodies didn't mean they lost their masculinity, it redefined it for them. Perhaps even made it more complete.

Reflection

If something changed your body, how would it change your sense of masculinity?

Key Summary and Reflections

- **The commoditisation of self:** Many men are always 'on', treating life as a performance, because it's the way they know how to prove their masculinity. The equation to them is: if they can look good and perform well, then they're more manly. But we can start to feel less like people, and more like products.

- **A range of performances:** Performance can come in many forms; perhaps acts, hiding of identity, or a need to compete. Performance isn't inherently bad, but it can often be used as a way of avoiding pain or insecurity.

- **Behind the mask:** We often miss what's happening *behind* the mask. We criticise or judge men for their external performances, their acts, their behaviours, not understanding that sometimes it's their way of trying to fit in and belong.

- **Less important than we think:** We are often performing in order to achieve a certain perception in other people's minds. In the vast majority of cases, they care a lot less about all of this than we think.

8
Breaking Point #5:
The Shame We Carry

No human wants to feel shame. It's a deeply painful emotion, carrying with it a visceral sense of humiliation and failure, and these things may often feel like a death sentence to men. Traditional masculinity has no room for shame. So it's an emotion many men don't understand or even know they have, and yet we can carry so much shame in so much of what we do.

Shame can come in many forms: in who we are, in what we look like, in our abilities. It will be a present force in many of the topics listed before this breaking point and after it, as it plays as the soundtrack to so much of human thought. However it surfaces, the feeling is so painful and alien to men that they do whatever they can to force it away, so sure that if we let our mask slip, even for a moment, that the world will see us for what we believe we are: failures, rejects, worthless. That in itself makes us feel enough shame to last a lifetime.

And so we carry it around with us like oversized baggage. Sometimes we know we're carrying it, sometimes we have no idea. But left unresolved and untreated, it grows, until it forces us down routes we don't want to take – withdrawal, addictions, acting out, or anything else to escape this feeling. Shame will present for men in different ways, but in the following chapters I've covered some of the most common places that it shows up for men.

Penis Size and the Myth of Manhood

It gets ingrained into boys and men that they aren't big enough, and therefore aren't good enough

—Dr. James Stevenson, Lead Physician, Bupa Health Clinics

When researching on this highly taboo topic, I came across threads from men who had anonymously posted that they've never even attempted to start an intimate relationship, assuming nobody would want them because of the size of their penis. Others talked openly about wanting to take their own lives.

For many men, the idea of what makes them 'good men' is deeply entangled with their penis, specifically its length. It's sometimes easy to underestimate how deeply a man's penis can impact him. Sometimes it can be a source of masculine pride, other times of unspoken shame. Sometimes both.

The penis is a focal point of most male jokes, and you'd probably be hard pressed to find a bloke that hasn't made some sort of phallus-related quip at some point in his life. I'd also be surprised if a man or boy hasn't at least once let their mind wander to their own size. Some studies have found that as many as 45% of the population have expressed dissatisfaction and anxiety over their penis size,[64] although I'd wager this number may be under-reported.

It seems strange really, doesn't it? To spend so much of our time worrying about the size of an organ. I'm sure we don't spend half as much time worrying about the size of our heart or lungs, two just as important, if not more so, organs. So why *are* we so overly concerned with penis size?

There are some biological factors. For example, testosterone plays a role in penis development during puberty. Although it has no impact on development in adulthood, there may be a belief that a larger penis equals more testosterone which equals more manliness. If men do think in linear ways, then there's almost no simpler equation than that. It's one of the simplest, and sometimes most misleading, equations. Bigger equals better, and bigger equals manlier. We aren't necessarily always taught it outright, but it's present; in conversations, in media, in jokes.

These jokes and conversations float from the playground to the pub, from teenagehood to adulthood. And it's not helped, of course, by the often exaggerated sizes and performances in porn, which is where many are getting their sexual education from.

How do you think a teenage boy or vulnerable man feels when comparing his size to that of a pornstar, sometimes someone 20 years his senior? The truth is, we don't yet truly know just how far-reaching the impact will be of what anxieties the next generations may carry into the bedroom.

Dr James Stevenson, a lead physician at Bupa, highlights how porn often features unrealistically well-endowed men: 'I've had quite a few patients come to me who are worried about the size of their penis, because it gets ingrained into boys and men that they aren't big enough, and therefore aren't good enough. I have to spend so much of my time re-educating boys and men that everyone is different, and you don't need much size for a healthy sex life'.

Much of what men believe about the size of their penis, and the shame they therefore carry with it, is a culturally and socially shaped narrative, reinforced through humour and in porn. They're not getting the correct education that they need, and then they're suppressed into not talking about their shame. But you only have to roll the historical clock back a few thousand years to see that things were different.

In Ancient Greece, small penises were associated with self-control, rationality, and wisdom. It's why when you take trips to local museums and see statues from these times, they're often carved with small, non-erect penises. On the other hand, larger penises were associated with barbarism, foolishness, and uncontrolled lust. That's why Greek art of grotesque figures generally depicted larger, more erect penises.

Clearly, the Ancient Greeks were onto something, and I'm not talking about size – I'm talking about values. They understood that intelligence and self-control were wise traits to value in their men and so perhaps it's no wonder they produced some of the greatest philosophical minds in Plato, Socrates, and Aristotle. These days it's much less common to hear men praised for their critical thinking on the form of the soul, save for perhaps academic circles.

As history progressed through to Medieval and Renaissance Europe, penis size often – particularly in Western contexts – became associated with virility, masculinity, and social power.

One of the more modern psychoanalysts, Sigmund Freud, placed symbolic importance on the phallus, associating it with power and dominance, and this idea influenced Western beliefs of masculinity, and no doubt played a part in shaping our cultural narratives today.

Freud also said young girls have penis envy, believing that they feel inferior because they don't have one, and also that boys as young as three develop unconscious sexual desires for their mother, and so harbour resentment towards their father – ideas which are often heavily criticised due to a lack of empirical evidence, and so perhaps his work is more revealing of a point in time, rather than definitive human behaviour.

But, wherever these beliefs originated from, we now live in a society that often cares more about the external than the internal. Whether it's conscious or subconscious, we place value on the materialistic and the physical, and that's how many men measure their worth – in the price tag on their watch or the size of their physical attributes. Shame doesn't travel alone, and whether intentional or not, it's often carried forward on the jokes we make, the conversations we have, and the things we value. But it doesn't need to be this way. As Dr James Stevenson said, 'the really important thing I want to get across is that everyone, no matter their size, shape, or gender, should be allowed to have a healthy sex life. But men often don't think that they're good enough'.

And why don't they believe they're good enough? Because they're measuring themselves up against what they've been told matters – physical attributes and external qualities. While there is a place for these, they often aren't measuring themselves for what's on the inside too. When a man equates so much of his masculinity with his penis, if he feels shame around it, that shame will haunt him constantly. We know that much of this is a societal construct, which has changed throughout periods of history. Perhaps we're due another cultural shift, one that remembers what's always mattered more.

Reflection

What would change for you if you no longer saw size or performance as a reflection of your worth?

Sexual Anxiety and Silent Shame

One in four men would rather end their relationship than talk about their erection issues with a partner

—*Dr James Stevenson, Lead Physician, Bupa Health Clinics*

A man's feeling of the need to perform in the bedroom, coupled with any shame he might feel about himself, can often present real challenges when it comes to sex. It can lead to erectile dysfunction, premature ejaculation, low libido, difficulties orgasming, and more – often with roots in psychological anxiety.

It's something that has probably impacted most men from time to time, even for a short period, and there's no shame in that. Or there doesn't need to be, at least. The issue for men is when it becomes a mental health challenge where a vicious cycle is created, the anxiety feeding into the performance, and vice versa. Sex requires you to be present in the moment but these issues can pull you away from that and into your head.

There are a few reasons it impacts men so deeply. One concept of masculinity distils it down into three core roles, called the Three Ps: Provide, Protect, and Procreate. Purely through the lens of this concept, the perceived inability to procreate can make some men feel 'broken'.

But sometimes a man's social status can also be measured among other men on not only how many people he's slept with, but how *well* he's done it too. The better the sex, the better the man.

These things aren't necessarily cured when in a relationship either, where in fact there can be a heightened pressure to satisfy expectations and be a 'good' partner. Shame and stigma at the perceived inability to meet these expectations well enough can often push men into a deeper hole, perhaps turning to drink, drugs, or other coping mechanisms – with these things, of course, only feeding into the cycle of hampering sexual function.

Dr James Stevenson, who has a wealth of experience across sexual function, highlighted some striking statistics:

Research we did with Bupa found that around one in five men have experienced a sexual dysfunction issue, sometimes one in four depending on the issue. But, one of the most shocking things that came out of it was that one in four men would rather end their relationship than talk about their erection issues with a partner. And almost half of men who reported a sexual dysfunction issue have never spoken about it.

This is, sadly, the weight of shame in action. Keeping a muzzle strapped tightly on not only men's mouths, but their experiences too.

More than that, we found that a lot of men try to hide it. A third of men have turned to the dark web for treatment, which can be so damaging, while around 25% of men may do things like drink deliberately and then blame the drink for any dysfunction.

None of this is to assume that men will read this chapter and suddenly feel comfortable discussing everything to do with their sexual function. It's a difficult, embarrassing subject. But Dr Stevenson said:

If we compare it to something like the menopause for women, I think often a woman is more comfortable speaking with a female clinician about it of a similar age because they expect it to be something they're all going through at that time, or something they're susceptible to. Whereas for men, they often seem to think they're the only ones in the world experiencing a sexual function issue.

The media doesn't help with how it perpetuates this stuff around physicality, well-endowed men, the hero image that men need to play. But when it really comes down to it, how often are women telling men they have to have better sex in order to be a man? It's unlikely. Generally it's men perpetuating this myth, men that perpetuate the alpha male stereotypes.

And when literal relationships are at stake, not to mention the wellbeing of the man experiencing these things, it's hard not to wonder if we're missing something. Particularly as there is a plethora of treatment options available, from medicine to therapies. It's often stigma, shame and embarrassment that stops men accessing them, because these things feel unmasculine and awkward. And so they suppress how they feel and do what they believe they must – sacrifice their wellbeing in order to maintain masculine pride, while shame lingers overhead.

Reflection

Where in your life has a feeling of shame convinced you to shrink and hide?

Mirror, Mirror: Men and Body Image

What a lot of individuals don't recognise is that something like body dysmorphia is an emotional problem

—*Professor David Veale, consultant psychiatrist*

One of the places that people feel shame most acutely is over their physical appearance. When we think of body image issues, we tend to think of women. The reasons for this are numerous, not least because of the obsessive nature we collectively hold over the 'perfect female body', while 'appearance anxiety' is considered a highly unmasculine trait, and so men have been conditioned to not talk about it.

But sometimes this can play into a harmful misconception that men don't need to care about the way they look, or perhaps that their bodies are free game for jokes or newspaper columns, as it won't impact them as much. A quick hop in the shower, a smidgen of moisturiser on the face and boom, they're all good to go. Any more than this – for example, a man who wears makeup – carries a lot of stigma and shame. Meanwhile women are expected to work their way through dozens of tinctures and potions.

But would you be surprised to learn that at least 69% of male adolescents are dissatisfied with their bodies in terms of weight?[65] A survey by the Global Equality Collective (GEC) found it to be higher, with a staggering 86% of men and boys *not* having a positive image of their bodies. As stated in the report, 'the most common themes influencing body image was the pressure to look muscular, lean and in shape. Many responses alluded to desiring "muscles, 6-pack abs, athletic physique . . . "'.[66]

Men are under enormous amounts of pressure to look a certain way. Picture an image in your mind right now, and you'll know the one I mean. Ripped abs, chiselled jaw, a brooding look in their eyes. This is the archetypal male, the image of perfection. Men will go to incredible lengths to achieve this, with some reports in the UK estimating that there are at least half a million male steroid users, with some sources putting it closer to one million.[67]

Many of these problems surface for boys who don't yet understand their bodies, who go through puberty and likely get comments from others on the playground. I've never been a stocky man myself, and frequently had jokes made about my body. Whether this is overtly present or not in the jokes, they have their basis in the perceived *lack* of something. The implication is that the perfect male build is about having an abundance of muscle and weight, while anything less is something to target.

What is the real-world impact of this on the men behind the masks? I interviewed Tommy Hatto, a model and actor who's starred in huge blockbuster films such as *Thor: The Dark World* and *The Maze Runner*. He's also a body positivity advocate, having been through a long journey with body image issues and eating issues.

He had to prevent his two worlds from colliding, modelling with Calvin Klein yet struggling with his body image. He kept it hidden for years, terrified that he wouldn't get picked up for work – the dual parallel of the outside, materialistic world in a battle with the inner mask a man wears.

I've always harboured resentments towards the modelling industry, because of my own body biases as I've never looked like the men I see on billboards. It doesn't bother me so much these days, but as a younger kid, it was a constant reminder that I wasn't masculine enough, simply because I didn't have enough muscles.

Hatto agreed there are challenges, and said:

---

the industry has a long way to go. But it is becoming more inclusive in terms of different body types and people. And I do think there's a responsibility to be more transparent about the life of a model. The person you see on the billboard with the 'perfect' body? They've been on a strict diet and fitness routine for a long time to reach that standard, it doesn't just happen. But people still buy into it, because we're drawn to good-looking things, whether that's a person or a product.

And he's right. The human brain fires off chemicals in our reward systems when we see 'attractive' things. It's what the modelling industry is built on. But it shows why it can sometimes objectify people to unhealthy standards and impact the consumer looking at it who doesn't see themselves reflected in the products.

For Hatto, who now runs his own agency and continues to model, he triumphs transparency. When he does his shoots, he's honest that he's been in the gym for six weeks to achieve this physique, or that an image may have been photoshopped or edited. And he really highlights the challenge of social media.

In the past, there was an acceptance that the models you saw on billboards were a certain type of person who sat in the 1%, and you didn't see these things all the time. But now, you're seeing it on your social feeds every day, with the algorithm serving up seemingly normal people who will always be 'better' than you in a way you'll laser in on: more abs, bigger biceps, bigger boobs, longer hair, bluer eyes, a better lifestyle, smoother skin, and so on – pick your poison.

These images work too, often attracting more social media likes or comments, all helping to fuel the cyclical belief that the better the body, the better the man. Social media now allows us to scroll through thousands of bodies in a short space of time, each image another rewire to our brain, telling us we aren't good enough.

Many people struggle with body image issues and body dissatisfaction, but this can manifest into body dysmorphic disorder (BDD), which is a mental health issue characterised by an obsessive preoccupation with one's own appearance. It can be hugely debilitating to the individual, sometimes to the point where they can't even leave the house.

Professor David Veale, a psychiatrist who specialises in BDD and obsessive compulsive disorder (OCD), told me that BDD affects around 2% of the population, with no significant gender bias, although men tend to be more worried about their nose, hair, or genitalia and whether they're masculine enough. A subcategory of BDD can develop – muscle dysmorphia, which primarily affects men. They may develop other problems like eating issues, abusing anabolic steroids or other performance-enhancing drugs, eating excessive amounts of protein or getting addicted to exercise.

Veale said: 'these men may feel that they're improving their appearance in some way, but it doesn't actually solve the body image problem. What a lot of individuals don't recognise is that something like this is an emotional problem. They view it as an appearance problem, and so try to fix it with something like a cosmetic procedure or to hide it. So you're not really treating it at its root'.

And what sits at the heart of things like body image issues, and many other issues that men face, is, in Veale's words, 'what we call internal shame. The individual is shaming themselves, putting themselves down because they don't think they're good enough or attractive enough. It's part of a lack of self-esteem and lack of self-compassion'.

This is what can happen when we condition men to value strength, muscle mass, and appearance above all else. This isn't to discount the role that these things can play. Working out, staying fit, and maintaining strength and mobility is obviously good for us, especially as we age, and if someone values these things in their life, that's great. But when masculinity is equated with *only* how we look, it can breed these unhealthy obsessions, and often at the expense of what's happening on the inside.

And, as Veale highlighted, men have been conditioned to take a fairly linear, physical response to the challenges in their lives, missing the hugely emotional and psychological components often at play.

From talking to Tommy Hatto, even once men reach these almost impossibly high standards, in many cases they're just as unhappy or self-conscious – they want to chase an even higher level of perfection. There's no summit, simply a ceiling which keeps getting higher and higher.

We are always going to be attracted to our own preferences of people and bodies, but that doesn't mean we can't bring a little more compassion into the conversation, to understand that men care about their bodies just as much as women, and to stop making them free game. And to understand that what a man looks like on the inside – his values, how he treats others, his ambitions, his empathy – is just as important as his muscles. And both things can contribute to a man's sense of masculinity. A focus on one at the expense of the other isn't a win, it's a loss.

Reflection

What's the harshest thing you've ever said to yourself in the mirror, and would you say it to someone you love?

The Hidden Eating Struggles of Men

The bulimia, the weight gain, the training, it was all to show other people what I thought a good man looked like. Even though on the inside I was miserable

—*Ryan Hopkins, author*

Eating issues can arise for numerous reasons, for example, body image issues, a way of coping, a response to bullying or a traumatic childhood. Again, much like with body image issues, we tend not to associate eating issues so much with men.

I spoke with Professor Janet Treasure, an academic psychiatrist and professor at King's College London who has specialised in eating disorders for around 40 years. She told me that anorexia nervosa, the medical term for what is more commonly referred to as anorexia, was first described in various medical sources 150 years ago. But it's only been since the 1980s that we've recognised overeating, known as bulimia nervosa, with episodic overeating and attempts to compensate for the effects of the food binge being first described by Professor Gerald Russell in 1979.

As to what causes an eating issue, Treasure explained that there isn't one sole factor, and it's a complex mix. She said that there's a definite genetic element, and development factors are important too. As are social factors, 'as was seen by the large increase in anorexia nervosa presenting for care during the COVID epidemic'. She also explained that different vulnerabilities can increase the risk of an eating issue, things like autism, OCD, or anxiety, for example.

Like with most things, it's a complex condition that doesn't fit into a neat category of 'if you do X, then you have Y', and it's relative. But generally speaking, does it impact differently based on sex?

Treasure said:

Female adolescents are at most risk, and it's been found that eating disorders are ten times more likely in women than men. It could be that a higher proportion of men go undiagnosed. It could also be that some of the symptoms, such as loss of sexual potency and function, are more worrisome to men, and so they're more aversive to eating disorders. And for women, we know this tends to be triggered by weight loss and calorie counting, while for men, it's more about muscularity. It's not so much about losing weight and the number on the scale, it's more about the ideal body.

Whatever the true picture of the gender split between those that struggle with an eating issue, we know that it *does* impact men. And yet the general awareness and support for men isn't as available. Treasure said: 'it's weighted more towards women, perhaps because the muscularity drive for men is much more culturally condoned and regarded as attractive, whereas extreme thinness everyone finds a bit frightening. This has been culturally set for a long time, you know if we think of history with gladiators and warriors, the emphasis is on a muscular body shape, and so this is what a lot of men strive for'.

How many men have you met in your life, or seen on the TV or social media, talking about having had an eating issue? Even after working in the mental health space for 10 years, I can't recall seeing many stories from men on this topic. Because, like with most things in this book, there is so much shame and stigma wrapped around the subject and masculinity. And often because if a man is eating to bulk up, that is typically glorified, not demonised, and he believes that's how he *should* look.

One man who has bravely talked about it is my good friend Ryan Hopkins, bestselling author of *52 Weeks of Wellbeing: A No-nonsense Guide to a Fulfilling Work Life*. When he was younger, Ryan fit into much of the stereotypical image of a man: he was loud, confident, had a few tattoos, and played rugby. But after an accident on the rugby pitch, he couldn't walk and lost his job as a tradesman, couldn't play sport, couldn't go out anymore. And so he turned to a source of comfort for him – food.

As things started to get better for Ryan and he was able to return to the gym, he wanted to lose his new-gained weight: 'I was training and reading bodybuilding articles. Then came the calorie counting. Eventually I was only having chicken and broccoli for dinner. A treat would be a piece of chewing gum, and then I started taking diet pills. It all led to me developing the most insane relationship with bulimia, where I'd just be binging and then purging. It was fucking relentless, and nobody knew'.

What really compounded the issue for Ryan is the way this new image of his was being received on the outside by others:

Everyone would say things to me like 'oh you look great', because this is what men are meant to look like, right? I'd be getting female attention, and it all just reinforced this feeling

171

> *that I looked the right way, even though I didn't feel right on the inside. All of it, the bulimia, the weight gain, the training, it was all to show other people what I thought a good man looked like. Strong, confident. I was doing it all for others, even though on the inside I was fucking miserable.*

This can quite easily play into a hidden addiction for men – fitness. Sometimes this is to maintain or achieve a certain body image, sometimes it's because of an obsessiveness around maintaining health. As fitness is an activity which is glorified in our society, an addiction can sometimes get missed. As we saw from Ryan, it's easy to get compliments on the external and the physical, while the interior is falling apart. It can perpetuate an already unhealthy relationship one has with their body, where they aren't giving it enough nutrients and sustenance, and illness, fatigue, injuries, and hormonal imbalances can follow. They may neglect relationships and social situations, obsess over what they eat, or abuse anabolic steroids to achieve the 'perfect' physique.

I asked Ryan how it feels to have both gone through that experience, and now talk about it openly, as a man:

> *I'm still learning how to tell this story, and it's new for me. But I wear it as openly as I can, because all people normally talk about is the burnout and the stress, that's the more commonly accepted mental health story. It's not so sexy telling people you used to get sick over a Murray Mint.*
>
> *I thought I was the only bloke in the world going through this. It took a long time to get better, and it was only by changing my environment and working on myself that things*

got better. Society and the environment around us has a lot to answer for. If a plant isn't growing, you don't get angry at the plant, do you? You move it to more sunlight, you give it some water. So it's rarely the human that's broken, it's the environment they're operating in. We're essentially all just house plants with complicated emotions; we just need a bit more sunlight, a bit more water and a bit more love. Nothing like some Instagram wisdom!

Ryan so perfectly summarised so much of what I've found in my research and in my other interviews. For men going through things, they often carry that shame and embarrassment on their own shoulders, in silence, berating themselves for not being good enough. Societal constructs loom large overhead, pushing them back down into those neat little boxes labelled 'masculine'. And yet we don't always stop, take a step back, and acknowledge that many of our problems start in the environment around us, not within the person struggling.

Most importantly, how is Ryan doing now? 'Look, I'm not the biggest, I'm not the thinnest, I'm not the fittest, but I'm the most comfortable I've ever been. I've got a little bit of love handles, probably always will, but I like to say I'm business up top, party down the bottom'.

Ryan carried his shame around with him for a long time. Solving that shame wasn't about scrambling harder on the hamster wheel to fit into society's definition of a perfect man or to strap the mask even tighter around his face. It was about making peace with himself and *his* definition of what it means to be a man.

> **Reflection**
>
> *Where did your ideas and beliefs of the 'perfect body' come from? Where have they served you, and where have they hindered you?*

Hair Loss: When Identity Falls Out

You have to follow a certain image, and that's the way it is

— *Justin Hopwood, former model, speaking on the modelling industry*

Male pattern baldness is a common pattern of hair loss and thinning in men. It's different to alopecia, which is a broader umbrella term that encapsulates any type of hair loss (including male pattern baldness), but can also be caused by things like autoimmune conditions. Depending on which study you look at these numbers might fluctuate, but it's generally thought that around at least 85% of men will lose their hair to some degree across their lifetime.

In short, it affects a whole lot of men, although to different levels. This is a personal one for me, having had to deal with a hairline slowly running away from me for the best part of a decade. I forked out a small fortune for a hair transplant in 2024 and it was one of the best things I've ever done.

A *huge* part of a man's image is wrapped up in the little bed of follicles that sits on the top of his head. To others that don't understand it, it might just seem like a few hairs are falling out. But to many men, it's a life-crushing experience to go through, one that develops over many, many years, as they watch their hair recede, wondering whether they're now less attractive, less cool, less of a man. It becomes his entire identity, his entire sense of self. It sounds dramatic, but it's how it feels on the inside for a man, and why jokes cut so deep. As the hair thins, shame can thicken.

And it's a slap bang reality check on our own mortality. You wake up and look at yourself in the mirror and see yourself as a little older, a little more fragile. Your sense of agency is stolen by a biological process you feel you have little control over.

I started sharing my hair loss journey online and I took a bit of stick from people, who, incidentally almost all of them older, bald men, told me to get over myself, that they've never had an issue, so why should I?

It perfectly captured for me the dichotomy of the image men *should* be adhering to, and the one that was going on below the surface. A bunch of people playing into tired stereotypes about men, suggesting real men wouldn't worry about their appearance, and would instead man up and get on with it. A *real* man would supposedly find solace in a razor and baldness, not introspection.

And so what happens? Men don't open up. Despite the multitude of treatment options available, they carry their shame around with them, they brush their hair a certain way, or avoid getting in photos, even avoid nights out, struggling in silence. They're in turmoil inside, but don't think they have a right to voice it on the outside.

Aside from the odd negative comment, I received a tidal wave of positivity and a *lot* of comments in my private messages, from men struggling with hair loss, searching online for miracle cures, feeling like they're the only ones in the world going through it. And from women who suspect their partner might be going through it because they never let them touch their hair, or will spend hours perfecting every little strand before being able to leave the house.

For many men, hair is more than just cosmetic. It's a window into his soul and a mirror which reflects his pride. Or his shame. Perhaps even his grief. A compliment or acknowledgement can make his day. Conversely, a joke can leave him wrapped in anxiety and shame for weeks, because so much of a man's identity sits with his hair, and it's not a leap to say that if we can have better conversations around hair, and the emotions that come with it, we'll be starting to have much better conversations around masculinity too.

I felt ashamed of my hair for the best part of a decade. And because of that, I carried a slice of shame over how I felt as a man too. I was with my partner for four years before she saw the extent of my hair loss. Four years. This is how deeply ingrained in us men it is that we can't talk about these things, that we have to hide and smile our way through it, all the while that shame is smiling and laughing back at us, thriving in the silence.

Reflection

What's the first emotion that comes up for you when you think about your hair? What does that feeling tell you about yourself, and does it feel fair?

Key Summary and Reflections

- **The feeling of shame:** Shame is a deeply painful, intense emotion that carries feelings of worthlessness and humiliation. However much we want to tell our men to suppress their emotions, shame still exists. Shame around their body, around sex, around not being 'good enough', around plenty of things.

- **Shame and masculinity:** Men have a difficult time coping with shame, because the feelings of failure and humiliation that come with it feel inherently unmasculine.

- **Suppression supports shame:** By forcing emotional suppression onto people, we are actually perpetuating shame. Shame works best when conversations stay hidden and it wants us on our own. It thrives in the shadows, in among the weeds. Forced emotional suppression isn't helping men, but it's certainly helping shame.

- **A solution for shame:** The antithesis to shame is connection, love, and community, and we can start to banish shame by encouraging emotional **expression**.

- **A source of information:** As with any emotion, shame is there to tell us something about ourselves. You don't have to embrace it like a long-lost friend, but do recognise it, acknowledge it, and name it for what it is. And then ask what it's trying to point your attention to.

9
Breaking Point #6: The Wounds That Don't Heal

All of this pressure that builds inside of men, this shame they carry around, it doesn't simply lie there dormant. It can cause deep cuts to their soul. We've created an image of traditional masculinity that values toughness and resilience, and the perception can be that men are emotionally bulletproof.

But the truth is, men are human, and feel things just as deeply and acutely as anyone else, and they can get wounded too. Forcing men into suppression and silence is like repeatedly ripping a scab off a wound that's trying to heal.

It can become a never-ending cycle, one slice of shame compounding another, cutting even deeper. The pressure doesn't relent until it gives way somewhere. Wounds can come in many forms and arise from many situations, and the next few chapters cover some of the rawest, exploring pain that sits deep below the surface.

The Hidden Grief of Male Fertility

So when, as a man whose role is to supposedly give the seed, can't do that, then what am I?

—Shaun Greenaway, male fertility coach

Given that many men have an innate belief that they are on this planet to provide, protect, and procreate, what happens when a man struggles with infertility? It can be a crushing feeling that the one purpose they feel they were put on this planet for, they've failed at.

Research shows that around half of infertility issues are due to male factors.[68] And the World Health Organisation estimates that fertility issues affect roughly one in six adults globally,[69] so chances are, there are a few people in your network struggling with this.

I had the privilege of speaking to Shaun Greenaway, a male fertility advocate who shared his own story of infertility. After struggles conceiving in 2017, he and his wife went to the doctors and after further testing, it was found Shaun had zero sperm.

I got the diagnosis over the phone and was sitting on a slab outside of work, I felt like I'd been chucked in a river. Most of the time that river was fast flowing, pulling me under, gasping for breath. Other times, it just stopped and I was in the doldrums and not moving.

When I asked Shaun why he chose to speak out about this topic, he explained the almost total lack of support that exists for men in this area, navigating through medical pathways and going round in circles. Two years passed by and he had very few answers. He had surgeries and other treatments, but was eventually hit with the reality that he'd never be a biological father.

He said to me: 'but this just isn't spoken about enough. One in fourteen men will have issues. Of the optimal fertile years between 18 and 40, 130 million men worldwide will face issues. And yet there's 10, maybe 15 people like me, worldwide, actually consistently talking about this. Men are under-represented on this issue in medical pathways, and they're under-represented in society too'.

And what of Shaun's sense of masculinity? He told me that it impacted him hugely:

It's sort of assumed that if men want to have sex, they can just go, and any fertility issues must be on the woman's side. So when, as a man who's been told that his role is to give the seed, can't do that, then what am I? What good am I? I had to not only grieve the life I'd no longer have as a biological father, but I had to grieve my sense of what it was to be a man too.

Greenaway's story really touched me, no more so because it was clear how much his suffering had been prolonged due to a lack of education, support, and general social acceptance for the things that men can go through, sometimes hundreds of millions of men around the world. Gender roles or expectations can be forced upon us and so when we struggle with things like procreation, we're often under-represented in support. We don't hear or see enough men that we can relate to going through similar things, and so shame piles onto us even further, making us tell ourselves that we've failed at one of the things we think we exist for.

How did Shaun make peace with himself and start to heal that wound to his masculinity? He started to research men who have done amazing things in their lives *after* they've had kids. 'Two I always remember are Nelson Mandela and Martin Luther King. They both had children long before the famous acts they've become known for, acts which went down in history. So if they can do that after having kids, then maybe a man's sole purpose on this planet isn't only about procreating. They changed history. And I thought to myself, maybe I still can too'.

It's a powerful message, and one we can all relate to. If there are instances of men doing things outside of traditional masculinity, then surely masculinity is more flexible than we sometimes make it. But I also couldn't help but feel the weight of the fact that Shaun has had to go through this journey silently, re-educating himself on what it means to be a man. And that's the point – there are options available out there. Shaun now has a wonderful family that he loves with children born via the use of donor sperm. His wounds have healed, but the journey of getting to that point was prolonged by a silence he felt forced to take.

Reflection

What messages have you been taught about your worth being tied to what you can produce, whether in your work, sex, family, or elsewhere?

Baby Loss: Grieving in Silence

I've spoken to some men who have lost a baby, and then they're back at work two weeks later

—*James Routledge, author*

There's a stereotype about men where while a mother can be viewed as a parent, fathers can be viewed as little more than glorified babysitters. Clearly this isn't right or fair, but it's a perception that *does* exist. In the event of a miscarriage or baby loss, do fathers get the right space to allow their own wounds to heal?

Clearly, the process of pregnancy and miscarriage is physically more traumatic for the bearer of the child, and there's a huge emotional and mental toll too, and none of this is to discount or dismiss that experience. Focusing purely on the side of the father, they'll have been preparing to become a father for the first time or again, spending months planning for a new way of living. They too will have to deal with loss, not only of the child, but of the life they were planning to lead.

So what place does that grief have among that of the woman who has borne the child? Men can be left feeling guilty for their grief, dealing with it in silence and not wanting to subtract from the experience their partner is having.

James Routledge, author of *Mental Health at Work*, has a personal experience of the loss of his and his partner Sarah's baby, Teddy. James not only couldn't wait to become a father, but it became a large part of his identity – the soon-to-be father who was looking forward to Sunday strolls with the pram to the local cafe in town.

> *Then we got to the 20-week scan, and we were told that the baby was majorly unwell and had quite significant structural abnormalities. We were given this long list of printouts: heart not in the right place, can't see the bowels, can't see the end of the spine, just loads of problems really.*

James said it was a strange feeling, because they went home and Sarah was still pregnant and their baby was still moving around. 'But we knew that probably in a week's time, we'd have to end the pregnancy. We knew we'd have no happy ending.'

I asked James how it felt going through that specifically as a man, and he explained that he felt like he was a spare part, knocking things over in the hospital room or getting in the way of the midwife. He knew he was playing a vital role for his partner Sarah, but he felt completely helpless.

And what about after the event itself, what do the healthcare and support pathways look like? James said:

> *There's not a lot of support for men in the hospital environment. The midwives asked how I was, which was lovely, but it was always right at the end, just as they were about to leave. And how do I answer that? In comparison to what my wife's just been through, I'm absolutely fine. But I'm not. And it's tough, because there's no league table on how you feel, but, the truth is, there is a league table, because someone in the room has had to physically put their body through something, while the other one has just watched.*

And James goes on to tell me that when they sought support on the outside, it was predominantly weighted towards women.

There is some support for men, but it's quite underground and there's a lot less of it. And men don't always know how to engage with these things. The most telling example for him was through the charity he accessed for support, who have a forum for women and a separate one for men, so there *is* a support function there. But the one for women was pretty active, while the one with men was almost silent.

James was 'lucky' in some respects in that he worked for himself. He downed tools immediately and took three months off work, not only to support his wife Sarah, but to support himself too because he was struggling. But many men don't get that space or freedom. 'I've spoken to some men who have lost a baby, their life fundamentally being flipped on its head, and they don't speak about it at all because they don't think they have the right to grieve. And then they're back at work two weeks later. It's madness that men have to go through that'.

And that's where we can do more for men, or for anyone who has been the non-bearer in a relationship that has suffered a miscarriage or baby loss during a pregnancy. We sometimes have reinforced the perception that men simply provide the seed, and then it's almost over to the women after that, to carry and then care for the baby. And what can happen is that men's grief is quietly layered on top of whatever other pressure they're carrying.

Many of us are carrying deep wounds, sometimes over the same shared experience, whether it's baby loss or something else entirely. But men can sometimes feel as though their wound isn't important, and they have no right to feel it. And so they suppress it, but it doesn't stop the bleeding. It's important that we show men that two things can be true at once, and we can make space and time for more than one person's wound.

When the Pressure Breaks

> **Reflection**
>
> *Where in your life have you felt like you didn't have a right to grieve or feel emotions?*

Bullying: The Bruises That Don't Show

Working under the weight of a 'wolf culture' damaged him beyond repair

—*Caroline Roodhouse, suicide awareness advocate*

Bullying, whether conscious or not, is about one person dominating another. It's a powerplay that creates a hierarchy where one takes control and another feels submissive and lesser, and this can come in many forms. Some bullying is rooted in banter, some in subtle digs, some in prejudices, exclusion, or microaggressions. It's not always overt, which can make it hard to clearly define and draw a line between bullying and not-bullying.

It's common to hear stories of bullying among kids in the playground, and indeed many people have a story of feeling bullied. But it can progress well beyond that into later life too, whether that's in the workplace, the home, or down the pub with mates.

The Office for National Statistics (ONS) found that in the year ending March 2023, around 34.9% of children aged 10 to 15 in England and Wales had experienced in-person bullying behaviours.[70] A study a few years prior found that cyberbullying affected almost a quarter of all Britons.[71]

Sadly, it's not uncommon to read stories in the news of young kids taking their own lives after being bullied; things which would once stay on the playground now following them home on social media too. Professionals who couldn't cope with how they were being treated at work seeing suicide as their only way out.

Bullying carries a lot of shame and stigma for men. It's so intertwined with the need to compete and win affection from peers, testosterone, to show strength, to shun weakness. For men, it's often not just about the act of bullying in and of itself, it's about how it makes them feel as a boy or a man. The very act of bullying takes away that feeling men have been told they must strive for – one of being in control, one of power and dominance. They feel emasculated, and how each person responds is highly subjective.

Some react with the one emotion they've been told to show: anger and rage. Others go inward and withdraw, showing the world on the outside it's not affecting them, all while a maelstrom gets whipped up on the inside, creating those internal wounds of shame and humiliation.

After many years working in the mental health space, I've come to develop a degree of compassion and empathy for bullies. Bullying doesn't always come from a place of malicious intent. It often comes from broken homes, or parents who mistreated them and that mistreatment becomes a learned behaviour. Or bullying is a way of dealing with someone's own inner turmoil and pain; it can be easier to bring others down rather than confront our own inner demons. It can often disguise deep-rooted anxiety, insecurity, and low self-worth that the bully is feeling.

I've had a lot of internet trolls over the years jumping into my public comments or private messages, and while it's never nice receiving it, I know that if someone feels so compelled to spend their time bringing someone else down, chances are they aren't in a great place, whether they know it or not.

For a bully who themselves is struggling with self-worth, a highly 'unmasculine' thing to admit to, how can he reclaim that? How can he prove his masculinity to himself and others? He can do what society has told him he should do – look for dominance and power.

To a lesser degree, it's often the same place where light-hearted jokes come from among friends. People often make jokes about the things they're scared of or insecure of, by putting others down to allow themselves to rise up.

But many, many boys and men will struggle to admit they're being bullied. The very act of admitting that you're feeling like you're being bullied is to imply, whether directly or not, that you are a little further down the pecking order than the bully. That the bully's push for control *is* working, and you're faltering under the power play.

That's why many men go inward. They can't admit to this weakness externally. Sometimes some don't even admit it internally. Many struggle alone. Others move away, looking for a new job, a new group of friends. Some take their own lives.

Earlier in the book I shared Caroline Roodhouse's story, who sadly lost her husband Steve to suicide. He left no note, and so she can never know the true cause. But Caroline places a large part of the blame on a toxic workplace, one which turned, in her words, 'a confident and motivated man to a frightened, nervous wreck with a shattered self-esteem. Working under the weight of a "wolf culture" damaged him beyond repair'.

This is the danger when we allow bullying to persist, and also when we have created a culture and a society that leaves people feeling that they can't talk about it, and one that doesn't value difference or empathy. Steve left behind two young girls who will always grow up wondering why. In the face of all of this, we have to ask what purpose this ideal of what it means to 'be a man' is really serving, and *who* it's serving.

Bullying can inflict one of the deepest wounds that someone can suffer. It carries with it a huge degree of shame, one that helps the wound to grow larger and to fester. It's not long before an infection can take over as the bullying begins to affect every other part of their life, the man's identity slowly degrading and breaking.

Reflection

When was the last time you pretended that something didn't hurt you, just to appear strong?

When Men Are Hurt at Home

As a victim, I was re-victimised by having these services tell me that I wasn't a victim, but I was a perpetrator

—*Earl Silverman, domestic abuse survivor*

In England and Wales over the time period 2022/23, the ONS reported that around 2.1 million people over the age of 16 experienced domestic abuse, which includes both physical and emotional. Of that number, almost a third were men. And yet in the same year only 4.8% of victims being supported for domestic abuse were men, so we can see the huge disparity in these figures; the number of men being abused versus the number of men actually getting support.[72]

There is no doubt that women are more disproportionately affected by abuse, and this is not to draw any attention, awareness, or support away from that. And while these statistics are UK-focused, I suspect the statistic that one in three victims being male will surprise people. It certainly did with me.

The trouble for many men is not only are they carrying the abuse and the ongoing threat of abuse with them, but they're carrying an added weight of shame and stigma too. We've been told for a long time that men are supposedly the strong ones, the dominant ones, the leaders in relationships and that women are 'weaker' and 'submissive'. The perception, therefore, is that a man being abused in a relationship, whatever the nature, sex, or gender of the people involved, 'shouldn't' happen, and if it does, he's weak for it.

I have to wonder if part of the disparity in figures of men suffering abuse versus those getting support for it is down to men not believing they have a right to open up about these experiences, to seek help, and admit that they're struggling.

A powerful advert from the domestic abuse charity The ManKind Initiative, released in 2014, showed two scenarios playing out on a public street in England, filmed with hidden cameras to get the public's reaction. It showed a man and a woman getting into a fake argument. In the first scenario, the man is shouting at the woman, grabbing her, pushing her up against a fence. Members of the public flock around them, asking the woman if she's okay, calling the man expletives, asking if she wants to come away with them to a safe place. The second scenario shows the roles reversed, with the woman abusing the man. The public's response? They ignore it, they continue eating their lunch, several people even laugh about it.

This is the reality that many men face. That somehow it's funny if they're getting abused, because it can't be that big a deal. There may even be a perception that if a woman is physically abusing a man, then he *must* have deserved it. And men certainly can't talk about it, because they're *meant* to be the strong ones. It shows how little we take abuse against men seriously, and a large part of that is down to these predefined gender norms we force onto people, that men are almost too big and strong to suffer abuse.

The harrowing Netflix documentary, *My Wife, My Abuser*, shows some of what men can face in the home, and how it can leave them after. Richard Spencer suffered two decades of abuse at the hands of his now ex-wife, and throughout the documentary you could see how withdrawn and broken he'd become.[73] When she was arrested, she tried to pin everything on Richard, saying that he was the abuser and she was defending herself. Luckily Richard had the foresight to secretly film his experiences but if he hadn't done so, there is a question over whether he may have ended up being prosecuted too.

Someone that I spoke to for this book told me that a male friend took his own life after he'd been suffering domestic abuse at the hands of his female partner for over a year. He'd reported it to the police, but it hadn't been taken seriously enough. And now he's left behind a child who no longer has a father.

It's hard to deny that there is something conflicting thinking of 'abuse' and 'traditional masculinity' together, and that somehow the latter negates the former. Where traditional masculinity heavily favours strength, it may not allow for the reality of a man being abused in his own home.

Some men try their best to 'man up' even in the face of vile abuse, because that's what they believe they're meant to do. But the reality is they may be suffering both physical and emotional wounds from their abuse, compounded with the wounds of shame and suppression. It can create a devastating hurricane of shame that attacks them from several angles, slowly making them feel smaller and smaller. Part of the resolution here lies in us changing our perception of men and masculinity, realising that, as we all exist on the same continuum, the pain men feel from abuse is just as valid and worthy of our support.

Reflection

If a male friend told you he'd been abused, would you respond with the same empathy and urgency as if it were a female friend? Why or why not?

Trauma: When It Doesn't Go Away

The last thing I was going to do, especially as a police officer, was show anyone any weakness

—*Gary Hayes, former police officer*

Trauma is a weighty word. If you were to picture a 'trauma' now, I imagine you'd think of something violent and dramatic. And in truth, these are the experiences we tend to associate with post-traumatic stress disorder (PTSD).

But in fact, we all experience trauma, likely on a daily basis, what some refer to as 'micro-traumas' – the small, cumulative stressors of everyday life. Fears that we hold, a stress on the morning commute, a difficult conversation at work, these are all minor traumas that have an impact on the body and our emotional system. These things are an everyday part of life which impact people to different degrees, although it feels highly 'unmasculine' in the traditional sense of the word to admit that we experience these.

While how we respond to these things is subjective, we do know that lifetime PTSD prevalence is higher in women than men (10–12% versus 5–6%).[74] Women tend to exhibit higher levels of acute stress reactions but, importantly, while women tend to lean towards emotion-focused approaches and seek social support for their trauma, men tend to lean more towards problem-focused coping strategies which can involve addressing the traumatic event head on. This means that they may help to reduce and lower their risk of both PTSD or the symptoms that result because of it.

But this coping or solving style isn't without risk, where men may address the physical parts of PTSD, but not the emotional scars, and men may not be able to self-identify and recognise symptoms of trauma. And, if they do, may not feel able to talk about it. We know some of the reasons this may be – not wanting to appear weak, not believing they have the right to feel the way they do or not being able to articulate the emotions they're feeling.

When these things are left unresolved, whether that's PTSD or any other type of life trauma we may face, the body can store these traumas, whether big or small. When that pressure cooker builds up and where it leads to can have heartbreaking consequences not only for the person suffering, but for those around them too.

I felt privileged to sit down with Gary Hayes, former soldier of the Royal Green Jackets and police officer, who, through his own experience of PTSD, established PTSD999 to offer support for emergency service workers.

Gary has been through enough traumatic experiences to last several lifetimes. It didn't surprise me when he said that it all culminated in him attempting to take his own life. This chapter contains some more graphic details of some highly traumatic experiences.

The military regiment I joined in the 80s was probably one of the toughest in the British Army. We went through hell to earn the right to wear our badge. About 170 of us joined the regiment, and when we came to the end of our training programme twenty weeks later, there were only 55 of us left. So showing any sign of weakness was certainly something I didn't want to do.

Gary eventually left the military and joined the police. 'Policing changed dramatically after 9/11. But then it happened here in London with the 2005 London bombings. I was part of a new anti-terrorism team at the time, but I was on paternity leave. One of the lads at work called and said "grab your kit bag mate, we need you. We've been bombed".'

And so Gary was pulled away from his paternity leave, his new child, and his wife, and saw things that nobody should have to see. By his own admission, he'd seen plenty of fatalities in his life, but the scenes of that day were devastating. 'People were unable to stay at the scene for any period of time, it was that horrific.'

He was told to keep as much emotional distance from the victims and their families as he could, and for good reason.

But a gentleman had come to view a body, it was obviously his young lad. He'd just lost his wife to cancer a couple of weeks prior, and that was his only son. I caught sight of this gentleman's bereavement card and then my world fell apart. I was wracked with guilt, because to me, I was part of the anti-terrorism team, I should have been able to stop this. I was going home to my two young boys and my newborn third son, and this man was going home to nothing.

What compounded the incident for Gary was how quickly he and the other frontline responders moved on. 'I finished up at the mortuary on a Thursday. Friday I was at Crown Court. Saturday I was off. And then Sunday, I was straight back into normal response work. No break, no talking about what had happened as a team. It was just another day at the office.' Like it was just another day being a man – back to work, emotions swept under the rug, mask on.

A few years later, Gary had been on a train when someone sadly took their own life. He was one of the first to respond, identifying himself to the driver as a police officer. It was yet another incident that piled on top of the trauma that Gary was collecting. But, what was worse, is that he had no idea this was building, like interest he was gaining on a large debt he didn't know he owed.

And it was a debt that he'd started gathering at a very young age. Gary was the victim of sexual abuse as a child by two different men. The first was his family babysitter. 'The stuff that he would say to me if I was to tell anyone filled me with dread. But I told myself, well if he's doing it to me, at least he isn't doing it to my brothers and sisters, so at least I'm protecting them. This abuser was a friend of the family and still to this day my parents don't know about it.'

Gary's second abuser was his football coach, someone who should have been in a position of caregiving and nurturing. Gary was the team captain, and saw himself as a strong character who was protective of others.

The abuse went on for years, but I didn't know that the coach was doing it to other members of the team, and the senior team too. I tried to stop it, but again I was told if I say anything to anyone, certain things would happen to me, to my family.

I carried so much shame around that, I didn't even tell my wife until 10 years after we were married. For years I blamed myself for everything that happened.

What happens when all of this builds? The trauma mixes with the shame, the guilt, the emotional burden to create a tinderbox of unresolved pain that's going to go off eventually.

In 2012 during the London Olympics, I was part of a specialist search team. I had just come off a 12-hour shift, and an off-duty situation developed in front of me. I ended up fighting with an individual down in a busy underground station. This individual had just tried to push two coppers onto a live train track. I eventually subdued this man, and it took five police officers to get him out of the station and into a police vehicle, where for 10, 15 minutes he was smashing his head against the police vehicle.

And then 17 months later, because of this incident, I'm gripping a rail at Crown Court on trial for an Actual Bodily Harm offence for what was deemed above an acceptable level of the use of force, with a very strong chance I was going to go to prison. Thankfully, the judge was on my side and sent me to see a forensic psychiatrist. And that was when the report came back that my change of character on that day was due to post-traumatic stress disorder, which was the first time I realised what I was going through.

It all began to make sense for Gary after that. For so many years he'd carried around so much shame and anger, anger which he said was directed at his wife and kids for all that time. He drank heavily, he blamed himself, he never opened up. 'I was this tough bloke, always the first to a fight if I needed to be, always there for people to lean on. The last thing I was going to do, especially as a police officer, was show anyone any weakness'.

Gary's story is obviously a dramatic one, containing many situations that many of us won't experience. But those feelings of shame, those deep wounds, that need to push incidents to one side and pretend we're fine – these are experiences that many men face. Some cope with addictions, some have unbridled rage, others take their own lives. Trauma is stored in the body, and while the traditional masculine stereotype image is one of silence, this doesn't clear our problems in the way that we think; it just lets them build and build.

And how does Gary feel now, sharing this story? 'It's cathartic for me. I carried an overriding feeling of guilt for such a long time over the people I couldn't help. But now I get messages and emails from people saying "thank you for saving my life". There's not many better feelings than that'.

Gary, like so many people I've spoken to in this book, is the *real* definition of masculinity in my eyes. Tough and strong, eager to protect their loved ones, no shortage of resilience. But also someone who has developed humility and humbleness, an acknowledgement of things he's got wrong, and, importantly, a new muscle he's worked on – one of vulnerability. Not only has it helped him to move through his own pain and develop stronger relationships, but it's helping others to do the same too. This is the ripple effect we can *all* have when we start to unpick these unhealthy, rigid masculine stereotypes.

The deep wounds that he carried came out in the worst possible way, driving a wedge into his relationship, almost landing him in prison, and almost resulting in him taking his own life. Luckily, he went down a different path, but the more we keep forcing our men into emotional suppression, the more we may be sending them down a path that they can't come back from.

Reflection

Are there any wounds you've tried to bury which might still be affecting you today?

Key Summary and Reflections

- **Feeling inadequate:** When men are taught to suppress deeply painful emotions like grief, trauma, loss, and bullying, it can have devastating consequences. It compounds with feelings of shame, humiliation, and failure – emotions that make a man develop a belief that he isn't good enough.

- **Space for emotions:** Men are often given less emotional space to process difficult events, or treated with the same level of respect. Their emotions can get missed in some events like miscarriage or infertility, or they can be seen as 'invincible' to things like domestic abuse.

- **Building up trauma:** Trauma left unresolved is stored in the body; it doesn't dissipate on its own. These difficult emotions are like sticking a lightning rod into the pressure cooker, until something breaks.

- **A right to feel:** Whatever emotions you're feeling right now, whatever your gender, you are allowed to feel them. You have just as much a right to feel them as any other human on the planet. Don't give yourself an extra burden to carry by shaming yourself for your natural human emotions.

Summary to Part Two

These six breaking points are some of the areas where we're seeing the pressure on men seep out, often without warning or their control. This list isn't definitive and there will be other hidden behaviours and taboos that men are knowingly or unknowingly using to cope and move through life, other areas where that pressure is building.

Men have internalised a learnt behaviour of emotional suppression, and often all we see is *how* that pressure is reaching an unmanageable level, and we criticise the man for it. We label the homeless person as lazy. We label the man struggling with an addiction as a mess.

This doesn't mean men don't have personal accountability and agency to change, but too often we rush to blame without asking what they might be carrying beneath the surface. Many are getting dragged into a rip current that they're furiously paddling against on the inside, while on the outside they smile.

These stories can get buried in statistics, studies, and sensationalist headlines. Which is why I've shared them – to show the reality that's going on for men, to show the humans behind the masks. They're the result of decades, centuries even, of emotional suppression, stigmatised vulnerability, and a rigid view of masculinity – men who tried to fit into that view, and cracked.

But I also deliberately shared such a range of stories to show how pointless it is to try and define masculinity as one small set of characteristics. Men are humans, and humans are complex, unique, and quirky. The more we keep trying to squeeze men into a small little box labelled 'masculinity' in order to satisfy society's perception of it, the more we'll keep creating stories like I've shared.

Men are coming up against the weight of not only the things they're dealing with, but also the almost unbearable weight of trying to hide it too. The hard news is that it's still happening today. The good news is that it's in our power to change it. And that's what we'll focus on next.

Part Three

Releasing the Pressure

'Man up'. Two words, but a lifetime of pressure. Phrases like this suggest masculinity is fixed and rigid, with a certain level to which they should man 'up' towards. But all this does is rob them of their agency to change and carve their own path. So many of the issues that men face are social constructs, human-made norms. Which means we can change them. Where there are harmful breaking points, there are also healthy release points.

There are some brilliant thought pieces and suggestions out in the world for how we can start to help men. For example, Richard Reeves's excellent book, *Of Boys and Men*, argues for, among other ideas, starting boys a year later in school than girls, as boys' brains tend to, on average, take longer to develop.[75] I've seen articles about recruiting more male therapists, getting more male teachers into schools, banning social media platforms for certain ages, or creating governmental departments for boys and men.

Many are smart, but they rely on political policy and entire societal restructures. Other fixes may take generations to unwind. In the face of this it can be easy to shrug our shoulders and let somebody else deal with it. If you're in a position of influence, be that government, business, media, education, or otherwise, I hope you'll use that position to drive the change that's needed. But for the rest of us, we don't need to wait for that. There are things that we can do right now to start to build a healthier idea of masculinity. We have agency and accountability over our own lives, and we need good people, particularly men, to start flying that flag of positive transformation.

There's no silver bullet. Life is unique and that means our responses are too. But we've seen what happens when that pressure builds. What would it look like to open the valve?

10
Release Point #1: Building Better Connections

Men need other people, there's no doubt about it. Strong friendships, healthy relationships, a solid community. Traditional masculinity can resist these things – shunning interpersonal connections and favouring independence.

But our bodies just aren't wired this way. Professor Paul Gilbert OBE said to me: 'in flourishing communities, where men feel valued and part of a community, levels of depression were quite low. Conversely, where there's no real sense of belonging or feeling valued, and when men feel on their own, they can often struggle as one thing the human brain doesn't like is social disconnection.'

Masculinity is co-created and relational, built together with others, with so much of our sense of self coming from how we connect with the people around us. The deeper those connections, the deeper we can know and value ourselves. And so a huge part of building a healthier idea of masculinity is about building stronger connections, ones with depth that value empathy, emotion, and closeness. These aren't soft skills, they're survival skills.

The Lost Art of Male Friendship

We can be really unfair and have all these misconceptions of men, that they can't talk

—James Routledge, author

Strong male friendships are critical for men, and yet they're often built on fragile foundations. We know that male loneliness is a silently growing epidemic, and a large part of this is down to the stigmatised perception of truly close interpersonal relationships between men, built on deep connection.

One research paper that looked at 148 different studies totalling 308,849 participants, found that those with strong social relationships have a 50% increased likelihood of survival and decreased risk of early mortality. This was true irrespective of age, sex, cause of death, and initial health status.[76] Put simply, we are social creatures, and those of us with stronger social connections are more likely to live longer.

When I really struggled with my mental health, I didn't tell any of my mates, my supposed best friends that I saw every single weekend. Because I let shame and fear silence me. When I eventually did open up, I found nothing but support. And yet I hadn't even given them a chance to try and help me. If that's where you're at, I get it, it's hard as hell. But we do have to give men more credit than they sometimes get.

James Routledge, who I interviewed about his experience of baby loss, summarised it perfectly for me:

I think we can be really unfair and have all these misconceptions of men, that they can't talk. But my mates were amazing

210

when I lost Teddy, and seeing how they rallied around me, it really made me question those misconceptions. But it was because I communicated well and kept them up to date. And it's made me think of other times in my life when I've been shut off and closed off about something, how do we as men expect anyone to help? Whereas when I was on the front foot with communicating and opened myself up to it, that support was there.

And we agreed that the conversation might be different, generally speaking, between groups of men and groups of women. James said that when he and his partner Sarah were going through it all, Sarah's friends were texting her constantly and very specifically, asking her things like 'what have you eaten today? Have you showered today?' James's friends weren't doing that as specifically, and probably (again, generally speaking) as men, those might not be the sorts of conversations we have; it could be something as simple as a text saying 'you good?'

That doesn't mean we don't care, and that doesn't mean we can't offer support in our own ways. But we do need to find ways of communicating that feel right to us. A few friends and I were getting frustrated with only waiting until everyone was horrendously drunk to have vulnerable conversations in dingy nightclubs at 3 a.m.

So a few of us get together occasionally for what we have unofficially dubbed 'mental health meet-ups'. It's generally still at a pub and generally still involves rounds of beer, but one of the first things we do is rate how we've been doing out of ten, and talk about why we've given ourselves that score. It all helps because we know we're meeting under the pretence of talking about what's going on for us. The shame, embarrassment, and awkwardness of how to start the conversation is removed. And where shame is banished, real connections can thrive.

I've also heard men encourage conversation around telling their male friends that they love them, in a platonic, non-sexual way. As in, specifically saying 'love you mate'. It may make you shudder a bit; it still does to me too sometimes. But that's that archaic, societal masculine construct kicking into gear, telling your body to feel awkward and your brain to run from this external threat to your manhood.

A book by friendship expert Dr Marisa G. Franco, *Platonic: How Understanding Your Attachment Style Can Help You Make and Keep Friends*, delves into how the increased under-valuation of friendship in our culture has led to an epidemic of loneliness. In the book, Dr Franco highlights that before the mid-1800s, friendships generally involved a comfortable level of expressing love for each other.[77]

There was something of a turning point after this period, par-ticularly in the West, fuelled by a shift in cultural beliefs. Sigmund Freud partly contributed with a framework that sug-gested that many friendships and attachments had underlying sexual drives and desires. Affection between same-sex friends started to be viewed through a different lens, and for friend-ships between men, this often meant a lens of same-sex attraction. American sociologist Professor Eric Anderson coined the term 'homohysteria' to describe the fear among men of being perceived as 'gay'. Much of it now permeates through our cultures and societies today, where men are taught to avoid behaviours that might see them labelled as gay.

We see again how a social construct, created at a moment in time, is clashing with our innate need for connection and closeness. Johann Hari, who wrote the book *Lost Connections,* argues that one of the roots of depression and anxiety lies in the connections that we have lost – to ourselves, to the world around us, to our purpose and, importantly, to people. The reasons for mental health issues are complex, but many agree that our increasingly disconnected world is contributing, at least in part, to some people's experiences.

The modern way of living, with things like longer working hours and a reliance on tech to communicate over face-to-face interaction, is causing a break in people's connections with each other, and that is causing deep-seated unhappiness. But then men are stigmatised against speaking about that unhappiness with those closest to them, and so the chasm widens. It's a self-perpetuating cycle of misery fuelled by a belief that we can't, or shouldn't, communicate.

Maybe you're not ready to pick up your phone and text your friend that you love him, I get it. But we can all find methods of communicating in ways that feel natural to us. Sometimes a message like 'how you been mate?' can mean the world for someone.

And meeting men in an 'active' environment can help. Sitting opposite them at a table, staring into their eyes and asking them to bare their soul might be a stretch too far. But, for example, perhaps meeting each other on a hike, walking side-by-side and talking that way can be a good way to connect.

Action

What man or men in your life do you value, but have never told? Send him a message telling him what you appreciate in your friendship. Maybe tell them what's been going on for you; connection starts with you.

What Masculinity Looks Like in Love

Many men worry about being good enough and so struggle with rejection, because they often believe something's wrong with them

—David Chambers, men's relationship coach

Depending on where you look, you'll find statistics that say around half of all marriages end in divorce – a staggeringly high rate of failure for one of life's most important decisions. There are numerous reasons for this, but here I want to focus on how men might be showing up in intimate relationships and how, if we better understand this, we can start to communicate better.

John Gray's book, *Men Are from Mars, Women Are from Venus*, found 12 key areas where men and women can differ in relationships,[78] such as in communication and language, emotional needs, and problem-solving. For example, women often talk about problems 'to get close and not necessarily to get solutions', while men 'mistakenly offer solutions and invalidate feelings'.

John's work is primarily focused on heterosexual couples, but of course every relationship is unique, and these principles apply differently based on the individuals. I share his work to highlight, however, that there can often be typical ways that a man's experience and his sense of masculinity can influence how he shows up in a relationship.

More often than not, we don't even realise that what we're doing can be the polar opposite to what our partner wants or needs. So, how does our sense of masculinity shape who we are in a relationship, regardless of the nature or sexuality of that relationship, and how can we understand it?

Masculinity in the Mirror of Intimacy

I sat down with David Chambers, a men's dating, relationship, and avoidance coach, and he said, 'What we commonly call "masculinity", or our sense of being a man and what it means to be a man, directly impacts our relationships and our ability to relate and connect with people'.

What this means is that it is likely very hard for any relationship involving a man to be healthy and sustainable unless all parties involved have a clear understanding of not only masculinity as a whole, but also how it specifically impacts and influences that man or men within the relationship.

Women in particular may often get frustrated at men because, in Chambers's words, men are often 'stunted in relational capacities and relational skills needed to create good and healthy relationships' and so we hear complaints that men aren't communicative or emotive enough.

Many relationships get caught in what's called a demand-withdraw pattern, where one side demands, pushing for change or resolution, while the other side withdraws, seeking to avoid or end a discussion. It's an incredibly destructive pattern and studies have shown it's a huge predictor of marital dissatisfaction and divorce. Research shows that the 'demand' role is generally played by the woman, and 'withdraw' by men, supporting Chambers's point around an emotional stunting in men.

There are various studies which suggest this is more of a problem in heterosexual relationships, where heterosexual men may have been socialised to suppress emotional expression, and you have women on the other side who aren't fighting against these same societal restrictions. For gay men, research tends to suggest that they have more emotional flexibility and are less constrained by traditional masculine norms, so are better at both expression and conflict resolution. As with anything in this book though, this will of course be different for each individual and their unique circumstances, and we are talking in general terms here rather than a hard and fast rule for everyone.

When communication breaks down over the lack of emotional expression, I believe there's often a misalignment on the reasons why. The assumption made by many is that men *can't* do emotion or expression. We know this to be untrue, and that it is more likely to be that they've never been shown *how* to 'do' emotion or expression.

Chambers explained that often many young boys are good at emotional expression, showing compassion, playfulness, and kindness. But by the time they get to around the age of 13, that's disappeared. Sometimes these traits aren't valued at home, or these traits are ones picked on by bullies. And so boys internalise a belief that these traits are wrong. David said:

Put simply, boys are often bullied out of their inner child and connection. But there's also a climate that young boys are seen as trouble within schools, and that they're going to hurt the girls. Girls can actually be very emotionally skilled at manipulation and cruelty, and can cause a lot of trouble for the boys. And boys, who are perhaps not as good at emotional articulation, react in a way that is more noticeable and overt, perhaps aggressive, and so they get in trouble while the girl gets away with it.

It's an interesting point that Chambers touches on, and it's easy to see how certain behaviours are reinforced, or toxic patterns perpetuated. This is not to place the blame at the door of young girls, but it's felt that they may develop emotional literacy earlier and more comprehensively than boys. And what can happen is that behaviours like gossiping can take place, and boys may react with anger or rage, which is often the only part to get punished. They may feel their reaction is justified, but if anger is the emotion they're familiar with, and only that gets punished, it can reinforce the belief that *all* emotions are bad.

So where do experiences like this in our youth lead and how do they end up impacting our relationships later down the line? While human life is complex, there does tend to be linear dots we can join from the playground to our relationships.

He explained that there are generally two distinct buckets of men who come to him:

There's one bucket of men who are anxiety driven and anxiously attached. They're reactive, prone to perfectionism, and so lack action and risk as they don't want to get things wrong. They're often fearful of intimacy. It hampers relationships because you have to take risks to be able to learn, but they've often not taken risks with their love life, for fear of getting it wrong or getting hurt. And in the other bucket we have men who are avoidantly attached, who struggle with emotional expression and end up in a lot of short-term relationships or there's a lot of cheating involved. They overthink a lot, they're very logical, they feel their emotions in their heads, not in their bodies. They can be charismatic and have no trouble meeting a partner, but when they get into a relationship, they feel suffocated by commitment. They fit the classic, archetypal view of a man, one that's stoic, emotionless, and action-orientated.

He was clear to stress that these are spectrums on which we all operate, and while we can't oversimplify and distil all men down into two simple boxes, it does help us to start to understand some behaviours and actions of men in relationships, particularly when at surface level we may only see them as emotionally stunted. And this can have real impacts on relationships in a number of ways.

Sex, Assertiveness, and Not Feeling Good Enough

Sexual intimacy is obviously a huge topic within relationships, and one of the key reasons that men come to Chambers. He sees men who are worried about lasting long enough, being big enough, how they stack up against previous sexual partners.

Many couples come to him over sexless marriages, where there is a sexual mismatch in the desires on both sides. 'A lot of what it comes down to with sex is this deep wound that men carry of not being good enough, and so they struggle with rejection. A lot of this can be triggered through intimate experiences'.

The reasons for this are likely complex, but for men who place a lot of value or self-worth on sex, while carrying a deep wound of not feeling good enough, sex can become the ultimate act on which they build themselves up, or tear themselves down.

David also explained that there's a prevailing narrative about men that they're either lazy and stupid, or predatory and dangerous. In the minds of many, there's often no middle ground. But when we talk in extremes and generalisations publicly, we end up harming men privately. A huge thing for men is not wanting to be predatory or dangerous, or to do anything that could even play into the perception that they are, and so many men over-index on being good.

But there can be a real challenge to this, as David said:

this can make them appear meek and passive which often is a turn off for women. Many women want a bunch of stuff that they probably aren't willing to admit out loud, but they do want a man who's assertive, who stands up for himself, has opinions, someone who can lead and take control. Some women I work with want their man to get angry at them, because they want to see a level of assertiveness.

The issue for a lot of men, is that this core wound of not being good enough combines with the fact that they want to do what they can to appear good to the person they're trying to attract. They believe if they're overly nice and good, it'll prove that not only are they a moral man, but that they're one worth mating with too.

But Dr Robert Glover's book, *No More Mr. Nice Guy,* shows why the statement 'nice guys finish last' sometimes can have some truth to it, particularly when it comes to relationships.[79] 'Nice guys' believe that, in Dr Robert's words, 'If I'm good, I'll be loved and get my needs met.' But actually, to people who may see it as passive, it can lead to rejection, but it can also lead to things in relationships like less sex, or none at all, arguments, resentment, and more.

Nice guys can sometimes be seen as lacking in energy and strength, but David said we're not helping our boys in this regard because 'as boys, we're taught to be nice to girls. We're taught that girls are soft and fragile, as though they're made of porcelain'.

Chambers and I also spoke about one of the biggest issues within a relationship, where 'we see the world and other people through a mirror of actions that *we* would take. So if I want connection, I might go and hug my partner. But if she wants connection, she might come and talk to me. Talking might not be as important to me specifically in terms of connection, so what is her bid for connection to her, is to me just an act. So I might not really engage in conversation with her, and then she feels hurt. We often don't realise people's bids for connection, because they don't match ours. And that's when problems can arise'.

My biggest takeaway from the chat with David Chambers is how often couples miss each other with their communication, often operating on different levels. And anger and resentment often arise because we expect our partner to be on the same level as us, or do the things that we'd do, and get annoyed at them when they aren't. But how often do couples adequately articulate their needs and bids for connection? My guess would be not that often and not that well.

And this is natural, humans are different. But when we layer on top of that the historic and societal gender pressures, which add a complex web of layers to these levels of connection that the other side may have no experience of, and that the man is unable to voice, then we have a problem.

A partner might complain that their man doesn't show enough emotion, but unbeknownst to both of them, it was because the man was bullied out of it as a kid. If neither side knows that or talks about it, the relationship will stay in arguments at the surface level, missing the decades of trauma and emotional baggage underneath.

What can be useful for us to learn, and I've had to learn this through my own journey too, is the place that men are often coming from. Calling them unemotional often doesn't paint the true picture. In many cases they're trying to avoid rejection and humiliation, sometimes on a subconscious level, and their natural bid for emotional connection has been hammered out of them from a young age. This doesn't excuse the need to communicate emotionally and in a way that a partner needs, and men must take responsibility for change; knowing our patterns and being able to talk about them isn't the same as changing them.

These aren't things we can solve overnight, but for any relationship that hits road bumps over things like communication or emotional misalignment, starting to unpack some of our historic experiences, and learning more about our partner's own bids for connection, are a good place to start and helps us to build bridges between our two communication styles and needs.

Start by researching your love language or do a personality test and ask your partner to do one. We can't always be so easily distilled into a short personality survey, but it's a start. Talk about what emotion means to you both; what's been your experience of it? How comfortable do you feel with it? What's the one thing your partner does that means the world to you? Conversely, what do they do that really grinds your gears? Where are you connecting through sex, and where are hidden tensions rising? It's conversations like these that can start to build those bridges.

Action

Make a list of all the ways you like to be appreciated, valued, and communicated with. Ask a significant person in your life to do the same, and then compare. Where do you overlap? Where do you repel?

Community: The Power of Belonging

Something about sitting in a room with a bunch of other men who've been through similar stuff to you . . . that's priceless

—Stuart Fawcett, ANDYSMANCLUB

It can often be easier to make connections and open up with people we don't know, people that aren't family or our closest mates, as they're the ones we're most worried about shaming us. That's where an external source can be a blessing. There are therapists and coaches dotted all around the globe, but for many men, opening up to them is just as scary.

And so there are some fantastic organisations out there which are taking a community-based, group approach to interventions that have connection overtly, or in some cases subtly, baked into their DNA.

One such example is ANDYSMANCLUB, a UK nationwide men's suicide prevention charity that offers free to attend peer-to-peer support in, at the time of writing, over 265 clubs. Sessions run every single week for men only, who attend, catch up over a brew and biscuits, before sitting in a circle and answering five questions – a mixture of personal ones like 'anything to get off your chest?' and more light-hearted ones like 'what's your favourite movie quote?'

Stuart Fawcett, a regional area lead at the club, told me 'if you don't want to talk, you don't have to. We get new guys that come along sometimes for a couple of months that don't answer anything, they just listen. But it's surprising how much that can change'.

It's a cleverly designed session, with breaks that allow men to decompress but, importantly, to bond with a group of people they might have only met for the first time. And Stuart tells me that they'll often have banter in those questions, which can be so important for male bonding and connection. I asked him what kind of people attend these sessions, and he said:

We get people from all walks of life. Office workers, construction workers, people with tattoos, massive beards, guys of all sizes, loud, quiet. I think a lot of people that come, and it was the same for me, don't always resonate with therapy. It can be powerful, but something about sitting in a room with a bunch of other men who've been through similar stuff to you, that you can have a laugh and a cry with . . . that's priceless.

I asked Stuart if he saw real change in these groups and real connections form:

We had the most magical moment last year. One of the regular attendees had an operation and hadn't been able to get down to his allotment, his safe space. He sat in the group and said he felt down and deflated. Weeds were everywhere, none of his winter veg was growing, he felt isolated. And the lads talked him through it. But then the following week, we found out that all the lads from the group took him down there the next Saturday, got everything sorted, planted his winter veg, and now every fortnight they go down there, take a few flasks, have some cups of tea and chat. And you've got guys that are unemployed, guys that are builders, guys that are directors of companies . . . all different walks of life, but they're all meeting up.

How often do you hear stories like this? Men meeting up over a cup of tea at an allotment to support each other's wellbeing? When men are given the space to be, and I mean *really* be, you'll find there's a lot of love and compassion underneath the surface.

But what if even this type of group still feels daunting to a man? As its premise is still, of course, shaped around talking and listening. I met with another wonderful organisation, MAN v FAT, a football league community for men who want to lose weight.

The league table is based not only on the weekly football results and goals scored, but on how much weight the men lose too; it's a nice way of building accountability, competition, and camaraderie into something like weight management, particularly as these things aren't changing what men enjoy, they're working with it. There is research to suggest that taking a more positive strength-based model on masculine norms could help engage certain men by affirming their masculine identities.[80]

On the surface, it's an organisation built around football and weight. But behind all of that it builds real friendships among men, creates a community and kick-starts conversations around life, work, mental health, and everything in between.

I met with Richard Crick, head of MAN v FAT and Siobhan Birbeck, the mental health and wellbeing lead, who took me down to my local MAN v FAT club for their weekly game night. I didn't know what to expect, but I'll admit I had my own preconceptions about the conversations I might have; these would be men who were there for football, not for talking. We entered the building and bumped into a member in the corridor just on his way out to get on the pitch. 'Been coming here a while?' I asked him.

'Yeah,' he replied. 'I took a break for a few months, my mental health got bad, I was struggling with suicidal thoughts and I needed some time for myself. But I'm back now and I love it. Right, I gotta go lads, I'm playing now!' His football studs clunked on the floor as he dashed out onto the pitch and I turned to Richard, both of us smiling at his complete honesty. I gave myself a mental slap on the wrists for having expected anything other than this before I got here.

And that wasn't the only conversation I had that night. I talked with members about their autism assessments, social anxiety, board games, weight loss, and the weekly walking group they'd set up. Another man told us we couldn't come near him as he was going through radiotherapy treatment and his immune system was low, but he wanted to come down to support the team, and because he wanted the connection with his teammates. They were rich conversations and I could see how tight the community was that had been built, coming together to support each other not only on weight loss, but in life too.

I asked Richard if these were normal stories from around the UK.

We had a man whose mental health issues got so bad, he couldn't leave the house for months. MAN v FAT was the only thing that got him out of the house, and now he's one of the most confident people we have here! Another man was told that he and his partner couldn't conceive because he was overweight. He joined us to lose weight, and six months later they fell pregnant. Someone else's father was in desperate need of a new kidney, and he was a donor match, but he wasn't healthy enough. He started coming to us to get fit so he could donate his kidney to his dad. He's so thankful for what we've done, he even missed part of his brother's wedding day to come to one of our events!

It was only a few short hours that I was there, but I felt really impacted by the community that had been built. Again, it reminded me of these preconceived ideas we're told about men. That they can't or won't bond. But here I found men that met over a shared love for football and desire to lose weight, and used that as a launchpad to have all kinds of conversations and life-changing impact.

This is only a snapshot of the countless groups around the world offering spaces for men. Some are about mental health and talking. Some are about fitness and exercise. Some will be pub crawls or sports teams, some will be about board and computer games. What matters is that there *are* spaces for men, and by men.

Connection doesn't always have to be about mental health and deep conversations. Sometimes it's just getting together with a group of people who like doing the same things as us. And sometimes that's enough to help show men that there are more ways than one to be a man.

Action

Think about something you enjoy – sport, music, food, art, games, anything. Is there a local group or community built around it? If not, could you be the one to start it? Community isn't something you have to wait for, it can start with you.

Key Summary

While traditional masculinity can often champion independence and resist strong interpersonal connections, humans are biologically wired for connection, community, and love. We are inherently social creatures, and to deny this in order to serve a perception of masculinity isn't good for us. So much of what we learn about ourselves comes through strong connections with others.

11

Release Point #2: Bridging the Gender Divide

It's not only strong bonds between men that can help to expand masculinity, but strong bonds with women too. Women have an incredibly important role to play in helping men to feel understood, seen, and valued, just as men must hold this role for women. But in some pockets of society, divides are growing wider at an alarming rate.

When I was at my lowest point with my mental health, it was my female partner at the time and my mum that spotted signs, started a conversation with me and got me into the right health-care pathways. Would I still be here today if it hadn't been for the intervention of two women? I'm not sure. I was so convinced I couldn't speak about any of what was happening to me, that I wasn't even questioning that silence, it was all I knew. Two women showed me it didn't have to be.

And I know women can have that impact for other men too. Both men *and* women have a role to play in building bridges between the two sexes which, ultimately, helps lift everyone up.

The Power of Female Allies

Men often find it easier to open up to women because their masculinity may not be challenged as much

—Michaela Wain, founder of Women in Construction Awards

Research suggests men may feel more comfortable opening up to women as they perceive women to be more empathetic and less judgemental. Where women aren't bound by the same social conditioning of emotional suppression, I believe they can show men that there is a different way and that expression isn't to be feared, and they can help to do this in households, friendship groups, online, and in boardrooms. Many women already are doing this and in many cases, women are often playing a quiet, yet crucial role in men's wellbeing.

For example, the doctors I spoke to for this book told me of studies which have shown women make around 80% to 90% of the healthcare decisions within a household. We saw earlier in this book how men are tracking worse in numerous healthcare statistics, and Dr Tim Woodman's own story of prostate cancer, which was caught after he was told to go to the doctors by his wife, highlights the role that women are playing.

But it's not just within the household where women can save men's lives, it's in our industries and societies too. Nowhere is this clearer and more stark than the male-dominated, construction industry, which is seeing devastating rates of suicide among its workers. I spoke with Michaela Wain, a finalist of the BBC's *The Apprentice*, and founder of the Women in Construction Awards. She's a powerhouse within the construction industry, and she's had to be, as she tells me it's an industry where only

15% of people are women. Is it too much of a coincidence that in an industry with such little female influence, and one that is overtly masculine, that more men are taking their own lives?

It's one of the industries struggling the most with a mental health crisis. Construction workers in the UK are 3.7 times more likely to take their own life than the national average,[81] with around two workers taking their own life every single working day. In 2021 alone there were 507 suicides in construction.[82] For comparison, in the same year that 507 construction workers took their own lives, this number was 33 for health professionals.[83]

What Michaela finds most tragic is that in the year of 2021, when 507 people took their own lives, there were also eight people who died from health and safety-related accidents. And yet she tells me there are eight major Health and Safety Executive accreditations (essentially meaning one accreditation per one health and safety-related death in that year), but how many accreditations are there for preventing suicide? None. Which is why she's working hard to launch an accreditation specifically around suicide in construction in 2025.

Aside from accreditations, one of Michaela's biggest beliefs for solving this issue is to get more women into the industry. She believes that the influence of more emotionally attuned leadership styles, often brought by women, will help ripple out through an industry that so desperately needs it. Because conversations aren't happening like they should on construction sites.

In some ways, the industry feels inherently masculine, which isn't surprising given the nature of the work. But it means that people are finding other ways of coping. For example, two in three tradespeople have misused drugs and alcohol as a way of coping with, and mitigating, symptoms of poor mental health.[84] Michaela said:

The construction industry has the highest suicide rates, highest divorce rates, highest mental health issue rates. And I do believe that more women in the industry will help because women often instinctively know when somebody isn't right, they have an empathy and an ability to read micro-signals. And I think men often find it easier to open up to women because then their masculinity isn't challenged as much. This isn't just about construction either, this is any industry, any friendship group, any home.

Michaela knows the importance of this first-hand. Her son's father, a tradesman, took his own life. 'I think a typical male response to the suicide statistics is "that's awful, but that's not me, that's them". Men will be respectful and polite of course, but then they often just crack on and ignore the statistics. I know men who have lost best friends to suicide, but it's hardly spoken about, because that's often the norm'.

Michaela, someone who sits outside of masculinity, perfectly highlighted the challenges that so many men face. 'Society often fails to protect men emotionally. They're taught to be completely different and they're often not getting support from their industries or from the authorities, and they're too embarrassed to open up to their friends and family. So what are they left with? They're left with suicide. And that's where I think women can play such a huge role'.

As with any statistic, there is nuance. It's tough physical labour and there's a lot of pressure. We know that more men take their own lives, so in an industry that is predominantly male, the statistics are likely to be higher.

But stronger female influence in our workplaces, our homes, and our lives can only be a good thing for men and masculinity. No more so in helping to unpick the conditioned emotional suppression in men.

None of this is to place the entire emotional burden and responsibility onto women. A new term has been popularised in recent years called 'mankeeping', which refers to the emotional labour women feel they're having to pick up for their male partners who may be emotionally stunted or have limited strong bonds elsewhere.

While the term is in danger of becoming an overused hashtag, its invention speaks to a sad reflection of where many men and women are at. Through emotional suppression, men's emotional support networks are often incredibly bare. And as the pressure builds inside them, and perhaps loneliness too, the females in their lives are often having to act as the emotional safety net. Many women are voicing frustration and exhaustion at this; they've been fighting their own battles for so long, and now feel they have to pick up men's battles too.

I want to acknowledge how tiring this can feel for women, and my hope is we can also acknowledge why this is happening for men, and meet somewhere in the middle. Men *do* have to take responsibility over this and the agency over their own lives.

They need to lead the charge, put arms around other men and build strong connections outside of the home. But we also can't leave all of this to personal agency alone. Much of the solution to the rising male suicide rate in recent years has been to tell men to 'open up'. And yet the suicide rate isn't coming down. Suicide is a complicated thing and we can't draw linear conclusions; however, this example shows where we *have* tried to give men agency, in owning talking, and yet alone it isn't the solution.

So that's why we also need the help of women who often aren't bound by these same cultural rules of emotional suppression. Maybe that *is* putting an arm around a man. Maybe it's role modelling good connections with other humans. Maybe it's a firm but fair word on personal agency. All I know is that if we only leave it up to men to solve this, many will find that their decades of suppressed baggage will stop them building the necessary bonds and connections.

Katie Maycock is a straight-talking stress and burnout coach, and one whose client base is predominantly male. I wanted to understand why Katie felt this was, as I believed there would be useful lessons for both men and women. Why do so many men choose to work with Katie over a male coach?

A lot of it is performative. Many men have an unconscious bias of peacocking with other men, where they expect to be judged or to have to compete. And traditional masculinity can fear interpersonal connections, but especially with other men, where they feel a connection has to have a value – they ask 'can this other man either save me or serve me?' So they're cautious, competitive and defensive. For some men these unconscious barriers are removed when talking to a woman.

It's sad, because the next question I asked Katie was, 'and what are these men coming to see you for?' And her answer was that pretty much all of them had their experiences rooted in similar struggles and feelings. So many men are feeling the same way, but this innate perceived need to compete and perform stops them sharing these feelings with other men, men who may be feeling exactly the same.

Men come to see me because of specific situations that happen in their lives. They spend around three months wearing a mask, telling me what I want to hear. Once we get past that, and go deeper into their belief systems, we find feelings there of not feeling good enough, of being scared of letting go of their stress, of having numbed out so much they don't feel happy or sad, of wanting to connect better with their family, but not knowing how to.

Everything seemed to distil down into two buckets: men not feeling good enough and men not knowing how to simply *be*, with themselves or their emotions. They don't step off the hamster wheel because they're scared of what they'll find. Katie said many of these people overwork, because it's the one thing they know how to control, and they need this feeling of being in control.

And I believe this is where women have such a powerful role to play, because men often perform to other men. They maintain this illusion of control; they control the narrative, control the mask they're wearing, control their emotions. This isn't all cases of course, but for some people, there aren't these same barriers when it comes to seeking support from women.

There was one other critical piece of advice Katie gave me:

---

one thing men could do is talk to women about how women have had to manage and survive through this society, through the patriarchy. The patriarchy doesn't only harm women, it harms men too, and the impact of that is why so many men come to see me. Women have been creating support structures for other women for a long time within this society, and perhaps women can role model to men how they can create these support structures for themselves, and men can take the time to listen and learn, in order to lead the charge for other men.

Masculinity isn't a rigid, fixed concept that's built in a vacuum. It gets shaped with others, and it gets shaped through connection and how we're both supported and challenged. Emotional support and challenge can come from anyone, but given the absence of traditional power hierarchies in many female friendships, women are often well positioned to hold this mirror up to men.

Action

Think of a woman in your life who has helped to shape you into who you are. Send her a message to tell her you appreciate her. Reflections and acknowledgements are bridge builders.

Men Leading the Change

To know love, men must be able to let go of the will to dominate

—bell hooks, author

There is a divisive gender war in many sectors of society. I see women blaming men, and men blaming women, and both sides perpetuating tired stereotypes. These harmful divides are appearing at an alarming rate all over the world. There is voting analysis evidence which suggests many women are swinging to more progressive politics, while men are swinging to more radical views on the right. The reality is, of course, there are plenty of good people who sit in the middle, but it's often the extremes at either end that grab the headlines.

Divides show up differently across different genders, relationships, and LGBTQ+ communities, but many of these patterns of disconnect are threaded throughout. And in many cases, it's all become far too binary and a zero-sum game which doesn't help either side to heal or communicate – it simply drives a bigger wedge.

Lee Chambers, a business psychologist who focuses on gender in the workplace, argues for greater allyship between people, regardless of ethnicity, sex, sexuality, or any other factor. He tells me that the word 'ally' itself comes from an old French word, *allié*, which means to combine and unite.

And Chambers explains it's that lack of unity that is one of the biggest issues harming everyone. 'People see the patriarchy and they see men. But the patriarchy is not a man, it's a social system, which has been upheld by men and women. But what it's created is this divide and narrative that men don't need women and women don't need men. Independence is the goal. But that's the biggest power play the patriarchy has and what it wants; us divided, because it's only by working together that we can dismantle it'.

So what's men's role in this? It's important that we step back, examine our own biases and ask where we might be furthering this divide. A divide which creates more of a battle, more noise, and more reason to cause men to retreat even further into traditional masculine ideals, often as a defence mechanism.

I once read a quote that said 'men are socialised to hate women'. I initially bristled at the ridiculousness of it, and then as I stepped back and brought more awareness to it, I realised that there probably *are* some uncomfortable truths within it. There's a lot of biological, societal, historical, and generational nuance to it, but books like *Men Who Hate Women* by Laura Bates highlight the fact that, often from a young age, many boys and men are exposed to cultural messages and online spaces which condition them to see women as inferior. One quote that Laura shares early in her book, from an incel forum, shows the extreme challenges that so many women face around the globe from some pockets of men. It reads 'since they deserve to [be] raped I cannot concern myself with the pain rape causes them'.[85]

Lee said to me that 'to say that we're socialised to hate women is quite strong, but I think the key point here is the "socialised" aspect. Men don't automatically hate women, and it's worth seeing that we've been swimming in a sea of misogyny for a long, long time. Generally, our society is quite degrading to women, and that water seeps into us while we swim in it, whether we want it to or not'.

So men have a huge role in unworking some of the cultural conditioning and bias we have between the sexes, particularly as the real-world impact is stark; it's women who are the ones who are more fearful of violence, stalking, aggression, and

240

sexism. Often perpetrated by men. If this feels like murky territory and a bit uncomfortable, that's because *it is*.

There was one person I met who perfectly voiced to me the need to actively work on how we relate to women so we can start to lessen the divide. I spoke to Spencer Matthews, *Made in Chelsea* star turned entrepreneur and founder of CleanCo, the alcohol-free spirit alternative brand. When we spoke, Spencer said 'I'm probably not the best person to speak to', in reference to masculinity as a whole and his expertise on it. 'I come from a very privileged background, and I have very top-level views on masculinity, which are probably irrelevant to a lot of people'. But I felt that Spencer was the perfect guest in many ways.

He acknowledged his past reputation on his time in *Made in Chelsea* and said 'I didn't always behave in the way that I would have liked to. Throughout my life, I'm certainly no saint, and I've upset people'. But he's also been clear that he doesn't like being known as Spencer from *Made in Chelsea*, and that he wished he'd cared more about what people thought of him at the time, where he often acted in ways that his friends thought was cool.

And there is always a great deal of context that gets missed when we watch short episodes of other people's lives while we're cosied up on the sofa, commenting on things that we, in reality, know very little about. Spencer was 19 in the first season of *Made in Chelsea*. You'd be hard pressed to find many a 19-year-old boy that isn't grappling with his sense of identity, puberty, trying to understand how to be 'cool' to his friends and to impress women, all under the weight of cultural conditioning and norms. Try shoving a camera, millions of viewers, and fame into that scenario too, as well as tabloids who hang on every word to find their next story, and you've got a potentially fiery situation.

The beauty of being human is that we're messy. We make mistakes and do things we aren't proud of. But we also have the capacity to learn from that past, and use it to become not only better humans, but better men. Spencer admits to a troublesome past relationship with alcohol, one that he has actively worked on. Spencer turned to fitness and currently holds a Guinness World Record for the most marathon distances completed on sand in one month, where he ran 30 marathons in 30 days!

He's also been through periods of deep trauma too, losing his brother, Michael, in 1999 when Michael became the youngest Briton ever to reach the summit of Mount Everest. But it was a trip he never returned from. Spencer filmed the documentary *Finding Michael* as he underwent a quest to search for Michael's body, and although he was unsuccessful, you could see his own healing journey playing out.

Notably throughout the documentary, Spencer doesn't cry, and it's something he commented on to me. 'I was brought up to not cry unnecessarily. It wasn't in a nasty way, but I've been brought up that crying isn't going to help me get on with it. If I see other men cry, I don't assume they're weak, but for me this isn't the focus of what we should be talking about with masculinity'.

It was here that Spencer argued for a way that we can help to expand masculinity, not only by focusing on emotional awareness, but in narrowing gender divides and building bridges between humans.

This isn't to say that men shouldn't express emotion, but I think we'd also be well served in trying to lessen the divide between men and women, and that's something I've really worked on as I've grown older and matured. I think if society looks at the population as a whole as just beings, championing equality without division, stopping this unnecessary labelling where everything has to be split by gender, and instead we just focus on people, I think that would go a long way in helping a lot of men. And humans in general.

If I take my own family life; I'm married to a fiercely independent woman who makes loads of money. I've known that from the beginning. So I just don't have that sense of needing to spend my time having to be the breadwinner, the provider, the protector. Our relationship feels incredibly even and, because of that, respectful.

The day that we had our interview was the same day that a tabloid was busy running a story about Spencer, and he said that it's a common experience for him, often dealing with false stories and fake accounts being shared. I saw the two opposing worlds at play in our interview; the one that the tabloids wanted to run, the one that perpetuates a certain image of men and masculinity. And then I saw the real Spencer in private, a man who, like many of us men, has a past that contains things they're not proud of, but one who has acknowledged wrongdoing, taken accountability for harmful habits, and forged a new path. And one who knows that half the battle of being a true man lies in having balance, compassion, and respect towards other humans, whatever their gender.

A real positive, authentic masculine role model for me is Walton Goggins, the actor. He's talked about having an impoverished childhood, where his mother worked all year round to earn like eight grand a year. When his career as an actor took off, he had a day where he made that same amount, in one day. He said it was the best, and hardest, day of his life. He was proud of himself but it felt hard for him too, thinking of his mother. Most people would just think 'fuck yeah, look at all this money', but for Walton he was caught in this beautiful dilemma because of deep love for his mother. And I just think that's peak masculinity right there.

For someone like Spencer, who has fame and wealth, who cares deeply about his fitness, who ticks a lot of boxes in the 'traditional masculinity' camp, it was refreshing to hear his more expanded, flexible view on masculinity too, and one that isn't only focused on emotional vulnerability, but also on treating humans with more respect and compassion.

Emotional expression and vulnerability are critical, and much of this book has examined how harmful emotional suppression has been for men. But this also isn't the only solution for expanding our sense of masculinity, and it's why it's not the only angle I've focused on in these chapters. Much of the public conversation I see happening on masculinity only seems to focus on high-profile, polarising influencers who sit at one extreme, or about how men should cry more.

While that's a reasonable argument, it's still another extreme, sitting at the other end of the spectrum. The reality is many well-intentioned men don't align themselves with radical influencers, but they also don't want to align themselves with an overemphasis on visible emotionality either. But if these are the *only* conversations we have, we'll be missing a huge portion of men.

So, the more we can expand out the conversation on masculinity beyond only emotion and vulnerability, and the more we can all work on treating humans with more compassion, the healthier I believe this world will be for everyone.

Action

Think about what biases you might hold about the opposite sex, and ask where they came from. Do they feel fair and grounded in fact? Try actively challenging it this week; have a new conversation or listen to something you wouldn't normally.

Key Summary

The concept of masculinity doesn't exist in isolation, it's co-created by how we show up in the world, how we treat others and how they treat us. This is in relation to other men, but it's in relation to the opposite sex too. A huge part of building a healthier concept of masculinity is by building bridges of respect, empathy, and collaboration between all genders.

12
Release Point #3: A New Space for Masculinity

Many men are feeling lost out at sea. There's noise at the extreme ends of the masculinity spectrum, noise which often grabs the headlines. But many men who are caught in the middle, who support equality and want to do good, can feel unsure of where they belong as their traditional role shifts. They're looking for a little direction and leadership. Sometimes they're scared to admit that or to ask for it.

At the same time, stereotypes persist, and men internalise and use them to limit or undermine themselves. Stereotypes are the antithesis to what it means to be human – they're rigid and simplistic, stripping away nuance. In reality, humans are unique, complex, and dynamic. For many men, the clothes simply don't fit.

The world is changing, but many of our perceptions of men are lagging behind. To change things for men we can start to change our language, our perceptions, and our beliefs, and help them find a new place before they get swept under by the wave of tradition clashing with modern change.

Beyond the Breadwinner

The rise of women and the securing of women's economic independence – which, I argue, is the greatest economic liberation in human history and an absolutely wonderful thing – has had the effect of exposing the fragility of male identity

—Richard Reeves, author and social scientist

For so long a man's image has often been equated with the Three Ps of Provide, Protect, Procreate. Many believe that this is the role of masculinity. In truth, society has reinforced these clearly defined gender roles for quite some time. It was only in 1918, under certain conditions, that women were allowed to vote for the first time in a general election in the UK. But inequality still thrives; 'gender apartheid' is commonplace in many countries around the world – girls being denied access to education and jobs, or having to request permission from their male partners to travel.

We see this play out at the highest echelons of society, where, as of the time of writing, women serve as head of state or government in only 25 of the 193 UN member states, and the number of Fortune 500 female CEOs often sits in the low double digits. Not only have some men been *told* they're the breadwinners, it's reflected in the most powerful positions on the planet. Although these numbers are starting to change, with the trend of more women gaining positions of power slowly tracking upwards. But I place emphasis on the word 'slowly'.

And we also see how this permeates throughout other areas of society; for example, with marriage between a heterosexual couple. Men, generally speaking, are expected to propose. The wife must wear her engagement ring, symbolising her commitment, while the man wears nothing. The wife-to-be is physically 'given' away at the wedding by her male father, while the speeches are dominated by men – father of the bride, best man, groom. We take it as 'tradition' but the underlying message is clear – men are in control, women are subservient, property even.

Some of these traditions might seem harmless, but who decides that, and for whom? And at what point does tradition become more like handcuffs? There have been plenty of instances throughout history of traditions which, while innately immoral, were upheld simply because that's the way it's always been.

While much of the example I've shared around marriage is symbolic, and doesn't directly correspond with things like structural inequalities in the workplace, it can be confusing for men when traditions linger and they're looking to balance old norms with new expectations. And it does all feed into a deeper question around who holds what kind of power in what relationships, and which are archaic traditions, and which are things we want to uphold. It's okay to argue for a man to lead the charge in relationships, but we also have to acknowledge the subtle, subconscious power play and hierarchies this invites in.

Decent men understand and respect the need for equality and equal opportunity. But it's understandable if it feels like a strange time for them and that their role is shifting. Two thoughts and two beliefs can be true at the same time. Many men carry a lot of shame and embarrassment if their female partner is the breadwinner. They're worried about hearing jokes like 'she wears the trousers', about seeming lazy or inefficient, or about the impact it will have on their self-worth. In fact, a study published in 2024 found that in heterosexual couples, when the wife earned more than her husband, there was a higher likelihood of poor mental health diagnosis for both spouses, but especially the husband.[86]

Consciously many men know this shouldn't and doesn't matter, but subconsciously many men have such a deep, visceral reaction to this. It's not for materialistic reasons, it's because every deep cultural signal they've been raised with is starting to sound the alarm bells, that not only are they not fulfilling their role as the breadwinner, but that their female partner seems to be doing a better job of being more masculine.

When it comes to masculinity in the modern world, we're rarely dealing with logic. We're dealing with emotional triggers and biological wiring so deep that it causes subconscious reactions that most men, having been taught to be emotionally suppressive, don't understand and can't explain.

Naturally, it's time to let go of these constructs that are no longer serving us. Historian Stephanie Coontz, who has looked at the history of family and marriage, wrote in 2013: 'there is no such thing as the traditional male-breadwinner family. It was a late-arriving, short-lived aberration in the history of the world, and it's over. We need to move on.'[87]

Although the perception does seem to be changing generationally, and many men do understand the need to 'move on', many are also struggling to know exactly what to move on to, or where to. Where feminism has had a rallying call in recent years of equality and empowerment, men haven't had this same banner to stick into the ground. Many are feeling displaced as the way of life they've always known changes, and while that's no bad thing in the push for equality, many haven't found a new place to occupy.

It doesn't help that they don't always feel they can voice it, where some sides are quick to push away how men feel because of historic oppression caused by men. Forgetting, of course, that the spoils of those at the top haven't been shared equally among men and many further down the ladder are suffering because of the actions at the top.

Lee Chambers, a business psychologist who focuses on gender within the workplace, said to me, 'if you're a man, then you do have a level of privilege. But privilege isn't binary. We're all privileged to an extent, it's just that some people have more keys to open more doors than others. But we all have a set of keys, and true progress comes from using these keys to open the doors of others, rather than trying to smash their door down.'

So, what can we do about it?

1. **Acknowledge:** We must first acknowledge inequality and widespread oppression that many groups have faced, and continue to face, whether that's due to sexuality, gender identity, race, or any other factor.
2. **Support:** With that acknowledgement in mind, we can't treat equality as a zero-sum game. True equality is about uplifting both sides, and also recognising where we need equality, and where we need equity. We can acknowledge the bad actors on both sides, and also realise they represent a minority. We win by doing it together, and we can support more than one group at the same time. This is not mutually exclusive.

3. **Celebrate:** Let's celebrate our men. There aren't too many positive messages out there for men at the moment, no rallying call, no statements of pride. Toxic influencers fill this void with their seductive messages. Let's shout about the good that men can do and the good that they are.

4. **Redefine:** It's worth expanding out what our definition of 'provider' means. None of us only provide in financial ways. We provide in the time we give to others, the love that we show, our acts of kindness and charity, what we put out to the world, the caring and respect that we show to our partner and others. For far too long, men have associated providing with only needing to earn more money, but men have a lot more than just that to give, and the people around us are looking for more than just what's in our bank.

5. **Expand:** Finally, let's encourage men to do whatever it is that they want to aspire to. We've made progress in recent years in encouraging women to take roles outside of predetermined gender norms, but we don't always see this reflected with men. We can encourage men to take roles that are typically seen as 'feminine', encourage expression, encourage stay-at-home dads.

Lee told me:

once we start to do this, it allows us to access parts of ourselves we may have shut off. It'll always feel fragile stepping outside of our gender roles, because society will punish you for it. And there's a lot to fear for men with this; getting it wrong, upsetting people, looking like a hero, looking incompetent. . .it's so multifaceted. But today's discomfort is tomorrow's growth, and while fear is the biggest barrier to change, it's also one of the greatest indicators to act.

This starts as a perception. Some men are feeling displaced because they're not filling the role that they've been told they have to. Let's help build them a new one they can be proud of.

Action

Write down a list of everything that being a 'provider' means to you, beyond only financial ways. Where did those beliefs come from, and which ones still serve you today?

Redefining Dad

I was diagnosed with PTSD after the birth of my child, but I never spoke about it

—Elliott Rae, fatherhood campaigner

The stereotype of the father isn't a pretty one. While mothers are seen as caregivers, compassionate, and a child's first point of call, dads are often joked about as being absent, clumsy, and lazy. They're seen as second-rate to the mother, a side dish to her main course.

These stereotypes *are* beginning to change, and Elliott Rae, a fatherhood champion who has been working in the space for almost a decade, and is the founder of Parenting Out Loud, highlighted how: 'Ten years ago, on films you'd have seen bumbling dads, the kind that when the wife goes out, suddenly the house descends into chaos. Essentially, that he's incapable. But that's shifting, and there's more acknowledgment of the capabilities of fathers'.

But in many ways, the stereotype of fathers being second-rate and predefined gender roles are reinforced societally through parental systems that understandably provide more physical recovery for women post-birth, but often also overlook the emotional and bonding needs of fathers. In some countries, men get *zero* time off after having a newborn child. For gay couples, there can be even greater inequality around the world, with both sides facing remarkably low levels of paternity leave. The expectation is men will provide, women will nurture. The traditional working system that many countries operate under is over one hundred years old.

Clearly, the world has expanded since our working systems were established. There are same-sex couples, women who are rightfully aiming higher in their careers and, in many cases, are the breadwinner in the family structure, and men who want to be stay-at-home dads.

But the perception hasn't changed entirely, and we reinforce it not only through policy, but with our language and beliefs. Unhealthy phrases like 'you're such a hands-on dad', while well-meaning, have clear subtle undertones. It implies that men aren't meant to be looking after the kids, and if they do, it's a surprise. It can be hard to be a 'hands-on dad' when they're forced back into the office after two weeks. Our society and policies create distance and emotional suppression and stereotypes reinforce it.

We allow these to persist because 'that's the way it's always been', but we rarely step back with enough critical thinking to ask 'is this right?' Particularly when the stereotype doesn't match up with the science.

Biologically, men are capable of nurturing and caregiving, with research showing that fathers can develop caregiving responses that are comparable to that of mothers.[88] This is not to underplay the huge role that women undertake in pregnancy, who clearly undergo a number of life-altering changes, both to their bodies and to their careers. But, if I purely focus on the male's lens, beyond pregnancy and women who choose to breastfeed, it's been found that men and women share remarkably similar levels of natural caregiving abilities.

Science shows that a father's testosterone reduces after he's had a child, and he becomes primed to have his reward system triggered when he interacts with his child. His brain physically changes, with the areas linked to affection, nurturing, and threat detection growing. If men weren't meant to be natural caregivers, then why do their bodies and brains change so meaningfully after having a child?

But Elliott tells me that fathers have to be given the chance for these abilities to develop, and that comes through time and bonding with their child:

If you are given the exposure to real caregiving responsibilities, your brain goes through changes. When men are given this chance, the risk of mental health issues for both themselves and their partners decrease, but also, they're in the rhythm of family life. Imagine family life is like a carousel, if you all get on that carousel early, then you're all in for the ride and in a rhythm. But if that carousel has started moving, which is what happens if that father doesn't have time off at the beginning, then he has to try and jump on midway when it's already spinning fast. And it's very difficult to assert yourself into family life a year later.

We also discussed a lesser-known, but crucial challenge that new fathers can face – that around one in ten men can suffer from postnatal depression. It's often not spoken about because of lack of knowledge, but at least 10% of all new fathers suffering from depression is a number which I'm sure will surprise most. Elliott told me:

> *one of the biggest risk factors for a father developing postnatal depression is when a dad struggles to bond with his baby. The figure of one in ten is probably modest, because that's only the number that has been reported. Our understanding of postnatal depression in men isn't old, we're talking only the last few years, so there isn't the language and there aren't services of support being advertised to men.*

What it highlights to me is how a vicious cycle has been created. We don't believe that men are the natural caregivers, and so we have created policies that reinforce this. But then the lack of time with their child stops their caregiving abilities developing, thus further perpetuating the stereotype that *we've* created. All while we run the risk of causing postnatal depression in men, which they often struggle with in silence. And as we know, this can have devastating consequences.

Elliott knows the reality of this firsthand. When Elliott's daughter was first born, she fell sick with Group B strep, something that one in ten babies pass away from. He didn't even know if they were going to make it out of the hospital with her. Thankfully they did, but then it was back onto the hamster wheel of life, where just a few days later, Elliott was back at work. 'But something wasn't right with me; I had insomnia, I'd be crying randomly on the way home from work, I couldn't even talk sometimes, I'd just be mumbling and in a daze. It was only later that I got diagnosed with PTSD from the incident with my daughter, but I'd never spoken about it'.

Elliott has been campaigning for better paternity leave policies for many years. Clearly there's an economic question here, and also the fact that the woman who has carried the child obviously needs more physical recovery and support. But to give some men around the world no paternity leave at all, or a measly two weeks, after his life has so fundamentally changed? Not only is it diabolically outdated, but it's not good for the development of the child, the man's wellbeing, or the partner in the relationship who suffers with a lack of companionship and support.

There are countries leading the charge, like Iceland, who offer six months of leave to both parents, regardless of gender or sexual orientation. Up to six weeks is transferable to the other parent, allowing for choice between the couple. Many other countries, and forward-thinking companies within them, are exploring more flexible, progressive, and inclusive policies in this area.

But policies to one side, we can start to change our beliefs too and how we talk about fathers. If the evidence shows that there is little difference in a man and woman's natural caregiving abilities, then it's worth asking where our beliefs are coming from. Perhaps they are being perpetuated by a system making it that way.

Elliott is clear to stress there is a two-way fix here: 'Clearly, parts of the system need to change. But I'm a big believer in empowerment too. Let's empower dads. Because of our ideas of who we are, we don't change'.

Campaigning for better paternity rights and support for fathers isn't to draw anything away from women or mothers. We must keep championing mothers, who face such a large physical and mental burden during pregnancy and post-childbirth. And the battles they've had to fight for decades over the clash between pregnancy and career progression.

But let's also change how we talk about men as fathers. They're dads, not babysitters. Let's give them more credit and give them chances to step into their role of parenthood. Many men will be carrying their own learned lessons of emotional suppression into their interactions with their child, so may already be starting by keeping emotion at an arm's length. If we help them to be more present and to connect with their child, then perhaps we can start to bring out their own compassion and break the cycle of emotional suppression.

The more that we can raise fathers up and campaign for better rights, the bigger knock-on effect it'll have for everyone. Fatherhood built on close connection, caregiving, and compassion can become a cornerstone of an expanded sense of masculinity for those who want to be or are fathers, in whatever form that fatherhood takes. And it's not only fathers – these same traits can exist in all men and in all forms of care too.

Actions

Think about what stereotypes you hold about fathers. Where have they come from, and do they feel fair?

A Bigger Box for Masculinity

What most men don't realise is that they have a competitive mode and a compassionate mode

—Professor Paul Gilbert OBE, psychologist

Masculinity isn't a fixed concept, and that means we can start to expand our definition right now. That's the core thread of this book, and the need for it is in every interview, but I want to include a specific section on it.

I don't believe in shutting down traditional masculinity, because there are some great traits and values that we can be proud of. Strength and resilience are going to be needed in plentiful amounts throughout life. Providing for your family and protecting those around you is a noble cause. Striving to be leaders and to take control of situations has value and indeed is attractive to many.

But there are also times for asking for help. For compassion, empathy, and connection. For emotional vulnerability and awareness. For softness and for love. To deny these things is to deny part of the natural human experience. And none of these things have to be mutually exclusive.

We can tell our men all we want to suppress their emotions, but it doesn't get rid of them. We've seen enough examples throughout this book of what the outcome of this can be. Professor Paul Gilbert OBE, the man who has decades of experience working as a psychologist, told me: 'what most guys don't realise is that they have a competitive mode *and* a compassionate mode. These two things are often seen as being in conflict, but actually these are two motivational systems which stimulate different brain systems'.

In short, our biological systems are wired for a much more expansive definition of masculinity than we currently allow, which has been defined at a point in time by a group of people, and then reinforced through cultural norms. We've told men for a long time to be independent, to fear interpersonal relationships, but Professor Gilbert said that 'men don't realise just how much a sense of belonging is important to them, because they've been told for a long time that they've got to be individual heroes. But actually they want to be cared about and valued'.

Each person's definition of masculinity will be unique to them, and I don't believe in one neat little blueprint that we can hand to everyone as though it were a local flier. Everyone will have different values and things they care about more than others. But we certainly have to lower this barrier that sits between 'masculine' and 'feminine' traits, and understand that there is far more crossover between these things than we realise. Often what we're talking about are simply 'human' traits, which *we've* separated out, but it's more of a spectrum than a separation, and one that we can take a balanced approach to. We will all place greater value and emphasis on some traits over others, and that's fine. This isn't about changing your core values, it's about expanding them and the traits that you allow in.

I'm not asking you to close this book and immediately change your definition of what masculinity means. These things are deeply held beliefs that can take years to unravel. Hopefully I've shown you throughout this book why it could be time to expand our definitions, as the statistics and stories are compelling.

There were two men who I interviewed as part of this process who emphasised that no matter how 'peak alpha male' we might have been, there is always room to change our definition and bring balance into our lives.

Both were from the military; an industry I wanted to tap into as emotional suppression is a core component of military culture, a culture which some would say leans towards 'hegemonic masculinity'. There are obviously good reasons for this in life-threatening combat situations in some of the most inhospitable parts of the world.

Many would regard military men as the ultimate masculine man. What I wanted to know is how much of this image persists after military life. Is there room for change? I spoke with two veterans; Mark Ormrod MBE, who I featured in the earlier chapter on disability, and Anthony 'Staz' Stazicker, former Special Forces soldier and star of the Channel 4 show *SAS: Who Dares Wins*. Staz was awarded the Conspicuous Gallantry Cross for combat actions conducted in Afghanistan in 2013.

Mark's thinking aligned with much of my own, and much of that was shaped by his experience of stepping on an IED. And when I asked Staz for his view on masculinity, he said: 'I'm conflicted personally. Part of me has one view on mental health and masculinity, and there's another side of me that has a completely opposing view on it.' Staz goes on to tell me about his childhood, how he was raised in an environment heavy with traditional masculine traits.

Staz went searching for a place of belonging where he could fit in, and he joined a 'big boys club' – the military. 'It was a proud day for me and gave me that purpose, which I think a lot of men need. That North Star, something they can aim towards and push themselves towards'.

He explained that the Special Forces is a very masculine world, one that is very alpha. Soldiers aren't walking around talking about their emotions, it often comes out through other mediums, like drinking. 'It has to be guarded and restrained, because of the work we're doing. We were exposed to real suffering and pain, and we were conditioned to operate in those environments.'

When Staz joined, those 10 years were arguably the highest operational output that the unit had ever seen, in Afghanistan. He said that at the time, it felt incredible. 'But would I do it now, knowing what I now know? Probably not. I lost a lot of friends along the way, I was involved in large, multiscale attacks, I killed people . . . but that was just the nature of the business.'

Staz explained how this journey and his experiences have given him these two sides to masculinity:

As men it's our job to carry that weight. If not me, then who? If we can't do that, who are we expecting to do that? It's a privilege to carry it. However, when it tips over the balance and that weight becomes too much to bear, at that point an individual needs to be able to recognise that and speak out. But because of social conditioning, too many men don't, and that coupled with societal, financial, and professional pressures, it weighs heavily on men. Life's not supposed to be easy, we're going to face struggle. It's why my company is called Thru Dark, and our mantra is 'endeavour through adversity'.

It's clear to see the traits of 'traditional masculinity' in Staz, and also where they've been shaped from. In his own words, 'my life has been forged in the fucking fire'. But, while he opened our interview by talking about these opposing views, all I heard was balance, two sides of the same coin. Both sides have their purpose and their unique design, but we're still talking about one coin, not two opposing ones.

His life has been shaped by experiences which many of us would define as the height of masculinity. But he's also suffered grief, not just losing his mother at a young age, but also comrades he lost in action, and as a father now, he knows the importance of the real meaning of stoicism; emotional control but through emotional understanding and articulation. He might take pride in carrying the burden placed on him, and there's nothing wrong with that. But what's important is that he's comfortable shouting when that burden becomes too much.

I wondered if the military would leave Mark and Staz permanently battle-hardened to the world, rejecting any form of emotional expression. To hear them both talk about balance and flexible masculinity, and being able to straddle the entire spectrum of the masculine experience, was refreshing.

We often create an image in our heads of the types of men that fit into this new wave of masculinity, which is why I deliberately wanted to include people who fit outside of that. I'm sure there will be plenty of other military men who would argue back against what I've written in this book. But if Mark and Staz, who have been to some of the toughest places on the planet, can still come back home and recognise that toughness and strength is only one part of being a man, and it's not something that has to be permanently switched on, then I think any of us can.

Does this make them any less masculine? I don't think so. In fact, I'd love to see the people who would dare accuse these two to their faces of being lesser men! Masculinity isn't a cage, it's a toolkit – one that we can add several tools to so that we're equipped for the complexities and challenges of life.

Action

Choose one core trait you've always associated with being a 'real man', especially one that might be stopping you from opening up. Spend a week actively challenging it, and see what happens.

Key Summary

Masculinity isn't a fixed object that we can point to and say 'that's what it is'. So much of our sense of masculinity is built from language, beliefs, norms, and stereotypes, many of which are outdated or limit us. But, that also means we can change them. We don't have to wait for policies or permissions to expand our sense of masculinity and it can happen right now, in the beliefs we hold, the language we use, and the way that we see ourselves. Masculinity can be a toolkit, one that we can keep adding to.

13

Release Point #4:
Reprogramming the Feed

Humans are impressionable creatures as it is, but for men who have been conditioned into emotional repression or suppression, a particular challenge can occur. It may mean that they don't have a clear steering on their internal compass, on the things they're truly passionate about, and without emotional fluency or self-knowledge, identity gaps can form.

And these vacuums are easily filled in a noisy world. Doom scrolling, algorithms, the rise of influencers, films, music, articles and so on – there are an endless amount of things competing for our attention and, ultimately, our identity.

The content we consume and the people we choose to follow is like holding up a mirror. And it reflects parts of ourselves that slowly shape who we become by rewiring our brain, and influencing our habits, values, and even our emotional responses. There are a lot of strong voices out there shouting at men how to be. A good place for us to start in building a healthier idea of masculinity is by changing what, and who, we're giving our attention to.

Unplugging to Reconnect

It's really important for men to be able to sit in peace and quiet, with themselves

—Tj Power, neuroscientist and author

The relationships we now hold with our phones are, in many cases, an addiction. I'm not going to tell everyone to throw their phone in the bin as the solution for masculinity issues, that isn't feasible or what most people want. That being said, I don't believe we are examining in enough depth the intersection between technology and masculinity. We're often focused on the impact on our dopamine, but not enough on the impact on men specifically.

Tj Power, *Sunday Times* bestselling author of *The DOSE Effect*, earlier said to me in the chapter on technological disconnection that our passive consumption of content is 'leading to a lot of men feeling isolated and falling deeper into a spiral of pain, depression and passivity. We are potentially creating a generation of young men who aren't necessarily great at contributing to their families and their work'.

There are a lot of variables at play which were covered in that earlier chapter. It gives easy access to harmful influencers, some of whom lie and manipulate. It can give a bad education on what it means to be a man; for example, a lot of men gain their education on sex and relationships through unrealistic porn content. In many ways, technology has become the new third space for men, with social media and dating apps now replacing pubs, parks, and gyms. And for men who may be emotionally suppressed, it gives them a way of reinforcing that habit further, avoiding difficult emotions by staying in the technological wild west.

So I believe that the first step is acknowledging and re-evaluating our relationships with technology so that we're in control, otherwise we know these platforms will control us. This means being aware of what we're doing and why we're doing it. I'm not advocating for a ban, but simply bringing awareness to our actions. When I'm feeling anxious, I often doom scroll on Instagram. I *know* that I'm doing it because I'm anxious and I'm trying to avoid that emotion. Awareness helps me make peace with it, and it also helps me to put a stop to the scroll earlier than I would.

Next, creating space from technology, particularly our phones, can be incredibly helpful. Tj said getting the phone out of the bedroom is a good step. He said that if he wanted to get me as addicted as he could to alcohol, he would leave a bottle of wine on my bedside table and make me drink as soon as I wake up. This is essentially what we're doing with our phones. 'You need to consciously develop the capacity to be someone that's confident and calm as a human being, who doesn't feel the need to have their phones all the time. When you have the capacity to physically separate from your device, the screen time plummets'.

By having this distance from our phones, we create the space that allows us to feel and process challenging emotions. Men haven't been taught to sit in peace and quiet with themselves and their thoughts. A lot of men struggle to do things on their own, without music, podcasts, or headphones, sitting with nothing but their own thoughts.

Many men have been taught that they should be active, busy, and doing something. It means that they lean away from things like boredom, and they lean away from difficult emotions too, like anxiety. Technology is the perfect vice for helping us to lean away even further, which is compounded by the fact that it's not fully satisfying our biochemical need for real connection.

Tj's own therapist advised him to practise spending more time alone, free of distractions and technology. Tj said it terrified him at first, but when he finally did, he started to get some very loud messages from his own thoughts on the various things that needed attention in his life: 'It's really important for men to be able to sit in peace and quiet, with themselves. It's a core part of being a strong and resilient man'.

This isn't about completely banishing phones or shaming ourselves for using them. It's about learning when we're using our phone because it's an activity we want to do, versus when we're using it to escape or numb out. Because it's sitting with those more difficult feelings, rather than avoiding them, where we can start to emotionally express ourselves more.

Action

Notice when you reach for your phone without thinking. Can you leave it behind the next time you go for a walk? See what surfaces in the silence.

Changing the Content Diet

Vulnerability Is the New Cool

—album title by Shocka, music artist

Regardless of what we decide to do with our phones, we will still be consuming content in some form. Things we read, what we listen to, and the conversations we have. It'll be impacting and shaping our perspective of masculinity, whether we realise it or not. And with the advent of social media, a certain degree of critical thinking and nuance seems to have slipped and our views can often be shaped simply by the last social media post that we read, particularly troublesome when the algorithms reward extremes.

Commercial content specifically around men often falls into two buckets. On the one hand, it leans heavily into traditional views of masculinity. Hollywood blockbuster films featuring heavily toned men, surrounded by beautiful women, able to complete logic-defying stunts and fight scenes. Or we see a plethora of fitness influencers and books on how to better pick up women.

In the other bucket, we see content that leans into the extremes of male behaviour, the ones that grab the headlines. Violence, aggression, and crime. For example, Netflix's hit drama, *Adolescence,* explores the online radicalisation of young boys, and did an incredible job of starting a conversation around the dangers that young boys are facing, but it also presented one view of them. Watched in isolation, it's easy to think that boys and men are coiled springs of rage, ready to explode at any moment. A lot of the reviews I read painted boys as things to fear, rather than people to celebrate.

I don't advocate for scrapping these two types of content, which many people enjoy, but instead to broaden our definition of masculinity by expanding the content that we're consuming, to bring in these other traits and qualities to balance one side with another, valuing strength *and* vulnerability.

As I began to consciously change my relationship with masculinity, I became hyper-aware of the over-masculinisation of much modern-day music. Lyrics that focused solely on wealth, drugs, and sexual conquests. There is room for this, but it was only ever one view of masculinity – the traditional view. I began to expand what I listened to and consumed, so that I could see a different type of man reflected in my content.

Someone who perfectly epitomises this conscious shift is Kenneth Erhahon, a rapper who goes by the stage name Shocka. He spent the early part of his career fitting into the traditional mould, rapping about big mansions, big cars, clothes, women, drugs. But a powerful story of a struggle with mental health changed him when he got dropped from his label in 2012 and fell into a breakdown, where he eventually had to be sectioned. Then his mother passed away, and Shocka acknowledged there were a lot of things he'd never got the chance to say to her, and regret that he still carries with him.

Everything changed for him after these experiences, and he began to focus his music and his art on making a difference, and on *real*, deep-level things that go beyond the superficial of money, fame, and sex.

In my conversation with him he said:

I had everything I wanted, my life was like a fairy tale. And then I had one of the worst possible experiences you can have, ending up in a mental health hospital. I was seeing real life things; people talking to themselves, people tormented by things spiritually. My family and friends are coming to visit me, crying, devastated. How on earth am I going to go through that and then come out and keep making music about designer clothes and trainers? So I started searching for more, started listening to old music and really paying attention to the lyrics and the meaning. Like Tupac's music, and I was like 'oh so that's what he means in his single Changes: "I wake up in the morning and I ask myself, is life really worth it? Should I blast myself?"'

He published his most recent album, *Vulnerability Is the New Cool,* in 2024, which featured lyrics such as 'I know guys dying inside, but they can't express themselves because they're too cool . . . I was just like you until I was in a mental home on my own, now it's time to break that cycle, generations depend on it'.

The songs include stories of his mother passing from cancer, his struggles with his mental health and the stigma of mental health in society. One of his biggest hits, *Self Love,* was shared by Snoop Dogg. But Shocka notes that he didn't know how bad the stigma was around mental health, and if he did then he wouldn't have shared his story.

I was ignorant to this stuff when I first started talking about it publicly. I didn't realise how severe the stigma actually was with me being sectioned. I saw an interview once where a guy got asked about all these inventions he made and how he did it, because he was breaking all these rules. And he said 'I didn't know the rules, so I was just making it'. And that's how I felt. I'm glad I didn't know all the rules and the stigma, because then I wouldn't have put this content out there, and we wouldn't be having this conversation now.

This is the cycle that we all end up playing into – men who experience everyday trials and tribulations that life throws at us, but we hold back from sharing, for the perception of what others might think. Most content from men stays at the surface level, and that's most of what we consume. And so the cycle continues.

As you bring awareness to new values, you'll be amazed at how often you notice those values more in the world. *Star Wars* is a great example – a fictional world where audiences can mentally switch off to the CGI, sci-fi action. But underneath all of that, the film has strong Buddhist teachings and philosophical leanings. Yoda's much-repeated, sometimes meme-ified, quote 'fear is the path to the dark side. Fear leads to anger, anger leads to hate, hate leads to suffering' shows these teachings in abundance. This quote can easily be applied to our sense of masculinity, where often we have been taught to fear things like vulnerability and connections, and that can lead us down dark paths.

Keep consuming the content you love and pursuing your passions. Sometimes men can get a bad rap for the things they do – consuming too much content on sport, gaming, or fitness. This is incredibly unfair and these things are a core component of masculinity for many men. But we can also expand the content we're consuming to bring in new edges to our definition.

And this means consuming a range of content, balancing the bad with the good, and looking at what we're consuming holistically. This is about expanding and growing, not limiting and reducing. Let's consume more holistic, balanced content, and put more of it out to the world ourselves.

But let's also challenge what we hear with critical thinking. Let's be curious and ask questions, and allow other viewpoints in. We can hold space for more than one belief, and far too often these days content becomes about us versus them, one solution to rule them all. More than anything, let's assume positive intent and have respect. There are some bad voices out there, but there are *a lot* of good male voices out there too. It's on us to elevate them.

Action

Audit your content diet, not with guilt, only curiosity. Is there anything you're consuming which you know, deep down, isn't good for you? What would it feel like to remove it?

The Role Models We Need

We have to show young men that character is more important than status

—*Gareth Southgate, former England football manager*

Everyone needs healthy role models they aspire to be like. Aside from troublesome influencers who are filling a void, the men most often in the limelight are tech billionaires, politicians, athletes, and actors. They're often valued for what we see as traditional masculine traits: influence, fame, wealth, or talents. Who do you look up to for who they are on the *inside?* For showing emotional vulnerability, for their ability to communicate with their loved ones, for their stance on compassion and empathy?

Of course, we can value someone that has both, but as a society we haven't valued emotional expression in men, so it's made it harder for those who publicly display these traits to rise to the top. More voices are beginning to emerge who do balance masculinity, but many struggle to name more than a few male role models in this regard. These men *do* exist, but it's on all of us to help give them a bigger platform and a louder voice.

So what kind of role models *can* we follow? Everyone has their own definition of what a role model is, and it's influenced by beliefs, hobbies, generations even. My grandad's role model was Winston Churchill, while the younger generation are following YouTubers and gaming personalities. So it's impossible to draw up one bullet point blueprint that we can give to every man and say 'follow this'.

However, I think there are general shared characteristics that we can expect from a 'healthy' role model. We are all going to value these things to a different degree, and I'm not advocating for everyone being exactly the same – life would be pretty boring if we were!

But for me, a healthy male role model ticks these boxes:

- **Expansive view:** Comfortable with and acknowledges the full spectrum of masculinity and human experience.
- **Emotional awareness:** Acknowledgement of the entire range of human emotion. This doesn't mean they have to always bare their soul in overt public displays of emotion, but it's someone who is aware of all their emotions, rather than denying them.
- **Adaptive and balanced:** Ability and comfort with bending and flexing of masculinity depending on the situation.

Realising there are times for strength, providing, and protecting. And realising there are times for vulnerability, compassion, or asking for help.
- **Respect for others:** Respect towards women and all other groups. Realising that true leadership isn't about dominance, it's about unity – and you can be passionate and competitive without ego and arrogance.
- **'Soft skills':** Kindness, compassion, and empathy are much undervalued superpowers.
- **Accountability:** Ownership of mistakes. Looking for a squeaky clean role model is a fool's errand. We've all made mistakes. Someone who holds their hands up, takes accountability, and learns from them is critical.
- **Critical thought:** The ability to show critical thinking, to recognise bias, and also to admit that they don't have all the answers.

Often with this debate on masculinity we can go too far in trying to rebuild it, but an extreme sense of gentleness isn't what most men aspire to have or be; somewhere in the middle feels about right. What is crucial is that we don't water down masculinity and soften it too much, because men will push back. What if we were to recognise men's differences, recognise they often have an innate leaning towards things like competition and perhaps strength, and celebrate what makes men great, while also enhancing and expanding our definition of masculinity, and the role models that fit within it?

Perhaps it's not about redefining masculinity as such, but more about the components within it. For example, realising that strength can be physicality, but it can be vulnerability too. Or that competition can mean winning, but it can also mean community too. Providing can be striving for a bigger salary, but it can be about giving others our time and love as well.

All of this is a complex blend and I think it's fair to say that there is a lack of role models who fit this bill. Whether that's because they don't exist, or because we don't value the traits enough and so don't give them attention, is the question, and I'd wager it's the latter. But it's well within all of our abilities to choose who we follow or what we listen to. If we only craft our feeds to be full of people who exhibit certain traits, then that's all we're going to see and consume.

Here are a few role models who offer a broader template. There are plenty of examples in modern pop culture. I've had several comments on my content in the past that Aragorn from *Lord of the Rings* is the peak male role model. Strong and a formidable warrior, but a compassionate leader that brings the best out of people. The films themselves show male camaraderie during good times and bad, open expressions of platonic affection between men, and a huge diversity of male physiques, each of them carrying a burden regardless of their shape, size, or physical prowess.

So these role models *do* exist in our contemporary mediums, although the personality traits are sometimes lost in between all the action scenes, and we watch to switch off, not engage in critical thinking on masculinity.

We've also seen a new trend explode in recent years called BookTok, where fiction books burst into the mainstream by going viral on social media. Female authors and a hybrid romance/fantasy genre have benefited hugely from this, while followers of the trend joke about their 'book boyfriends', the men who star in these books.

Beneath the humorous tones of the trend, it's easy to see why this is happening. Many of these authors are women, and they're writing the male characters from a female's perspective. Often these men display many 'traditional masculine' traits of strength, power, and leadership, but they almost always have a soft side and a huge level of respect and compassion for their female counterparts. Not that masculinity is about proving anything to the opposite sex, but if we look at these books picking up steam, we may learn how the version of masculinity that men think is important is different to that of the one women hold.

It's not just fiction where these role models exist. They *are* out in the real world too, we just have to search for them and elevate them. Spencer Matthews mentioned that Walton Goggins is one of his. One of my role models is Ben Stokes, the England cricket captain. He displays a lot of traditional masculine traits in spades – physically tough, ultra-competitive on the field, a winner that gives it his all, and has won more than one World Cup. He's also made mistakes – he got into a brawl after a night out and faced criminal charges. He may have been defending two gay men who were suffering homophobic abuse, but there was still aggression there. But importantly, he took full responsibility and learnt from this. He talks honestly about the mistakes he made, and says never again. He threw every extra ounce he had back into his professional and personal life, using the experience to shape him. He talks about mental health and a hair transplant he had, and the players underneath him talk of how incredible a leader he is.

For me, this is perfect masculinity. Strength and vulnerability. The fact we are messy and make mistakes, but use them to mould us into someone better. Priding yourself on lifting others up.

We do need more and better role models, but it's also on us to find them. We have billions and billions of minutes of content available to us at our fingertips, with thousands of good men sharing content on all manner of things. It's never been easier, or more important, to choose who we follow and what we listen to.

Action

If who you follow shapes who you become, then who's been leading you, and what have they been serving? Think about who your first role model was, and ask why. Can you actively search out a new role model who shows a more expanded sense of masculinity?

Key Summary

We often treat content like background noise – passive and harmless. But the truth is, what we consume is being stored in our brains and bodies, slowly shaping our beliefs, actions, and behaviours. There's room for all different types of content and influences, and balance is often key. But if we want to expand our definition of masculinity, then expanding and transforming what we're consuming can be a good place to start.

14
Release Point #5: Talking and Healing

Men are often told to 'open up' or 'just talk', but the reality is that talking is really quite difficult. It's hard enough as it is to voice vulnerabilities or to have difficult conversations. But when you have men who may have decades of conditioning to *never* express their emotions, it's going to take a while to dust off those cobwebs.

The good news is that it is entirely possible. The brain is malleable and just because something has always been one way for us, it doesn't mean it has to stay that way. And while opening up isn't always everyone's solution, or it might be one of the last things they come to, it's still a critical tool to help us process our emotions, to build stronger connections with people, and to break this harmful cycle of emotional distance and suppression.

The Power of Talking and Listening

Communication leads to community . . . to understanding, intimacy, and mutual understanding

—Rollo May, psychologist

Talking – and I mean *really* talking with depth, compassion, and empathy, is a skill, and one we learn and continually develop. It's also something that's co-created with another person or a group; we must feel safe, to know our words are going to be heard and accepted, not shamed or shunned. We have an innate biological need to be part of a tribe and a community, and the perceived threat that men may feel with talking is that they're going to be excluded from the group.

So we all have a part to play in this, learning how to talk more openly but also learning how to listen better too. Although talking is hard, it has a lot of benefits. We're social creatures that thrive off connection, and it can help to reduce stress, fear, depression, anxiety, and more. It helps us to process difficult emotions and experiences, stopping that pressure valve from building so quickly. Put simply, it's good for us and our bodies.

I met with Wendy Robinson, the director of services at the excellent mental health charity, *Campaign Against Living Miserably,* or CALM. Founded in 1997, they've been at the forefront of helping to redefine the conversation around not only suicide prevention and mental health, but talking as a whole. We discussed some of the ways that we can encourage people to have better conversations.

The first thing Wendy said to me is that it's important to redefine our relationship with our emotions. They are natural body functions, and it's important to understand that:

our emotions are simply energy, in motion. That's what the word means, e-motion. Emotion is motion, and we're often afraid to have feelings because we think we're going to get stuck in them. We think if we let anxiety, for example, have its way, we'll be stuck with it forever. But actually the opposite is true, by really going into it, it starts to move. Like if you cry, you eventually stop, and you feel better for it.

This fear or lack of knowledge that we hold around emotions means that we generally don't always know *what* we're experiencing, or why. Which can make it hard to articulate them.

The link between mental health and emotional expression is such an important one. We probably have something like five hundred words to describe our emotions, and yet we use such a limited amount, maybe five or six – you know, I feel angry, sad, tired. Brené Brown says the closer you can get to the nub of the feeling, to describe exactly how you're feeling, the more relief you'll get.

The easiest way to get closer to this feeling is to flip yourself back to the inquisitiveness of your childhood, where you no doubt (to the annoyance of your family) questioned every single thing around you. Keep asking yourself 'why?' What's making you feel a certain way? Why is it doing that? Why has it started now, and what situation triggered it? Take the approach of a healthy observer to your own emotions, questioning them, but not judging them.

Remember that emotions aren't good or bad, they're simply sources of information from our body that it's asking us to pay attention to. Humans have unhelpfully placed emotions into two buckets: good and bad. But emotions aren't moral, they're simply messages from the body. If we weren't meant to feel them, there's a good chance evolution would have stamped them out of us a long time ago. So try not to label emotions, but pay attention to them instead, free of judgement.

Wendy notes that men 'tend to reach out for their services at points of transition, like going from feeling younger to older. So it's important to understand your transitions, the physicality of what happens to us and our bodies, how we feel, and understanding that you have a right to be feeling this way, and to talk about it'.

But, perhaps Wendy's most important piece of advice is that changing from emotional suppression to expression has to start from within and how we talk to ourselves.

Hardly any of us would ever talk to someone else the way that we talk to ourselves. We tell ourselves we're crap at what we do, that we aren't good enough, that we're not worthy, that we don't belong here. Would you ever dream of saying that to someone you love? Start showing more compassion and positive self-talk to yourself.

I recall my interview with David Chambers on relationships, where he says that the core wound for many men is about being not good enough. We hold ourselves up to impossibly high standards, ones that have been set for us long before we were born. If we start by telling ourselves that not only are we enough, but that we have a right to whatever feelings we have, it can help us voice them.

Talking is great, but we need understanding, self-esteem and emotional expression underneath as a foundational layer. So, start there. Self-esteem is critical, because that's going to be your shield for what life will throw at you.

For me, talking has been instrumental on my own journey. But it took me a long time to build up to it, so long that I kept everything a secret for over a year before I even voiced anything to anyone, even myself.

So my main message is: talk when you're ready. And talk in a way that suits you; that could be face-to-face, it could be over a message, it could be through journalling, it could be a chatbot. In this context, talking is less about an actual verbal conversation, but it's about the process of starting to understand your emotions and articulating them. *If you are in immediate crisis, then please do seek help from a medical professional. I have signposted some organisations at the back of this book.*

Talking isn't always easy, I still find it hard now. But we know that emotional suppression is more of a muzzle that has been forced onto men. So much of what we've seen in previous chapters, like shame, addiction, and loneliness, thrive in silence and suppression. So much of what men struggle with comes not only from what they feel, but from what they believe they can't say. This is a mask that we can all unstrap, and we can learn a new path of expression.

Action

Try journalling today, in whatever form works for you. Notepad, phone, or laptop. Diary entry or long paragraph of stream of consciousness. Get into the habit of noticing your thoughts and feelings, and starting to articulate them. Getting them out of our brains and putting them somewhere else can really help.

Rewiring the Brain

The brain is a far more open system than we ever imagined

—*Norman Doidge, psychiatrist*

Neuroplasticity, a fun-sounding word, became a linchpin for my recovery. In fact, learning about the neuroplasticity of the brain might be the point at which my recovery pivoted from one of hopeless despair to one of finally finding the light at the end of a very long, very dark tunnel.

One pervading thought that persisted when I was in my darkest depths was that I was broken beyond repair. Not only an unfixable man, but an unfixable human too. This was the chief reason that I was considering suicide; because I didn't see any other way out. I would have the same negative thoughts and self-talk running through my mind all day, as I spiralled around like one of those coins in an arcade vortex machine.

Then I read about neuroplasticity. In simple terms, it's the ability of the brain to change and adapt. It can physically rewire itself and create new neural pathways. That thought you keep having over and over again? Or that habit you can't seem to drop? It can change. It's one of the central tenets of cognitive behavioural therapy (CBT), which is that you can change your thinking to change your behaviour, and vice versa, to ultimately change how you feel.

Imagine you live near a beach and you go down there every single day. Everyone always walks the same path along the beach to the sea, so much so that the sand has been crushed down and a thick path has been created. What do new people do? They follow the same path. This is what your thoughts will do – go down the path most trodden. But you can create new paths and walk a different route down that beach. It'll be a light path at first, but gradually that one will become thicker and thicker and wind will cover the old one. Your brain isn't a fixed circuit board, it's more like clay, ready to be moulded. This is what you can do with your thoughts.

Things can change. Your brain can change. Your sense of masculinity can change. Where you are now doesn't have to be where you are in a year, if you don't want it to be. It's not always easy, but it is possible.

Katie Maycock, the burnout and stress coach I interviewed for an earlier chapter, highlighted the importance to me of empowering ourselves with personal agency to change and avoiding getting into what she calls a 'victim mindset'. Once we place ourselves into this mindset, we essentially lose all of our agency for change. She said:

> *It might be a crap pill to swallow, but it's also one of the most empowering things we can do, to say 'I do have accountability and responsibility over this'. Going into a victim mindset is actually an easy thing to do, because you don't have to do anything about it. You don't have to find the energy, resources or solutions. The harder option is choosing not to be a victim.*

None of this is to dismiss the severity of things that people go through, and the emotions that come with them. We're allowed to feel the things that we do, and changing mindsets isn't as easy as simply flicking a light switch. Life can be hard as hell sometimes, and it's okay to struggle. But for many experiences in life, we are presented with a fork in the road, where we can't choose what happens to us, but we can choose how we respond to it. Katie continued: 'The self-fulling prophecy is rooted in science; if you believe you're a victim and you can't do anything about it, then you're telling your brain that's what you believe. And then your brain will give you back all the information to reinforce that belief. And then that reinforces your actions, habits and behaviours'.

On a more societal level, Katie believes this victim mindset has led to the rise of incels, which is a term used to describe mostly male, heterosexual groups who claim they're unable to find a sexual partner, and so blame and shame women and girls as a result. Katie said: 'while many may be struggling with loneliness or rejection, their mindset can become dangerous and weaponised. And then you have toxic influencers who prey on this mindset, convincing people that you can escape through violence and oppression'.

One of the worst (and best) things about being human is that nothing is set in stone. Healing is rarely ever linear, and we have ups and downs. But just because you have a particular thought or belief now, doesn't mean it always has to be so. A brain that has been taught emotional suppression can unlearn this and relearn emotional expression instead. Some of these unhelpful societal beliefs which act more like handcuffs than aids can be worked back, and we can change our relationship to our emotions, our bodies, even ourselves. Sometimes all it starts with is curiosity.

Action

What's one belief you have about yourself that feels worn into your brain like an old path? What might a new path look like? Try to walk it at least once a day.

Let's Talk About Men's Health

Often men have to almost relearn their masculinity as they go through a health challenge

—*Professor Prasanna Sooriakumaran, urological surgeon*

A lot of men wait too long to go to the doctor. Many are going once something feels seriously wrong, fearing anything before that might make them appear weak. So it's clear that we need to have better and more well-rounded conversations with men about their health. And to understand that health professionals aren't there to judge, laugh, or finger point. They've seen it all a million times before. Many times when a man goes to see a healthcare professional, he's carrying embarrassment and shame, convinced he's the only person in the world experiencing this thing. What he often forgets is that it's highly likely this healthcare professional has dealt with this thing many times before, often even on the same day.

I spoke with Professor Prasanna Sooriakumaran (Professor PS), who works as a professor of urology and a consultant robotic prostate cancer surgeon across several of the world's leading clinics. He also works as the chief men's health officer for Smart About Health and has been cited over 7,000 times. The point is, Professor PS has a very decorated career.

But it has come with challenges. I've suffered a lot with my mental health and while my CV might look great, it's come with significant costs. And that's what makes me human, and that's what I bring to my patients. What keeps me doing this job that I love is the interaction I have with patients, going on that individual's journey with them to help them get to the destination that they want.

Knowing that Professor PS works so heavily with prostate cancer, something that can be awkward for men to discuss, I asked him how often he notices a man's sense of masculinity coming into treatment too. He told me of a finding that men would rather lose a leg than their erections, because to them, if they aren't sexually active, then they aren't men. This is how deep a challenge we're dealing with. But that's where healthcare professionals can play such a critical role. Professor PS said: 'we *know* this is how men are feeling when they come in and we want to help men preserve their sense of masculinity while we work through this challenge'.

He also tells me that many men come in to deal with and work on a physical problem which they think needs only a physical response. We've seen plenty of examples in this book where there is often a huge part of the puzzle that requires an emotional and mental response, but men need guidance in understanding that, and solving that part of the puzzle.

Often men have to almost relearn their masculinity as they go through a health challenge and change their relationship with their own masculinity. But it can be powerful when men do. Men will be able to have conversations with their healthcare professional that they won't with family or mates down a pub. And whatever is important to you, it's important to me. Because it's important to you. I go to football matches and play golf with some of my patients. Why? Because of the journey we've been on together.

We know how critical it is that we get this right. As we've already looked at from the statistics, there are a host of areas in health and wellbeing where men are disproportionately being negatively affected, whether that's life expectancy, cardiovascular disease, cancers, suicide, and more. Men often haven't had healthy conversations about their bodies early enough, they haven't had the right education, and they've often been conditioned out of seeking help until it's too late.

For men, knowing that their health professionals have seen these challenges dozens of times before can help to relieve some of the embarrassment. And then on the other side, the more we can talk about these things in groups, families, and between friends, the more it will help to remove shame from the bottom up too.

Action

Is there one aspect of your health you've been avoiding? Could you speak to a friend about it, book an appointment or even read more about it? The more that we can have these conversations, the more we can normalise them and expand what masculinity means.

Key Summary

The brain can change. So much of what we're dealing with when it comes to masculinity, and what we believe about ourselves, are societal constructs. We can have new thoughts, we can have new conversations, we can talk more about our health. It'll all help to change our experiences, rewire our brains and build a new, broader sense of masculinity for us.

Summary to Part Three

This isn't an easy fix, and it's not something we're going to solve overnight. So much of what we're talking about here is so deeply woven into the fabric of society that it will take generations to unravel it. It's not a case of snapping our fingers and implementing a couple of political policy changes. We're talking about deep-rooted beliefs, ancient laws, and outdated working structures. There are changes that must be made in government policy rooms, corporate boardrooms and school classrooms, and sometimes it can feel a little helpless thinking about it all.

That being said, there are plenty of things available to us to start changing things immediately, if we want to. We can make changes in our own lives, with the content we consume, with how we communicate, with our relationships, and with what we define as masculinity. Pick one, or pick several. Start small, or start big. Find a therapist, or find a blog article. Find a group to play football with, or ask your friend if he fancies watching the game together this week.

There's no right or wrong answer here. The main thing is that we start to make a conscious shift and, importantly, expand what our definition of masculinity means to us. There will be strong, noisy external messages for a while that tell men to stay quiet, to puff out their chests, and to force their emotions away. But it's in our power to say 'thanks, but no thanks'.

Conclusion

'Be a Man About It'. I want to finish this book by coming back to its title. To one of the many flippant phrases we throw about, thinking we're doing our men a favour, when often we're simply pushing them into a current that they're struggling to swim against. Hopefully throughout this book I've shown you the danger that a simple five-word phrase like this can have.

For far too long we've put men into neat little boxes that have a few traits and characteristics that supposedly make them 'a man', as though there is a simple seven-point checklist that they must tick. All the while we miss any sense of nuance, the grey areas, and the complexity of humans.

We've mixed biological wiring with cultural norms and male tradition, mob mentality with critical thinking, certainties with beliefs. We condition men to fear emotion, connection, and interpersonal relationships not because that's the way of things, but because that's the way of things that *we* know, decided at a point in time, not since the beginning of time. But then we collectively gasp when a man takes his own life, wondering why he didn't open up.

Conclusion

So much of the damage done to men doesn't start from within, it comes from the external. Unrealistic expectations, the perpetuation of stigma and shame, a warped sense of world order. A desperation to uphold 'traditional' values which are clashing with a world that is moving on without them. Men face challenges and struggles, they go through changes and upheavals, they suffer breakups, grief, and loss, they have aspirations, hopes, and dreams. But they've been told not to talk about any of that. They've internalised many of these beliefs and habits, reinforcing them, sometimes for decades.

A pressure cooker builds as a man does what he's told, rejects natural human experiences and emotions, none the wiser that his body can only store so much. We saw plenty of examples of where this pressure reaches breaking point, sometimes claiming men's lives.

We've found ourselves in a place of being in danger of watering masculinity down and forgetting some of the values that make men great. But we're also in danger of not doing enough, of allowing men to continue to find solace in bottles and drug packets, in delaying health checkups, in taking their own lives.

We only see the external action, and often criticise a man for it, forgetting to ask two important questions: 'what's going on below the surface that is making them do this thing, and what's going on in their environment that has made them feel that way in the first place?' The good thing about all of this is a lot of what we're dealing with are societal constructs. Deeply ingrained and hard to change, but not impossible.

There isn't one singular definition for how a man should be. I want him to make his own choices, not shackled by unhelpful stereotypes and societal beliefs. I want him to realise that masculinity is a spectrum and one that we can slide up and down depending on the situation and the response it requires. Too often we see this scale as a binary battlefield, two opposing armies trying to crush the other. But we forget we're all on the same team, trying to achieve the same goal.

It's on all of us to start making this change, to expand our definition of masculinity and to start unpicking these unhelpful beliefs and stereotypes. There will always be a new phrase or definition. 'Toxic masculinity' is popular at the moment, although it's a phrase I personally don't like and think does more harm than good. I've argued for 'flexible' or 'expanded' masculinity, while some are pushing for a 'bronaissance'.

In all honesty, I don't have much love for short phrases in the same way I hold little love for flippant clichés like on the front cover of this book. They often lack nuance and get taken by pockets of people, beaten and bent out of shape, misused, and become overused hashtags. Many of them try to summarise the whole human and male experience into a nice-sounding two-word phrase.

So instead let's focus on expanding our definition of human experience, talk about the good and bad, acknowledge mistakes and our ability to learn. Let's celebrate our men and build them up. Men have the capacity to do incredible things, to *be* incredible. To be loving, caring, and compassionate. To make others feel wanted, needed, and special. To build things, whether that's inventions or families. To live lives of fulfilment. They *do* want to connect, to talk, to feel belonging, to have value, and to give value. They've often just not been shown how to, or made to feel that they're not allowed to.

We've spent decades, centuries, longer even, forcing men into a small, compact shape like a piece of metal in a workshop. We told ourselves that this shape is malleable, meaning able to be hammered without cracking. That men could take it.

But the truth is, men *are* cracking. Quietly and privately, and in far greater numbers than we like to admit. That's why we need a new version of masculinity. Not an even harder metal, but something more flexible and elastic. One that can change, expand, adapt, and bend, without breaking under the pressure.

Much of this isn't ancient biological wiring or fate. It's cultural, societal, and traditional norms and beliefs that we reinforce. We built it, and so we can rebuild it. We have the agency to do so, right now. We don't need to wait for anyone else to say 'go'. Let's stop hammering, and let's start healing. We simply have to start; for men, for boys, and for our generations to come.

References

1. Dattani, S., Rodés-Guirao, L., Ritchie, H., Ortiz-Ospina, E., and Roser, M. (2023). Life expectancy. Published online at OurWorldinData.org.

2. Ramsay, D. and Bunn, S. (2023). Men's health. UK Parliament, December. https://post.parliament.uk/research-briefings/post-pb-0056/.

3. World Health Organisation (WHO) (2024). Cardiovascular diseases kill 10 000 people in the WHO European Region every day, with men dying more frequently than women. 16 May. https://www.who.int/europe/news/item/15-05-2024-cardiovascular-diseases-kill-10-000-people-in-the-who-european-region-every-day--with-men-dying-more-frequently-than-women.

4. Office for National Statistics (2023). People experiencing homelessness, England and Wales: Census 2021. https://www.ons.gov.uk/peoplepopulationandcommunity/housing/articles/peopleexperiencinghomelessnessenglandandwales/census2021.

5. Ramsay, D. and Bunn, S. (2023). Men's health. UK Parliament, December. https://post.parliament.uk/research-briefings/post-pb-0056/.

6. Office for National Statistics (2025). Homicide in England and Wales: year ending March 2024. https://www.ons.gov.uk/peoplepopulationandcommunity/crimeandjustice/articles/homicideinenglandandwales/yearendingmarch2024.

7. UK Parliament Committees (2018). MHM0020 – evidence on mental health of men and boys. https://committees.parliament.uk/writtenevidence/99613/pdf/.

8. NHS England (2022). Mental Health Act statistics, annual figures, 2021–22. https://digital.nhs.uk/data-and-information/publications/statistical/mental-health-act-statistics-annual-figures/2021-22-annual-figures/data-quality.

9. Health and Safety Executive (2025). Fatal injuries. https://www.hse.gov.uk/statistics/fatals.htm.

10. O'Dea, R.E., Lagisz, M., Jennions, M.D., and Nakagawa, S. (2018). Gender differences in individual variation in academic grades fail to fit expected patterns for STEM. *Nature Communications* 9 (1): 3777. https://www.nature.com/articles/s41467-018-06292-0.

11. GOV.UK (2025). Statistics on women and the Criminal Justice System 2023 (HTML). https://www.gov.uk/government/statistics/women-and-the-criminal-justice-system-2023/statistics-on-women-and-the-criminal-justice-system-2023-html.

12. Government of Canada, Statistics Canada (2025). Suicide, self-harm, and suicide-related behaviours in Canada. https://health-infobase.canada.ca/mental-health/suicide-self-harm/suicide-mortality.html.

13. Centers for Disease Control and Prevention (2025). Suicide data and statistics. Suicide Prevention. https://www.cdc.gov/suicide/facts/data.html.

14. Office for National Statistics (2024). Suicides in England and Wales: 2023 registrations. https://www.ons.gov.uk/peoplepopulationandcommunity/birthsdeathsandmarriages/deaths/bulletins/suicidesintheunitedkingdom/2023.

15. Movember (2025). About us. https://uk.movember.com/about/mental-health.

16. hooks, b. (2004). *The Will to Change: Men, Masculinity, and Love*. Atria Books.

17. Brizendine, L. (2010). *The Male Brain*. Bantam.

18. Butler, J. (1990). *Gender Trouble*. Routledge.

19. Weigard, A., Loviska, A.M., and Beltz, A.M. (2021). Little evidence for sex or ovarian hormone influences on affective variability. *Scientific Reports* 11 (1): 20925.

20. Chaplin, T.M. and Aldao, A. (2013). Gender differences in emotion expression in children: A meta-analytic review. *Psychological Bulletin* 139 (4): 735–765. https://doi.org/10.1037/a0030737.

21. Vingerhoets, A.J.J.M. (2013). *Why Only Humans Weep: Unravelling the Mysteries of Tears*. Oxford University Press.

22. Vingerhoets, A.J.J.M. (2013). *Why Only Humans Weep: Unravelling the Mysteries of Tears*. Oxford University Press.

23. van der Kolk, B. (2015). *The Body Keeps the Score: Brain, Mind, and Body in the Healing of Trauma*. Penguin Group USA.

24. Anderson, A., Chilczuk, S., Nelson, K. et al. (2024). The myth of man the hunter: Women's contribution to the hunt across ethnographic contexts. *PLOS One* 19 (8): e0309543.

25. World Health Organisation (2025). Suicide. https://www.who.int/news-room/fact-sheets/detail/suicide.

26. GOV.UK (2022). Men urged to talk about mental health to prevent suicide. https://www.gov.uk/government/news/men-urged-to-talk-about-mental-health-to-prevent-suicide.

27. Ramsay, D. and Bunn, S. (2023). Men's health. UK Parliament, December. https://post.parliament.uk/research-briefings/post-pb-0056/.

28. GOV.UK (2022). Men urged to talk about mental health to prevent suicide.

29. Guild, H., BBH Labs (2020). Puncturing the paradox: group cohesion and the generational myth. https://www.bbh-labs.com/puncturing-the-paradox-group-cohesion-and-the-generational-myth.

30. Ramsay, D. and Bunn, S. (2023). Men's health. UK Parliament, December. https://post.parliament.uk/research-briefings/post-pb-0056/.

31. Movember (2024). The Real Face of Men's Health report: understand the true state of men's health. https://uk.movember.com/movember-institute/the-real-face-of-mens-health-report.

32. NHS England (2021). Summary report: outpatient appointments by gender – NHS England Digital. https://digital.nhs.uk/data-and-information/publications/statistical/hospital-outpatient-activity/2020-21/.

33. Movember (2019). #KNOWTHYNUTS. https://uk.movember. com/story/view/id/11829/this-april-knowthynuts-for-testicular-cancer-awareness-month.

34. Smith, D.T., Mouzon, D.M., and Elliott, M. (2016). Reviewing the assumptions about men's mental health: An exploration of the gender binary. *American Journal of Men's Health* 12 (1): 78–89.

35. The National Confidential Inquiry into Suicide and Safety in Mental Health (NCISH) (2021). *Suicide by Middle-aged Men*. The University of Manchester. https://sites.manchester.ac.uk/ ncish/reports/suicide-by-middle-aged-men/.

36. NHS England (2025). Adult Psychiatric Morbidity Survey: survey of mental health and wellbeing, England, 2023/4. https:// digital.nhs.uk/data-and-information/publications/statistical/ adult-psychiatric-morbidity-survey/survey-of-mental-health-and-wellbeing-england-2023-24/methods.

37. Office for National Statistics (2024). Deaths related to drug poisoning in England and Wales: 2023 registrations. https://www .ons.gov.uk/peoplepopulationandcommunity/birthsdeathsand-marriages/deaths/bulletins/deathsrelatedtodrugpoisoninginengl andandwales/2023registrations.

38. GOV.UK (2024). Adult substance misuse treatment statistics 2023 to 2024: report. https://www.gov.uk/government/statistics/ substance-misuse-treatment-for-adults-statistics-2023-to-2024/.

39. World Health Organisation (2024). Over 3 million annual deaths due to alcohol and drug use, majority among men. https:// www.who.int/news/item/25-06-2024-over-3-million-annual-deaths-due-to-alcohol-and-drug-use-majority-among-men.

40. Committees – UK Parliament (2019). Written evidence submitted by Gambling With Lives. https://committees.parliament.uk/ writtenevidence/118437/html/.

41. Oates, W.E. (1972). *Confessions of a Workaholic: The Facts About Work Addiction*. Abingdon Press.

42. Bodó, V., Horváth, Z., Paksi, B. et al. (2024). Work addiction and personality organization: Results from a representative,

three-wave longitudinal study. *Comprehensive Psychiatry* 134: 152513.

43. Ince, C., Albertella, L., Liu, C. et al. (2024). Problematic pornography use and novel patterns of escalating use: A cross-sectional network analysis with two independent samples. *Addictive Behaviors* 156: 108048. https://doi.org/10.1016/j.addbeh.2024.108048.

44. Martellozzo, E., Monaghan, A., Davidson, J., and Adler, J. (2020). Researching the affects that online pornography has on UK adolescents aged 11 to 16. *SAGE Open* 10 (1): 215824401989946. (Original work published 2020).

45. Oxford University Press (2024). 'Brain rot' named Oxford Word of the Year 2024. https://corp.oup.com/news/brain-rot-named-oxford-word-of-the-year-2024/.

46. Judiciary.uk (2022). Molly Russell - prevention of future deaths report. https://www.judiciary.uk/wp-content/uploads/2022/10/Molly-Russell-Prevention-of-future-deaths-report-2022-0315_Published.pdf.

47. Hall, R. and Keenan, R. (2025). More than half of top 100 mental health TikToks contain misinformation, study finds. *The Guardian*. https://www.theguardian.com/society/2025/may/31/more-than-half-of-top-100-mental-health-tiktoks-contain-misinformation-study-finds.

48. *The Social Dilemma*. Directed by Jeff Orlowski. 2020. Streaming on Netflix.

49. Google Keyword Planner, accessed 20 July 2025.

50. Rodway, C., Tham, S.G., Richards, N. et al. (2022). Online harms? Suicide-related online experience: A UK-wide case series study of young people who die by suicide. *Psychological Medicine* 53 (10): 4434–4445.

51. Daoust, P. (2024). The loneliness trap: it is said to be as bad as smoking. So will it shorten my lifespan? *The Guardian*. https://www.theguardian.com/lifeandstyle/article/2024/jun/16/the-loneliness-trap-it-is-as-bad-as-smoking-15-cigarettes-a-day-so-will-it-shorten-my-lifespan?

52. Berwick, I. (2023). What's the problem with men?*Financial Times*. https://www.ft.com/content/cd2a8967-e9ba-48ce-91ed-131e1809bed5.

53. YouGov Plc (2019). One in five Britons have nobody to open up to about problems. © All rights reserved. https://yougov.co.uk/society/articles/23023-one-five-britons-have-nobody-open-about-problems.

54. eClinicalMedicine (2023). The epidemic of loneliness. *EClinical Medicine* 66: 102395. https://doi.org/10.1016/j.eclinm.2023.102395.

55. Movember (2025). Young men's health in a digital world. https://us.movember.com/movember-institute/masculinities-report.

56. YouGov Plc (2022). Father's day | YouGov Poll: June 8–13, 2022. © All rights reserved. https://today.yougov.com/society/articles/42860-fathers-day-yougov-poll-june-8-13-2022.

57. Cleary, A. (2022). Emotional constraint, father-son relationships, and men's wellbeing. *Frontiers in Sociology* 7: 868005. https://doi.org/10.3389/fsoc.2022.868005.

58. Solmi, M., Radua, J., Olivola, M. et al. (2022). Age at onset of mental disorders worldwide: Large-scale meta-analysis of 192 epidemiological studies. *Molecular Psychiatry* 27: 281–295.

59. Tanis, J. (2016). The power of 41%: A glimpse into the life of a statistic. *The American Journal of Orthopsychiatry* 86 (4): 373–377. https://doi.org/10.1037/ort0000200.

60. Office for National Statistics (2025). Sexual orientation, UK: 2023. https://www.ons.gov.uk/peoplepopulationandcommunity/culturalidentity/sexuality/bulletins/sexualidentityuk/2023.

61. Pachankis, J.E. and Bränström, R. (2019). How Many Sexual Minorities Are Hidden? Projecting the size of the global closet with implications for policy and public health. *PLOS One* 14 (6): e0218084.

62. UK Health Security Agency (2017). Mental health challenges within the LGBT community. https://ukhsa.blog.gov.uk/2017/07/06/mental-health-challenges-within-the-lgbt-community.

63. Shuttleworth, R., Wedgwood, N., and Wilson, N.J. (2012). The dilemma of disabled masculinity. *Men and Masculinities* 15 (2): 174–194.

64. Niu, C., Ventus, D., Jern, P., and Santtila, P. (2023). Associations between self-reported anatomical characteristics of the penis and sexual dysfunction in men. *Sexes* 4 (4): 622–637.

65. Quittkat, H.L., Hartmann, A.S., Düsing, R. et al. (2019). 'Body dissatisfaction, importance of appearance, and body appreciation in men and women over the lifespan'. *Frontiers in Psychiatry* 10: 864. https://doi.org/10.3389/fpsyt.2019.00864.

66. The Body Image Report by the GEC (Global Equality Collective), the world's largest EDI collective of educational experts, founded by Nic Ponsford, 2022. https://www.thegec.education/body-image-report.

67. House of Commons, Health and Social Care Committee (2022). The impact of body image on mental and physical health. https://publications.parliament.uk/pa/cm5803/cmselect/cmhealth/114/report.html.

68. Huang, B., Wang, Z., Kong, Y. et al. (2023). 'Global, regional and national burden of male infertility in 204 countries and territories between 1990 and 2019: An analysis of global burden of disease study. *BMC Public Health* 23 (1): 2195. https://doi.org/10.1186/s12889-023-16793-3.

69. World Health Organisation (2023). 1 in 6 people globally affected by infertility. https://www.mlo-online.com/disease/article/53056534/1-in-6-people-globally-affected-by-infertility.

70. Office for National Statistics (2024). Bullying and online experiences among children in England and Wales: Year ending March 2023. https://www.ons.gov.uk/peoplepopulationandcommunity/crimeandjustice/bulletins/bullyingandonlineexperiencesamongchildreninenglandandwales/yearendingmarch2023.

71. YouGov Plc (2019). Cyberbullying afflicts quarter of Brits. © All rights reserved. https://yougov.co.uk/technology/articles/23017-cyberbullying-afflicts-quarter-brits.

72. Office for National Statistics (2023). Domestic abuse in England and Wales overview: November 2023. https://www.ons.gov.uk/peoplepopulationandcommunity/crimeandjustice/bulletins/domesticabuseinenglandandwalesoverview/november2023.

73. *My Wife, My Abuser; The Secret Footage*, 2024. Directed by David Andrew Ward. Streaming on Netflix.

74. Olff, M. (2017). Sex and gender differences in post-traumatic stress disorder: An update. *European Journal of Psychotraumatology* 8 (sup4): 1351204. https://doi.org/10.1080/20008198.2017.1351204. PMCID: PMC5632782.

75. Reeves, R.E. (2022). *Of Boys and Men*. Swift Press.

76. Holt-Lunstad, J., Smith, T.B., and Layton, J.B. (2010). Social relationships and mortality risk: A meta-analytic review. *PLoS Medicine* 7 (7): e1000316. https://doi.org/10.1371/journal.pmed.1000316.

77. Franco, M.G. (2024). *Platonic: How Understanding Your Attachment Style Can Help You Make and Keep Friends*. Bluebird.

78. Gray, J. (2018). *Men Are from Mars, Women Are from Venus*. Harper Thorsons.

79. Glover, R. (2022). *No More Mr. Nice Guy*. Sanage Publishing House LLP.

80. Ramsay, D. and Bunn, S. (2023). Men's health. UK Parliament, December 2023. https://post.parliament.uk/research-briefings/post-pb-0056/.

81. UK Parliament – Committees (2023). Written evidence submitted by Mates in Mind (IMH0057). https://committees.parliament.uk/writtenevidence/124379/pdf/.

82. UK Parliament – Committees (2023). Written evidence submitted by Mates in Mind (IMH0057). https://committees.parliament.uk/writtenevidence/124379/pdf/.

83. Office for National Statistics (2023). Deaths by suicide of medical doctors 2020 to 2023. https://www.ons.gov.uk/aboutus/transparencyandgovernance/freedomofinformationfoi/deathsbysuicideofmedicaldoctors2020to2023.

84. UK Parliament – Committees (2023). Written evidence submitted by Mates in Mind (IMH0057). https://committees.parliament.uk/writtenevidence/124379/pdf/.

85. Bates, L. (2020). *Men Who Hate Women: From Incels to Pickup Artists, the Truth About Extreme Misogyny and How it Affects Us All.* Simon & Schuster.

86. Getik, D. (2024). Relative income and mental health in couples. *The Economic Journal* 134 (664): 3291–3305.

87. Coontz, S. (2013). There is no such thing as the "Traditional Male Breadwinner". stephaniecoontz.com.

88. Sharma, N., Chakrabarti, S., and Grover, S. (2016). Gender differences in caregiving among family: Caregivers of people with mental illnesses. *World Journal of Psychiatry* 6 (1): 7–17. https://doi.org/10.5498/wjp.v6.i1.7.

Signposting

There are hundreds of incredible organisations around the world doing amazing things across the dozens of topics covered within this book, and while I can't include them all here, please do consider researching if you feel you'd like to learn more or get specific support.

For those seeking more immediate help, here is a list of sign-posted organisations:

United Kingdom

- **Mind:** the UK's largest mental health charity offering a wide range of services, information, and support avenues for anyone struggling with their mental health – mind .org.uk.
- **Campaign Against Living Miserably (CALM):** a suicide prevention charity that provides support for anyone who needs it, not just men – thecalmzone.net.
- **Samaritans:** a charity dedicated to reducing feelings of isolation and disconnection that can lead to suicide, with a free helpline day and night (116 123) with volunteers ready to listen – samaritans.org.

United States

- **988 Suicide & Crisis Lifeline:** free support for anyone in emotional distress – 988lifeline.org.
- **Crisis Text Line:** a text-based service with trained counsellors – text HOME or HOLA to 741741 or visit crisistextline.org.

Australia

- **Lifeline Australia:** a national support line for anyone in crisis – call 131114 for 24/7 crisis support or visit lifeline .org.au.
- **Beyond Blue:** offers mental health support for anxiety, depression, and suicide prevention – beyondblue.org.au.

Global

- **Befrienders Worldwide:** a global directory listing suicide prevention helplines by location – befrienders.org.
- **Find a Helpline:** a global directory which also helps you find mental health helplines worldwide – findahelpline.com.
- **Movember:** an international charity that has become famous for turning the month of November into Movember and encouraging men to grow a moustache, all to support men's health issues like suicide, prostate cancer, testicular cancer, and more – movember.com.

Acknowledgements

I've always wanted to be an author. When I was at my lowest point, over a decade ago, I started making a vision board on my phone of things I'd love to do one day if I ever got better. I still didn't believe recovery was possible, so this vision board was more wishful thinking than an expected reality.

I know this sounds a little like a make-believe story, but the thing that sat at the top of that list was 'publish a book'. It feels weirdly full circle that, not only have I now published a book, but it's on something so related to those struggles all those years ago.

So I want to say a huge thank you to you, the reader, first and foremost. Writing this book has been a genuine highlight of my life, and I'm grateful if you've taken the time to pick it up and read it. I hope there's been something useful in here for you.

None of this would have been possible without my amazing publishers, Capstone and Wiley. Alice Hadaway, Annie Knight, Nick Mannion, Katy Smith, Richard Samson, Sunnye Collins, and the rest of the team, it's been a joy working with you all. A particular thanks to Alice for the speculative LinkedIn message that started it all!

Acknowledgements

A large part of this book has been made by the guests that were willing to give up their time to be a part of it. I started my interviews hoping for a few quotes here and there to supplement my material, but as I listened to people's unique insights and life experiences, I quickly realised these were going to provide far more than just the bones. I'll shout out each of the guests in the section that follows this, but I want to say a huge thanks to JAAQ and many of the great colleagues I met there, including John Reynolds, Dan Cook, Paul Smith, Ryan Hopkins, Joanna Watts, Dan Mason, and Roxanne McCarthy, as well as Dr Laura David from Smart About Health, for your support and making so many introductions to the amazing array of people included in this book. You've all been instrumental in helping it come to life.

Also, thanks to Stephen Middleton, Sam Percival, Daniel Sullivan, Alex Conn, and everyone else at Bupa for your support and for giving me access to some brilliant experts. And thanks to all the references and data sources who granted me permission to reuse their material in this book. This blend of expertise and external research has added an important edge.

A big thanks to my early readers who gave me critical feedback and told me when to stop waffling from my soapbox. But, more importantly, for giving me boosts of encouragement when I was letting imposter syndrome convince me the book was useless! Thank you – Ameena Altaf, Josh Brown, Alex Hammond, Michael Hiscock, Simon Jay, Connor Jennings, Robert Knight, Alex Lynch, Pruthvi Odedra, James Routledge, Shana Sexton, and Tunde Yusuff.

Hopefully I've convinced you all by now that masculinity isn't something fixed, but is something that is forged with others.

Acknowledgements

So, thanks to my mates. We do all the usual banter, beer, football chats, and all that malarkey, but we've also talked about grief, loneliness, depression, relationships, purpose, and so much more. Having a good group of men around me has helped me find that balance within myself, and to write this book. You're a bunch of legends.

A special shoutout to James Routledge. So much of my thinking on men, masculinity, and even myself has been shaped by our regular (sometimes slightly too philosophical) chats on men over the last ten years or so.

And last but not least, of course, I've got to say a special thanks to those closest to me. My grandad was a former journalist, and he always wanted another writer in the family. I'm gutted that he passed away not long before I got this book deal, but I know he's somewhere, perched in an armchair and a whiskey in hand, pulling me up on my overuse of the comma and already asking what book two will be about!

Massive love to my mum, dad, and brother. They were a huge support for me at the time I was struggling most, and this book genuinely wouldn't have been possible without them. They've always encouraged me to do the things that will make me happy rather than the things that seem to make other people happy, and honestly, I think that's helped make me into the man I am today and has shaped so much of this book.

Finally, huge love and a big thank you to my partner Sally for her support, patience, and words of encouragement that helped me make this book a reality. The book became a bit of a third wheel in our relationship and I would have struggled to finish it were she not as understanding and supportive as she was for how much attention my laptop was getting! Acting as a part-time sounding board, part-time editor as I paced around the house talking about men and masculinity really helped. I think me promising to book her a trip to Disneyland Paris as a thank you probably made it easier. I also want to acknowledge that choosing to write a book at the same time as buying our first home together was, in hindsight, not the best idea I've ever had. But we made it work, right?!

Contributors

A huge thank you to all of the guests who gave up their time to be a part of this project. Your insight, expertise, and willingness to share stories has added something really special. In alphabetical order:

- Alice Hendy MBE – ripplesuicideprevention.com
- Amelia Wrighton – suicideandco.org
- Andrew Jenkins – @andrewjenkinsofficial
- Anthony 'Staz' Stazicker – @stazthrudark
- Caroline Roodhouse – daddyblackbird.com
- David Chambers – @theauthenticman_
- Dr Dan Nicolau – kcl.ac.uk/people/dan-nicolau
- Dr James Stevenson – bupa.co.uk/health-information/health-blog/author-profile/i-l/james-stevenson
- Dr Naveen Puri – bupa.co.uk/health-information/health-blog/author-profile/m-p/naveen-puri
- Dr Ravi Lukha – bupa.co.uk/health-information/health-blog/author-profile/r-z/ravi-lukha
- Dr Tim Woodman – bupa.co.uk/health-information/health-blog/author-profile/r-z/tim-woodman
- Dr Zac Seidler – zacseidler.com and movember.com
- Dwain Chambers – @dwainchambers
- Elliott Rae – elliottrae.com
- Gary Hayes – PTSD999
- Isabel Berwick – ft.com/isabel-berwick

- James Routledge – jamesroutledge.co
- Jeremy Lipkowitz – jeremylipkowitz.com
- Katie Maycock – gystwellbeing.com
- Kenneth Erhahon (Shocka) – @shocka_artist
- Lee Chambers – leechambers.org
- Luke Tarrant – @luke_tarrant
- Mark Ormrod MBE – markormrod.com/
- Matt Morton – @themattmorton
- Michaela Wain – @michaelawain1
- Nick Conn – @dadinrecovery
- Paul Merson – @paulmerseofficial
- Professor David Veale – veale.co.uk
- Professor Janet Treasure – kcl.ac.uk/people/professor-janet-treasure
- Professor Mark Griffiths – www.ntu.ac.uk/staff-profiles/social-sciences/mark-griffiths
- Professor Paul Gilbert OBE – compassionatemind.co.uk
- Professor Rory O'Connor – gla.ac.uk/schools/healthwellbeing/staff/roryoconnor/
- Professor Prasanna Sooriakumaran – uclh.nhs.uk/our-services/find-consultant/mr-prasanna-sooriakumaran
- Richard Crick and Siobhan Birbeck (MAN v FAT) – manvfatfootball.org
- Ryan Hopkins – theryanhopkins.com
- Shaun Greenaway – @knackered_knackers
- Spencer Matthews – @spencermatthews
- Steve Phillip – thejordanlegacy.com
- Stuart Fawcett (ANDYSMANCLUB) – andysmanclub.co.uk
- Tj Power – @tjpower
- Tommy Hatto – @tommyhatto
- Wendy Robinson (CALM) – thecalmzone.net

About the Author

George Bell is a London-based writer and author who has spent 10+ years working in the mental health space, supporting several global brands and businesses on their mental health provisions for employees. He has written frequently on mental health and masculinity for many years, online, across publications and for several UK-based charities. He is the co-founder of JACK, a men's publication and platform for men's issues and experiences which aren't spoken about enough, but should be.

Connect with Me

You can find me in the following places:

- **Website:** www.georgebell.co
- **Instagram:** @georgeybell
- **LinkedIn:** https://www.linkedin.com/in/george-bell-10317184/

Index

women, 162, 164, 231
  as breadwinners, 251–252
  comfort of men in opening
    up to, 232
  communication in
    relationships, 214
  in construction industry,
    232–233, 234
  and demand-withdraw
    pattern, 215–216
  eating disorders in, 170
  female allies, 232–238
  gender roles of, 27–28,
    115, 250–251
  hate of men towards,
    240–241
  healthcare utilization by, 50
  and impact of porn, 87
  labels of femininity, 7
  and male-centred historical
    narratives, 25, 26

mankeeping, 235
and men, biological
  differences, 5–6, 8
PTSD in, 195
role in healthcare
  decisions, 232
suicide by, 62
therapists, 59–60
Woodman, Tim, 53, 54, 232
work
  addiction, 81–83
  remote, 109
  workaholism, 81
World Health Organisation, 74
wounds
  baby loss, 185–188
  bullying, 188–191
  domestic abuse, 191–194
  male infertility, 182–184
  trauma, 194–200
Wrighton, Amelia, 59